GRASS ROOTS

GRASS ROOTS

A History of Cannabis in
the American West

NICK JOHNSON

Oregon State University Press   Corvallis

Library of Congress Cataloging-in-Publication Data

Names: Johnson, Nick (Nicholas Michael), 1989- author.
Title: Grass roots : a history of cannabis in the American West / Nick Johnson.
Description: Corvallis : Oregon State University Press, 2017. | Includes
    bibliographical references and index.
Identifiers: LCCN 2017030868 | ISBN 9780870719080 (original trade pbk. :
    alk. paper)
Subjects: LCSH: Cannabis—West (U.S.)—History. | Marijuana—West
    (U.S.)—History.
Classification: LCC HV5822.C3 J64 2017 | DDC 362.29/50978—dc23
LC record available at https://lccn.loc.gov/2017030868

Oregon State University Press
121 The Valley Library
Corvallis OR 97331-4501
541-737-3166 • fax 541-737-3170
www.osupress.oregonstate.edu

For Nancy, who always said I was going to write a book.

Contents

Preface

A Note on Terminology and Sources

Cannabis is a complex plant that comes with a huge assortment of cultural and linguistic baggage, so it is necessary to explain how I refer to it. Throughout the book I use the uncapitalized term "cannabis" to refer generally to "marijuana," or psychoactive cannabis. I also use the phrase "drug cannabis" and mix in some of the plant's colloquial names, including "weed," "pot," "herb," "grass," and, less often, "dope."

By far the most common word for drug cannabis in the United States today—the one used most often by public officials, the media, the cannabis industry, and even the medical community—is "marijuana." Recently, this word has been the subject of debate and scorn among some in the cannabis industry. Many growers and aficionados feel that it is improper to continue using a term that the media and public officials appropriated from the Mexican American lexicon in the 1930s in order to exoticize and demonize the plant.[1] As a law that was at least in part devised to control populations of Mexican and black Americans, cannabis prohibition had undeniably racist origins. I'll admit that, as a historian sensitive to issues of social justice, I initially sided with those who found the term outdated and improper, and even considered railing against it in this book. But the word "marijuana," which is Spanish for the name "Mary Jane," is not inherently racist. In fact, as cannabis historian Chris Duvall has pointed out, it actually has African origins.[2] And while it is true that drug cannabis was most often referred to as cannabis indica in the United States before federal prohibition began in 1937, weed culture has since reappropriated "marijuana"—what, after all, would American cannabis culture be without iconic pot ballads such as Rick James's "Mary Jane," or Tom Petty's "Mary Jane's Last Dance?" And pop singer Halsey's 2015 hit just wouldn't sound the same if the "New Americana" was high on legal "cannabis" instead of "legal marijuana." Add the fact that nobody, no matter how well-articulated the argument, can stop people from using a word that is so well entrenched in the popular lexicon, and there is really no debate: the term "marijuana" is here to stay, regardless of how many aficionados—or historians—disdain it. Although I believe that "cannabis" more clearly conveys an agricultural context—technically, "marijuana" is the product that comes from the cannabis plant—I do use the term "marijuana" throughout this book.

In addition to dealing with fraught terminology, I also had to grapple with the fact that, compared with other crops, reliable primary source material on cannabis is frustratingly hard to come by.[3] Until the 1960s, marijuana use in the United States was concentrated among lower-class and marginalized people, such as minority farmers, transients, and laborers. Because most of these people were busy trying to survive, they did not have time to write about their experiences with weed in the way that some middle- and upper-class French and Americans did in the nineteenth century. Also, because cannabis has been outlawed in many states since 1913 and federally prohibited since 1937, there are no impartial USDA statistics to tell us how much cannabis was grown in a given year, or what the dominant agricultural practices were (though available evidence allows us to guess).

Even when the plant was legal, in the nineteenth and early twentieth centuries, it was not popular enough to warrant a steady stream of official or professionally published material. Law enforcement statistics on arrests and plant counts increasingly become more available throughout the twentieth century. Although they cannot be considered impartial—reporting larger plant seizures was a reliable way for law enforcement agencies to secure funding—law enforcement numbers might nonetheless be strangely accurate. There's no way any agency found every pot grower on a given campaign, so the number of plants a department reports, even if it is exaggerated, might actually be closer to the actual number than not.

Fortunately, cannabis did come up in the newspapers now and then in the nineteenth and early twentieth centuries, and the plant became one of the press's favorite sensationalized subjects by the mid-twentieth century. In the absence of plentiful official or personal sources, this book leans heavily on these newspaper accounts. While the sensational prose is great fodder for cultural analysis, this book tries to excise factual information from these articles—details that authorities and reporters had little reason to manipulate or sensationalize. These details include, for instance, where a certain crop was found and who was cultivating it. I also highlight authorities' estimates for the black-market price of certain crops; although estimates, they nonetheless give a general idea of the black-market price at a given time. Plus, law enforcement did a lot of undercover work to bust cannabis growers, dealers, and users, so the prices they gave to news reporters may be reliable more often than not.

Acknowledgments

Like all books, this book is the work of many, not one. For the early stages of research I thank the staff at the Denver Public Library; staff at the National Archives in Denver; Mason Tvert of the Marijuana Policy Project; Lincoln Bramwell and Daryl Rush of the US Forest Service; Greg Smoak of the University of Utah, as well as my advisors at Colorado State University: Mark Fiege, Jared Orsi, Adrian Howkins, and Michael Carolan. Other CSU faculty who helped inform my thinking on this project include Jodie Kreider, Janet Ore, James Lindsay, Ann Little, Sarah Payne, and Thaddeus Sunseri. Thanks also to Claire Strom and Annabel Tudor at Rollins College in Florida for inviting me to the 2014 Southern Forum on Agricultural, Rural, and Environmental History, where I received valuable feedback from a group of excellent PhD students and professors.

In California, I thank Anthony Silvaggio and Elizabeth Watson at Humboldt State University; Scott Greacen at Friends of the Eel; Dale Sky Jones, Noah Hirsch, and Aseem Sappal at Oaksterdam University; Jenny Hodge at UC–Davis; and the staff at the Oakland and San Francisco Public Libraries. In Colorado, I thank Nick Hice, Kayvan Khalatbari, and Ean Seeb of Denver Relief Consulting; John-Paul Maxfield of Waste Farmers; Steve Ackerman of Organic Alternatives dispensary in Fort Collins. In Oregon, I thank Richard Reames; Chelsea Rose at Southern Oregon University; the staff at the Pharm to Table dispensary in Medford; Greg Paneitz at Wooldridge Creek Winery; Scott Jorgensen of the Oregon state legislature; and the staff at the Southern Oregon Historical Society. In Nevada, I thank Aron Swan of Silver State Relief. In Washington, I thank David Rice at San Juan Sun Grown and Alex Cooley of Solstice Grown.

I am also indebted to the five anonymous reviewers who provided invaluable feedback and criticism of early drafts, as well as Chris Duvall and William Wei, who reviewed an early draft of a chapter. John McPartland provided crucial insight on cannabis taxonomy.

For the bulk of the research in this book I owe a great debt to the many journalists, past and present, who wrote about marijuana-related issues and events. We would all be lost on this subject without their careful reporting, lively writing, and many sacrifices.

Special thanks to those who donated to my research fund that sent me to Oregon in the summer of 2015: Betty Jo Brenner, John Carmon, Melanie Fleming, Jill Franck, Dirk Hobman, Kevin Jermyn, Eric Johnson, Marnie Lansdown, Shawn Lee, Jason O'Brien, August Ore, Michael Reidy, Joel & Paula Scherer, Tina Tray, William Wei.

Jared Orsi read every page of the first draft of this book and provided invaluable feedback, encouragement, and food for thought; he also chipped in to my research fund. Mark Fiege did more than his share to make this happen by putting me in touch with Oregon State University Press and making a substantial donation to my research fund.

My family in Chicago has encouraged and supported me in this project from the beginning. Last and most importantly, Nancy Gonzalez has put up with more than I could have ever asked her to with this project, from coffee-shop all-nighters in Denver to road trips through California to my general irritability as I tried to coax the right words and ideas from my brain. Over the last four years she has been nothing but supportive, loving, and encouraging, and her faith in me kept me strong. I could not ask for a better friend or life partner.

All errors in this book are my own.

Grass Is Not Greener

Full Pipes, Empty Streams

It would be a tall order to find someone more passionate about his local environment than Anthony Silvaggio. Even though it's a Saturday afternoon in late July, the fiery PhD sits in his office at Humboldt State University in Arcata, California, launching salvos of facts about the local marijuana industry. Silvaggio is a sociologist who studies cannabis farming as part of HSU's Interdisciplinary Institute for Marijuana Research. He explains that the cannabis plant has been the lifeblood of northern California's economy, and a hallmark of its culture, for at least the past twenty years. "We wear this on our shoulders," he says. "This is a badge that we wear. Humboldt County, since the early eighties, has been the place for the best marijuana in the world."

But soon after Silvaggio arrived in the 1990s, he began to notice some troubling things about the industry, in particular its effects on the region's true lifeblood—its watersheds. Those watersheds, he says, were first hammered by decades of logging, which silted up rivers and streams and decimated fish populations. Then, just as the environment was showing some signs of recovery, California legalized medical marijuana in 1996, and cultivation of the cash crop blew up on an industrial scale. "At one time it was small mom-and-pop stuff—twenty or thirty plants, no problem. But now it's hundreds and thousands of plants," Silvaggio said, visibly agitated. "It's horrible for the environment. We have an impaired ecosystem here, from over one hundred years of horrible federal and state land management policies. . . . And now we have industrial agriculture on the marijuana plantations."[1]

In other parts of the country, to describe local pot farms as "plantations" might be a slight exaggeration, but not where Silvaggio is from. California's Humboldt, Mendocino, and Trinity Counties are collectively referred to as the Emerald Triangle, the de facto weed-growing capital of the United States. Here—in stark contrast to the rest of the nation—if you don't grow,

Eel River, May 2013. The Eel River in northern California is a primary habitat for coho salmon, but it faces many threats related to human activity. One major factor in the decline of salmon habitat is the region's thousands of illegal marijuana grows, which divert water from the river's tributaries and clog it with dislodged sediment. Photo by Scrubhiker, Flickr (https://www.flickr.com/photos/scrubhiker/11429006005).

trim, or sell weed, or supply the cannabis industry, people wonder what you're up to.

The area, however, does not need cannabis to live up to its emerald nickname. From the air, the region appears a stunning deep green, and on the ground, one can easily disappear into the brambles, get lost, and never be seen again. Thick forests cloak the winding paths of the principal rivers—the Eel, Klamath, Mad, and Trinity. The northern California forests are some of the most ecologically diverse in the nation, home to more than twenty different species of conifers alone, as well as what botanists call "relic" plants—plants that have been extinct in other parts of the nation for more than a million years.

Near the coast, a thick fog rolls in from the cold waters of the Pacific, delivering extra moisture that makes possible the rare and famous redwood forests. White, red, and Douglas firs; tanoak; laurel; maple; oak; and several kinds of pine are also well represented in the region's canopy, while a dense tangle of madrone, shrubby willow and dogwood, bunchberry, and ferns grow below. Woodpeckers hammer away at tree trunks while bald eagles shriek in the skies above. Elk and mule deer meander through the trees, chewing on leaves and grasses. Among the denizens of the forest floor are salamanders, chipmunks, squirrels, and small carnivorous mammals called fishers. Trout and salmon splash in the streams, which are also home to a variety of turtles, frogs, and even river otters. This whole teeming, verdant tapestry rolls across a rugged landscape of wrinkled hills formed by millions of years of tectonic collisions far beneath the surface.[2] The hills are still being pushed upward today, meaning that the area's trees and other vegetation play a critical role in holding the soil down and keeping at bay the erosive forces of wind and rain.[3]

Cannabis, a sun-loving, wind-pollinated annual that thrives in open landscapes, is not native to the region and finds no natural niche within these dense forests. But it does have a long and storied relationship with humans, who came to this landscape in record numbers beginning in the mid-twentieth century. They felled trees to make room for homesteads and towns, and clear-cut the old-growth forests to support the nation's postwar construction boom. These activities effectively prepared the landscape for the introduction of the psychoactive herb, first brought by homesteading hippies in the 1960s and 1970s. As Silvaggio notes, these first couple generations of growers had little impact on the local ecology, but today satellite images show these forests pockmarked with unnatural clearings cut out just for cannabis.[4]

The California Fish and Wildlife Department estimated in 2014 that there are about ninety thousand cannabis plants growing in the region each year.[5] The actual number is probably far higher. Besides clearing vegetation to make room for their invasive herb, many cannabis farmers maintain crude pipe systems that illegally divert water from streams. On average, depending on plant size, growing technique, and local climate, a single cannabis plant consumes between four and six gallons of water per day; larger plants have been reported to guzzle as many as fifteen.[6] Using the six-gallon-per-plant estimate, a conservative calculation puts the daily water usage of the Eel watersheds' cannabis crop at more than half a million gallons.[7] The watersheds of northwest California may flow through some of the wettest climates in the state, but a punishing drought from 2012 to 2017 took its toll, and many of these streams will simply not be able to sustain excessive, unchecked cannabis farming for much longer.[8]

Erosion from traffic on old dirt logging roads that lead to remote grow sites also poses a problem for northern California's streams. While relatively light for most of the year, the traffic sometimes includes heavy loads, such as full water tanks, and it intensifies during harvest time in late fall. The vehicle stampede over these dirt roads triggers erosion that further silts up the river system.[9]

But dirt isn't the only thing that unregulated pot growing puts into the area's rivers. As in mainstream agriculture, cannabis farmers often apply fertilizers and pesticides to their crop, which wash into nearby streams or soil.[10] Farmers also often scatter rodenticide pellets around their plants to protect them from small mammalian predators. The anticoagulants in these pellets won't kill the vole or rat that eats them for a couple days, so if another animal, such as the housecat-sized fisher, eats enough of those smaller animals, it will die. This happens more often than one might think. In 2014, poisoning of fishers from pot growers' rodenticides was widespread enough for the US Fish and Wildlife Service to propose adding the fisher to the endangered species list.[11] The mammal was ultimately left off the list, as the various threats to its habitat from both logging and cannabis farming were deemed exaggerated.[12] Still, the unnecessary poisoning of California fishers goes down as another troubling side effect of unregulated cannabis farming.

Nor is the fisher the only animal hurt by these practices. The clearing of easily erodible land, the water diversion, the heavy use of dirt roads, and the pesticides also threaten the habitat of the Eel River's most iconic and treasured fish, its most telling indicator of ecological health—the coho salmon. The fish can't reach their spawning grounds if the water has been diverted away or if it's choked with sediment; they can't breed if their spawning pockets are too shallow and thus overheated; they can't live if fertilizers produce oxygen-sucking algae blooms in the water, or if it is poisoned with pesticides.

In sum, the watersheds of the Eel and other rivers in northern California are on life support, and cannabis growers are helping pull the plug.[13] Of course, cannabis farmers are not the only guilty party here—industrial logging and other farming activity pose similar threats to salmon—and growers are operating in a legal environment that is as unclear and uniquely hostile as it is profitable. Unlike other farmers in the region, most weed growers try not to talk too much about their crop—cultivation of even one cannabis plant is a federal felony punishable by up to five years in prison and a $250,000 fine.[14] Others will tell you that their plants are legal, destined for medical marijuana patients or for the state's recreational market, which voters approved in 2016 and is just beginning to take shape as this book is being published. But in reality, only a fraction—it is impossible to tell how much—of their product will be used by California patients or buyers in legitimate dispensaries.[15] The rest is funneled into the nation's massive black market in drug cannabis, an industry with an estimated value that varies considerably but is rarely reported to be under $10 billion.[16]

As if outdoor cannabis cultivation wasn't putting enough stress on local watersheds, the region's cash crop is helping to strangle the Eel River in another, far subtler way—indoor cultivation. Powered by a symphony of fossil-fuel fixtures such as high-intensity lights, air conditioners, and generators, today's indoor cannabis growing began during a crackdown on outdoor growing during the 1980s and evolved into a sophisticated botanical art. Growers found that they could hybridize different varieties of the plant to emphasize certain desirable attributes, such as greater potency, a shorter growth habit or particular taste or smell, or even a distinct kind of high.[17]

The indoor revolution turned American cannabis into some of the most highly regarded weed in the world, but plugging in to produce a premium pot crop had its own environmental consequences. In 2012, a study published in the *Journal of Energy Policy* found that indoor cannabis production accounted for 3 percent of California's total electrical usage and pumped as much CO_2 into the atmosphere as three million American cars.[18] This is but a drop in the ocean of CO_2 that human activity currently releases into the atmosphere, but it also represents data from just one state in a nation with hundreds of thousands of indoor cannabis grows. More importantly, since that report was published, Colorado, Washington, Alaska, Oregon, and California have all legalized—and in many ways encouraged—the indoor production of cannabis with barely a second thought.

Meanwhile, the carbon dioxide from indoor cannabis farms joins emissions from automobiles, power plants, and other industrial sources, contributing to the overall warming of the planet. The effects of climate change are being felt in California, an already dry state that only recently pulled out of one of its driest stretches in recorded history.[19] Governor Jerry Brown declared a state of emergency in January 2014, and from then until April 2017, most Californians were under some kind of water-use restrictions.[20] The ecological effects of the drought are still being tabulated, but at one point some fifty-eight million of the state's giant trees, including Humboldt County's famous redwoods, were at risk of perishing, along with the watersheds that course through them.[21]

The rapidly expanding cannabis industry in northern California seems to be beyond the control of regulators, and it may be too late to prevent the extinction of the coho salmon and the ultimate degradation of the Eel River watershed.[22] However, the end of the drought should help at least delay that disaster, and officials and growers in the Emerald Triangle have started to address some of the environmental impacts of cannabis agriculture. In October 2014, nearly three months after my visit to Arcata, Humboldt County commissioners approved a land-use ordinance that was developed in collaboration with growers. The regulations limit indoor growth to fifty square feet and cap grow light wattage at twelve hundred. They also require that outdoor growers submit cultivation and operation plans that demonstrate efficient water use, disclose water sources, and consider habitat impact.[23]

Silvaggio believes the rules are a step in the right direction, as they address issues that other environmentalists have pointed out for years and reflect a new willingness among growers and public officials to work together on regulation. But enforcement will still be difficult, he argues, since there are not enough officers to police the region's ten thousand growers. There's a similar enforcement problem in mainstream agriculture, he points out. Plus, as long as federal prohibition continues, environmentally negligent growing will be a problem. "Will we see the same kind of nefarious behavior on public land, on private land? The answer is yes, because of the inflated price," Silvaggio said. "The price is still going to be lucrative enough for people to do bad things."[24] This will likely remain the case even though California has now fully legalized marijuana.

So progress is being made, but will it be enough to save the Eel River and the coho salmon? Beyond California, will efforts to manage the environmental effects of cannabis farming be successful in other emerald enclaves such as southern Oregon, Seattle, or Denver? The answer, it would seem, depends on whether state and local officials can both craft *and enforce* legislation that will effectively regulate an industry that remains federally illegal. As Silvaggio notes, there is no precedent for such a thing in American history.

Untold Stories

There is, however, a precedent for cannabis *agriculture* in American history, one that has been overlooked and underexamined in most attempts to understand our relationship with this controversial plant. The history of cannabis, like the history of anything, is useful because it reminds us of things that can help us plan for a better, or at least a saner, future. For instance, cannabis's agricultural history reminds us that weed was grown legally in this country as a medicine in the early twentieth century; that the nature of people, plants, and birds has undermined cannabis prohibition since it began; that indoor cultivation only exists because of the war on drugs; and that most of the states that have legalized the mass cultivation of cannabis rely on overappropriated and ever-shrinking water sources.

Forty-one of fifty states, plus the District of Columbia, have either decriminalized cannabis possession or legalized some preparation of the plant.[25] Leading the way are Colorado, Washington, Nevada, Oregon, Alaska, and California, all located in that vast expanse of plains, deserts, and mountains generally referred to as the American West. While every part of the country has a long history with drug cannabis, focusing on the plant's story in the American West makes for a particularly enlightening case study. For one, California and Oregon have been the epicenter of cannabis culture and primary centers of cultivation for more than forty years. For another, westerners in those and other states have led the push to relegalize cannabis on some scale since 1996. Finally, the story of cannabis in the West is tied to some of the region's most definitive and interrelated themes, including borderlands conflicts, aridity and reclamation, extraordinary ethnic diversity, boom-and-bust economies and tourism, and an ingrained sense of self-determination that stems, at least in part, from a powerful myth of rugged individualism and a disdain for federal power.[26] The West offers an excellent setting to explore the origins, development, and environmental effects of cannabis agriculture, and with legalization unfolding across the region, there is no better time than now to delve into those stories.

The history of drug cannabis is routinely written by journalists, and rarely by historians or other academics.[27] With few exceptions, these books are generally framed around the social and political histories of the drug marijuana. While some devote pages or sections on cultivation or the plant's genetics and spread, none to date have offered a history focused on the plants in the ground. *Grass Roots* seeks to fill this gap by examining the myriad ways the cannabis plant found itself growing in American soil over time. It engages, if not answers, several critical questions: Where and how did cannabis grow? Who cultivated it—and how and why? What did the plant mean to them? How did cannabis fit into broader American attitudes about race, class, nature, and the distinct history of the West? And finally, how did we end up with a domestic cannabis industry that is, in its current state, environmentally negligent? While far from comprehensive, *Grass Roots* aims to tell the story of the complex human-cannabis relationship as it unfolded in one section of the country with the goals of informing current discussions about cannabis and drawing lessons from its past that may guide us toward a more responsible relationship with the plant.[28]

While it is the primary setting for this book, the American West is not an isolated region, nor was it the site of all significant events in American cannabis history.[29] In the early twentieth century, for instance, the US Department of Agriculture oversaw some of the earliest plantings of drug cannabis in South Carolina and Virginia.[30] Rather than argue for some essentially western cannabis experience, this book's focus on the West stems from a desire to acknowledge the region's critical role in the development of the American cannabis industry, as well as to encourage westerners—many of whom live in states where cannabis farming is legal—to think about marijuana as a crop first and a medical or recreational drug second. As the example of Humboldt County shows, cannabis is nothing if not an energy- and water-intensive crop that, like others, has barged its way into deceptively fragile ecosystems in a region that is dealing with water crises and controversial energy development. That fact alone injects the issue of cannabis agriculture with urgent relevance.

Farming Cannabis

So what kind of crop is cannabis? Generally speaking, it is a wind-pollinated, annual herb that comes in many different varieties, depending on its use by humans. Its closest relative is the hop plant (genus *Humulus*), another crop that humans use for the production of mind-altering substances. Historically, people added hop cones to beer to prevent it from spoiling, but today they are added for the huge variety of flavors and aromas they add to the brew. Both hops and cannabis belong to the family *Cannabaceae* and are naturally wind-pollinated, dioecious plants—meaning that individuals are either male or female.[31]

Botanists and plant geneticists agree that cannabis is part of the *Cannabaceae* family, but from there all bets are off. There is general agreement that drug-producing plants, commonly known as marijuana, are genetically distinct from fiber-producing plants, commonly known as hemp.[32] The question is how distinct—are drug and fiber types different species, or merely different varieties of the same species? Recently, cannabis geneticist John McPartland analyzed DNA "barcodes" from drug and fiber *Cannabis*, finding that the genetic makeup of the plants was not different enough to warrant categorization as separate species.[33] McPartland argues that all cannabis is *Cannabis sativa* (*sativa* is Latin for "cultivated") with a variety of subspecies that are capable of producing both drugs and fiber.[34] This breaks from the dominant taxonomy outlined by geneticist Karl Hillig, who argues for a multiple-species model. In Hillig's taxonomy, *Cannabis sativa* is hemp, and *Cannabis indica* includes all varieties of marijuana.[35] Clearly, the taxonomy question is far from settled, so for the sake of simplicity this book uses "cannabis" to refer to all drug-producing varieties and "hemp" to refer to fiber types.

Grass Roots is primarily an agricultural history of drug cannabis. While hemp is historically and presently an important plant with a stunning array of beneficial uses, drug cannabis is the most widely cultivated species in the country today.[36] As such, drug varieties are (for now) the only cannabis types with a discernible environmental impact. Drug cannabis is also the primary subject of most of the new cannabis laws being drawn up in many states, and it is those policies, as well as the general public, that this book seeks to address and inform.

Cannabis is one of the world's oldest domesticated crops. The ancestor of all modern *Cannabis* varieties evolved between 135 and 110,000 years ago in Central Asia. By the time humans migrated to that region, around 35,000 years ago, an earlier period of glacial activity had divided that ancestor between two different geographic refuges: fiber types in southeast Europe, and drug types in south Asia.[37] Botanists Robert Clarke and Mark Merlin note that when early humans gathered along stream banks and cleared the land to make shelter, "they helped create one of nature's relatively rare environments—the 'open habitat:'"[38]

> Camp-following *Cannabis* was among the first plants to colonize newly opened habitats . . . Humans provided *Cannabis* with a suitable habitat and soon learned to utilize plants growing on or near their waste piles rather than traveling to collect them. Different plant parts were used as sources of fiber, food, seed oil, medicine, and mind-altering drugs.[39]

Based on this description, early human experiences with cannabis were a lot like their first experiences with corn, wheat, and other crops: first, people alter the landscape in ways that disturb wild plant habitats, like clearing brush or setting fires. This creates open spaces that are colonized by seed plants. Humans then decide what, if any, qualities of these plants they like and artificially select for the plants that possess those qualities. They eventually decide to store seed and sow these "camp followers" at other sites.[40]

Early humans may have discovered the psychoactive properties of drug cannabis when they accidentally inhaled smoke from plants burning in natural or human-set fires.[41] Since then, people in many parts of the world have used drug cannabis as a medicine, recreational drug, and spiritual accompaniment, while hemp has provided food, rope, textiles, sails, birdseed, and other items. Its ability to serve humans in so many forms has afforded *Cannabis* the largest geographic range of any crop.[42]

While the plant comes in many different varieties, or cultivars, two major groups of marijuana plants have developed: one adapted to tropical or Mediterranean climates, and another adapted to colder, high-altitude environments.[43] In general, the drug product from each produces a different kind of psychoactive effect, or "high": the effect of the tropical varieties is more stimulating and cerebral, while the effect of the mountain varieties is more relaxing and felt throughout the body.[44] Innovations in cannabis breeding since the 1980s have resulted in thousands of crosses between these two major varieties.

Like growers of hops, coffee, coca, or poppies, farmers of drug cannabis carefully stimulate the production of a naturally occurring compound that helps the plant survive in the wild. In the wild, cannabis begins from seed, but today, since only female plants produce a drug, most growers begin by planting cuttings from mother plants called "clones." Hops are reproduced in the same way. Marijuana growers plant the cuttings in a loose, well-drained soil, often amended with a range of nutrient-rich additives, such as worm castings, peat moss, and bat guano. Some growers don't even use soil at all, choosing instead to run a constant stream of nutrient-rich water over their plants' roots—a technique called "hydroponics."[45]

Growers call the initial growth phase the "veggie" stage, as the plants gain height and branch out sets of odd-numbered, serrated leaves. These first sets of leaves are generally larger than subsequent leaves and act like solar panels, charging the plant with energy as it prepares for the flowering process. Female plants look identical to their male counterparts until they detect a shortening of daylight hours and begin flowering.[46] Outdoors, the flowering process begins naturally with the shortening of days in midsummer. Indoor farmers use a technique called "light-dep" (light deprivation) to trick female plants into flowering. This involves leaving the plants in a darkened room for up to twelve hours. Many growers have automated this process by attaching timers to lighting systems.[47]

Female plants begin the flowering stage by pushing out small white or orange hairs called pistils from nodes along the main stem and branches. Eventually, these pistils are joined by miniature leaves and small, round flower clusters, creating hairy, circular inflorescences (hop cones and grapes develop in a similar way). Instead of inflorescences, mature male plants produce tiny green pollen sacs that eventually burst open, scattering pollen to the wind. As the female's inflorescences grow into large, lumpy buds, the plant coats them with tiny resin glands called trichomes. These glands secrete a sticky resin that contains cannabinoids, unique compounds that help the plant retain moisture, protect the flowers from UV rays, and encourage propagation by catching pollen released from male plants.[48]

Delta-9 tetrahydrocannabinol, or THC, is the primary psychoactive cannabinoid found in the resin of female plants. It likely evolved to mirror a

Mature cannabis flower (marijuana). Flowers of the female cannabis plant are the primary source of the medical and recreational drug popularly known as marijuana. The flowers are covered with a sticky, psychoactive resin, which in a natural setting protects the flowers from UV rays and predation, retains moisture, and helps catch pollen released from male plants. Author photo.

similar compound produced in the bodies of some of the plant's predators, who become dazed and disoriented by its effects. The trichomes also secrete aromatic chemicals called terpenes—defensive oils produced in many plants—that help repel predatory insects and give the plant its distinctive, skunky smell.[49]

Overall, the more of this resin the grower can coax out of the plant, the more potent and aromatic (and valuable) the end product will be. In the wild, a female plant only produces resin until it is pollinated; then it refocuses its energy on seed production. When mature, the seeds drop to the ground and the plant dies. However, if the plant is not pollinated, it will continue to produce resin for several weeks until it expends itself, pining desperately for pollination. This is why growers use the cutting technique— it guarantees an all-female crop that will live, flower, and die without being pollinated, producing the maximum amount of resin.[50]

Healthy cannabis plants are generally well equipped to ward off pests and diseases. But genetic variation, as well as environmental stressors such as excessive heat or moisture, can leave plants vulnerable to infestations of spider mites, gnats, and aphids, as well as to a range of molds and mildews, including leaf spot and gray mold (*botrytis*).[51] Botanists have also theorized that modern cultivation methods force the plant to spend more energy producing cannabinoids such as THC instead of terpenes, its most effective insect deterrent.[52] In this way, the modern cannabis crop is more dependent on humans for protection from disease and infestation.

While there are plenty of organic insect repellents, such as neem and peppermint oils, many cannabis growers use chemical fungicides and pesticides to combat disease and infestation. Among black-market growers, who still dominate in most of the United States, some of the most popular chemicals are mildly toxic substances that are only approved for use on ornamental plants and have not been tested for combustion or inhalation. These include the insecticides Abamectin (sold as Avid) and Bifenazate (sold as Floramite), and the fungicide Myclobutanil (sold as Eagle 20EW).[53] Regulators of legal cannabis markets in Colorado, Oregon, and Washington have left these substances off their lists of approved pesticides.[54]

Although its basic principles have remained the same for hundreds, if not thousands, of years, cannabis agriculture has undergone massive changes over the past four decades. As the example of pesticides shows, some of these changes have paralleled similar shifts in legal agriculture. But other changes are the result of cannabis's illegal status, such as the guerilla grows that siphon water from streams in California and elsewhere, and the clandestine indoor grows that sap the electric grid. Socially and politically, cannabis's status as a federally illegal drug has overshadowed its status as a crop. This has delayed and distracted efforts by states and the federal government to contain some of the problematic elements of modern cannabis agriculture. With this agricultural history, I hope to speed up those efforts by demonstrating that the history of marijuana in the United States should be seen as nothing if not the history of a crop.

Like hops or grapes, when the cannabis crop comes out of the dirt—or hydroponic system—workers cut the stems and collect the flowers, which are then dried, trimmed, and sold, either in plastic baggies out of the pockets of street dealers or out of glass jars at legitimate weed stores, called "dispensaries." Like the hop industry of the late nineteenth century, which relied on the seasonal arrival of Native American laborers to pick the crop, many growers in today's legal and illegal marijuana industries rely on a highly transient population of trimmers and other laborers.[55]

Many legal cannabis processing facilities extract THC from the buds to use in concentrates, such as hashish and hash oil, or for baking into edible cannabis products. After making the purchase, the consumer will eventually pack the weed into a pipe, roll it into a joint, or eat it in a cookie, candy bar, or any number of edible preparations (one can even drink it in a soda).

In Bodies and Societies

Smoking THC delivers the effects instantaneously, while it takes between forty-five minutes and an hour to fully feel the effects of ingested THC. When smoked or ingested, THC interacts with receptors in the brain that are part of the body's endocannabinoid system, which regulates, among other things, experiences of pain, stress, hunger, sleep, body temperature, intestinal activity, and memory retention.[56] Though it is the primary psychoactive cannabinoid, THC is just one of many cannabinoids found in the plant, and the different ratios of these compounds in each plant makes the "high" difficult to predict. Just as botanists and geneticists have wrestled over cannabis taxonomy, doctors and pharmacologists throughout American history have struggled to completely understand the cannabis high, a fact that continues to complicate medical dosing, categorization, and regulation. A person's experience with cannabis hinges not only on the plant's cannabinoid profile, but on other factors, including "set"—the person's natural brain chemistry and disposition—and "setting"—the cultural, social, and physical environment in which the drug is taken.[57]

Over time, the psychoactive effects of cannabis have produced different cultural reactions. Some cultures, particularly in India, Central and North Africa, and some parts of the Middle East, have viewed these effects as a relatively inconsequential enhancement to everyday life or a gateway to spiritual connection. Others, particularly in the industrialized nations over the past one hundred years, have seen psychoactive cannabis as a detrimental distraction at best, and a menace to public health at worst. Yet the plant's therapeutic effects were once embraced and studied by medical professionals in Britain and the United States.

Since cannabis and other mind-altering drugs aren't a necessary part of life, some might argue, why should we spend water and other precious resources on them? Wouldn't it be better for everyone if people just gave up using mind-altering substances, especially if they are depleting water supplies and contributing to climate change? It might, but humans everywhere (as well as other species) have long sought out altered states of consciousness. They have reached them via natural routes of all sorts, from plants to toads to fungi.[58] Obviously, not all of these experiences have proved beneficial. But psychoactive cannabis has been used for thousands of years without causing a single death from ingestion alone, and despite the fact that the drug has been used by millions of Americans for decades, we have yet to see any evidence of widespread, cannabis-related illness.[59] In addition, cannabis users have found that being high often alters one's thinking and perspective in ways that foster insight or creativity. This experience—seeing or thinking about things a bit differently—certainly provides meaning or value to many cannabis users.

This does not mean cannabis is harmless. As with any mind-altering or medicinal drug, there are risks and side effects associated with use. Prolonged, heavy use of high-THC cannabis, especially by people under the age of twenty-one, can result in cognitive impairment, and it is estimated that some 9 percent of cannabis users become dependent (a real condition despite its routine dismissal by many cannabis advocates).[60] In people who are genetically predisposed to mental illness, heavy use of cannabis during adolescence can potentially lead to earlier onset of psychotic conditions, although the science on that connection continues to evolve.[61] However, there do not appear to be any major risks associated with occasional or moderate cannabis use by adults. One recent study concluded that "health problems due to cannabis use can be effectively treated."[62]

While recreational use is widespread, cannabis also has an array of therapeutic properties. Scientific studies have provided evidence that cannabis can at least partially treat nausea, AIDS, cancer, epilepsy, neuropathic pain, Post-Traumatic Stress Disorder (PTSD), glaucoma, and myriad other conditions.[63] Anecdotal evidence from thousands of patients and regular users alike corroborate the sparse clinical evidence of these effects—and clinical evidence is only sparse because the federal government blocks many proposals designed to study the medical potential of cannabis.[64] As the experience of cannabis is highly subjective, the plant is not guaranteed to offer therapeutic relief to everyone. But it is nonetheless a bastion of medical potential that awaits concerted, comprehensive study.

Since it arrived in the United States more than a century ago, drug cannabis has meant many things to many different people. And it remains both a helpful medicine and a potentially harmful vice. It is still a pathway to new ways of thinking, still a creative tool. It is still a symbol of freedom, of federal lunacy, and of youthful rebellion. It is certainly still a cash crop. And in spite of the current, unfortunate effects of its cultivation, cannabis remains for many Americans a symbol of hope for a more sustainable future. To truly understand the unique American identity of this plant, one needs to grasp its entire story—not just from the top of the plant, where the trippy flowers bloom, but from the roots up.

CHAPTER 1

From Medicine to Menace

Drug Cannabis in the Southwest and Beyond, 1851–1935

In September 1897, while overseeing a group of Mexican convicts working on a building in downtown Yuma, Arizona, a prison guard by the name of General Schriver discovered six small bags of apparent contraband.[1] Believing that the sacks "had been cached in reach of the convicts to be smuggled into the prison," Schriver picked them up and turned them in to his superintendent. Each of the small bags contained two ounces of what the *Tombstone Prospector* referred to as "mariguana . . . a kind of loco weed which is more powerful than opium. . . . Mexicans mix it with tobacco and smoke it in cigarettes, which causes a hilarity not equalled by any other form of dissipation." According to the *Prospector*, had the "mariguana" breached the prison walls, its value would have increased from fifty cents to four dollars per ounce.[2] While the report does not mention whether Schriver actually saw any of the Mexican workers trying to retrieve the drug cache, there was reason enough to suspect they would—not only was the drug common in Mexican prisons during the late nineteenth and early twentieth century, but in 1894 two Mexican prisoners were punished for "smuggling marihuana" into the very same prison.[3]

Clearly, in border towns such as Yuma "mariguana" was considered a terrible scourge of Mexican prisoners and "a dangerous thing to fool with."[4] But remarkably, that same plant took on a completely opposite identity the farther one got from the border. In 1899 the local newspaper in Holbrook, Arizona, some 220 miles northwest of Yuma, declared that "cannabis indica (Indian hemp) is one of the best additions to cough mixtures known; it quiets the tickling of the throat and does not have the bad effects of morphine, which is so frequently used in 'cures.'"[5] The earlier report from Yuma did not mention "cannabis," but it did state that "[t]he owner" of the confiscated drugs "can secure his property by calling at the office of the prison"—an

implicit admission that the bedeviled drug "mariguana" and the legal medicine "cannabis indica" were the same thing.[6]

Thus, in the hands of Mexicans along the border, cannabis was "dangerous" and "more powerful than opium," but away from the border, in the
hands of Anglo-American doctors, pharmacists, and patients, it was a useful medicine that was actually *less* harmful than morphine, a more powerful
derivative of opium. The fearful assumption that darker-skinned peoples
were misusing an otherwise valuable plant represented a fusion of the
plant's sinister reputation in Mexico with much older European assumptions about the so-called Orient—a collection of fanciful ideas about Asia
and the Middle East—and hotter climates more generally.[7] This union of
racial and environmental stereotypes fit nicely with Anglo-Americans'
growing disdain for Mexicans around the turn of the century and marked
the beginning of the "reefer madness" myth in the United States.[8]

As these examples from Arizona suggest, Americans have struggled to
understand drug cannabis from its earliest arrival in the country. This is
not surprising, as we still fail to completely understand the plant today.
You won't see this book next to similar books on rice or wheat—two other
plants that were domesticated in Asia thousands of years ago but fail to pro-
voke anything close to the level of inquiry or controversy that drug cannabis does today. Why? The old Asian weed remains an enigma, a status that
both rice and wheat shook off eons ago. Lacking complete knowledge about
something, humans tend to fall back on folklore, half-truths, and anecdotal
evidence. This is exactly what has happened with cannabis, both drug and
nondrug, in the United States. A plant confounding a society is nothing
new, but the story of cannabis in the United States is particularly notewor-
thy because Americans have a disturbing history of tying negative perceptions of drug use to stereotypes about marginalized people and then cod-
ing those attitudes into laws that affect people's lives. Cannabis was already
powerful, but criminalizing it resulted in granting it an unnaturally large
influence over the lives of people who grew, sold, and used it.

Journalist and cannabis historian Martin A. Lee wrote that the plant and
its history are "all about doubles, twins, dualities: fiber and flower, medicine
and menace."[9] The conflicting reports about the same plant from Yuma and
Holbrook, just two years apart, confirm Lee's observation. They also mark
the beginning of the cannabis plant's transformation in the United States

from medicinal herb to menacing drug.[10] As the Arizona reports suggest, the transformation began in the Southwest around the turn of the century and was aided by prevailing ideas about race and class in both Mexico and the United States—specifically, about Mexican soldiers, prisoners, and laborers. Use of drug cannabis by black laborers and white prostitutes in the United States also began around the same time and helped shift American perceptions of the plant, but ideas from and about Mexicans were by far the biggest drivers of the "menace" narrative in the United States.[11] As Mexican immigration increased and anti-vice attitudes became more prevalent in the first decades of the twentieth century, fear-driven notions of marijuana eclipsed a rational and scientific—if incomplete—understanding of cannabis, and the plant and people who used it became outlaws.

It wasn't just cannabis. Vice in general was under attack in the early-twentieth-century United States. Groups such as the Anti-Saloon League and the Women's Christian Temperance Union (WCTU) campaigned for alcohol prohibition and eventually won it in 1920, while pharmacists, physicians, and local politicians became concerned about the misuse of popularly prescribed medicines such as morphine, especially among poorer and minority populations. In this context, Mexican marijuana smokers fit in as the latest misusers of these drugs, preceded by Chinese opium smokers and African American cocaine users. The federal Pure Food and Drug Act of 1906 required detailed labeling of many drugs, including opium, cocaine, and "cannabis indica."[12] In 1914 Congress passed the Harrison Narcotics Act, which outlawed the nonmedical use of opium and cocaine. While some high-ranking federal officials sought to include cannabis in the new law, successful lobbying from the drug industry kept the plant out of the Harrison Act.[13]

While the federal government opted for cannabis regulation in the early twentieth century, many states chose to outlaw the plant as a preemptive strike against an alternative to already outlawed substances such as opium or alcohol. This was the rationale behind California's decision to enact the nation's first statewide ban on nonmedical cannabis in 1913.[14] As more states began implementing voter-approved alcohol bans, some local law officers and lawmakers called for bans on cannabis. For example, one Phoenix officer opined in 1920 that "since the passing of the saloon, marihuana has been responsible for more than one-half of the crimes committed in the city."[15] Preemptive bans on drug cannabis were enacted in Utah in 1915 and Colorado in 1917. Four northeastern states—Maine, Massachusetts, Rhode Island, and Vermont—outlawed nonmedical use of the plant between 1914 and 1918. Nevada, New Mexico, Oregon, and Washington passed similar laws in 1923.[16] By 1933, twenty additional states—well over half the country—had outlawed nonmedical distribution of the plant.[17]

Although most early anti-cannabis laws were passed in anticipation of increased use, some were passed in direct response to a known population of users.[18] The desire to curb cannabis use among Mexicans and Mexican Americans was the rationale behind local anti-cannabis ordinances in New Mexico and Arizona during the 1910s, as well as Texas's statewide ban in 1919. These local concerns about "marihuana" began to spread beyond the Southwest during the 1920s, often cropping up in cities and states with large populations of Mexican laborers.

Another factor in the decline of medical cannabis in the early-twentieth-century United States was its ambiguity as a medicine. Just as they do today, varying cannabinoid profiles in the plants produced inconsistent effects in users, which complicated attempts by physicians and pharmacists to nail down proper dosage recommendations and made it impossible to draw broad medical conclusions based on anecdotal evidence.[19] In this way, the plant's natural complexity made it impossible for nineteenth-century physicians and pharmacists to properly categorize what they called "Cannabis indica." But if cannabis defied official medical categorization, it remained a valuable medical and recreational substance to many outside professional medicine, a fact that made attempts to control the plant all the more futile.

As they were in the early twentieth century, Latinos remain more likely to be arrested for cannabis violations than whites, even though both groups currently use it and other drugs at about the same rate.[20] Moreover, the strategy that local authorities used to criminalize cannabis in the early twentieth century—connecting the plant to crime and perpetuating established tropes about its use by dark-skinned foreigners—gained traction among federal authorities in later decades and became a core argument for the national prohibition of cannabis in 1937. Thus, the racial, environmental, and class-tinged origins of marijuana, the "dangerous Mexican weed," remain especially relevant today.

Medical Musings

It is not known when drug cannabis first arrived in the United States, but it first entered the American pharmacopoeia in 1851.[21] By the late nineteenth century it had been the subject of multiple medical investigations and was sold as a remedy for corns, asthma, and insomnia. Authors of these investigations used several names for the plant, including the Latin *Cannabis indica*, the English "Indian hemp," or hashish, a word derived from literature on drug cannabis in the Middle East and Southwest Asia. There was also by that time a general awareness of the plant's intoxicating properties, although it spurred neither fear nor outright condemnation amongst physicians, scientists, politicians, or the general public.

Among the first Americans to document the effects of cannabis was Fitz Hugh Ludlow of Poughkeepsie, New York. During the summer of 1854, at the age of seventeen, Ludlow ingested multiple preparations of cannabis that he obtained from a local pharmacy.[22] Among other sensations, Ludlow described feelings of great elation and great terror. At one time the drug put him in a state of "unimagined bliss" and he "glowed like a new-born soul"; after another dose on a different day, he awoke after midnight in a "realm . . . terrible with an infinitude of demoniac shadows."[23] Although the next day he reported that he was "as vigorous and buoyant as I ever was in my life" and "felt assured that I had done myself no injury," the terrifying visions troubled him so much that he resolved to "experiment with the drug of sorcery no more."[24] Ludlow eventually declared the drug "an improper pathway" to a state of divine knowledge.[25] In 1857 he published a book about his experiences titled *The Hasheesh Eater*. The book kick-started Ludlow's literary career, as he went on to write a travelogue of the American West entitled *The Heart of the Continent*, as well as many essays, news articles, and short fiction pieces.

Ludlow was no physician, but in taking cannabis and documenting its effects he was using exactly the same methods as the American Provers' Union, a group of disgruntled doctors formed in Pennsylvania in 1853. Like Ludlow, these doctors were curious about cannabis's effects, but their experiment was part of a larger mission to change Western medical practice. The Provers' Union was founded by German physician Constantine Hering, a disciple of Samuel Hahnemann, the founder of homeopathy. Hering and the other Provers objected to bloodletting and other standard medical practices of the day, believing instead that physicians should test a remedy on themselves—to "prove" its effectiveness—before prescribing it to a patient.[26] In 1859 the Provers published a report on cannabis in which they claimed that the herb was an effective treatment for "Paraplegia," "Delirium tremens," "Trismus" (jaw spasms), "Tetanus," "Epilepsy," and "hypochondria."[27] They also reported what have since become widely known effects of cannabis, including "thirst," "excessive sleepiness," "uncontrollable laughter," and "increased appetite."[28] Strangely, the Provers also reported pain in just about every part of the body, a side effect that is virtually unheard of today; indeed, cannabis has been shown to be a relatively effective pain reliever.[29]

In an 1881 treatise titled *Drugs That Enslave*, Dr. H. H. Kane wrote that cannabis helped one of his female patients cope with anxiety and alcohol addiction. He did report that the patient, who smoked the drug in a pipe, occasionally suffered from vivid, disturbing dreams.[30] But vivid nightmares and paranoia figured more prominently in Kane's account of Horatio Wood's experiment with cannabis, in which Wood, a botanist, orally ingested a "very large dose."[31] Again, widely known effects of cannabis were observed, including "forgetfulness" and an altered perception of time—"days have enlarged to years and ages."[32] Later, in an 1893 edition of *Science,* E. W. Scripture of Yale University reported a similar distortion of time, along with "faint illusions," under the influence of orally ingested cannabis.[33]

In all, although they found it helpful for some conditions and much safer than opium-derived medicines, it seems that nineteenth-century physicians and scientists found the effects of drug cannabis to be largely unpredictable, and they were unable to come up with a reliable dosage regimen. This was the lament of an anonymous New York druggist in 1890, who wrote that "there is but little call for [cannabis], even in prescriptions, for the reason, I think, that invaluable as it is when fresh, of full strength . . . its active principle is so volatile that you never are sure of what its effects will be. Could it be depended upon it would be one of the least injurious and most agreeable of the intoxicants."[34]

Almost two decades later, the medical handbook *Modern Materia Medica and Therapeutics* echoed these concerns. After reporting that cannabis is most often used as a "mild" pain reliever and sleep aid, its fifth edition noted that "as the preparations of cannabis indica vary considerably in strength, and as some individuals are far more susceptible to the action of the drug than others, it is always advisable to begin with small doses and to increase them gradually."[35] American physicians published this advice in 1909, and unlike a lot of other medical advice published then, it remains good advice today. The Colorado state government advises cannabis eaters that "THC can affect people differently, so be aware of the amount you consume and its impairing effects," and states that it is best to "start with less than one serving and wait before using more."[36]

In addition to being the subject of scientific and medical experiments, cannabis was included in various home remedies around the turn of the century and sold in tinctures at drugstores. In 1898, Dr. F. H. Cassells of the Washington Medical Veterinary Association included "cannabis indica" as part of his remedy for acute indigestion in horses.[37] The same year, the *San Francisco Call* named "Indian Cannabis," along with opium and chloral, as a sleep aid.[38] In 1901, a section of the *Commoner* in Lincoln, Nebraska, prescribed a mixture of "cannabis indica," salicylic acid, and collodion as a cure for corns.[39] Similar remedies appeared in the *San Francisco Call* in 1901, the *Morning Oregonian* in 1907, and the *Spokane Press* in 1910.[40] Pharmacists, meanwhile, focused on perfecting cannabis extraction and preserving drug quality, as was evident in a 1910 discussion of the plant in the *Pacific Pharmacist*.[41]

How does the understanding of cannabis in the nineteenth and early twentieth centuries compare with what we know in the twenty-first? There is in fact evidence that cannabis can be an effective treatment for epilepsy and other spastic conditions; this may include delirium tremens, as there is also evidence that alcoholics can use cannabis as a substitute drug to wean them off the bottle.[42] Despite the claims of many turn-of-the-century advertisements, topical cannabis solutions are not considered to be an effective remedy for corns. Drug cannabis has been observed to induce paranoia.[43] When ingested orally, THC, the plant's principal psychoactive compound, is metabolized by the liver and becomes 11-hydroxy-THC, a more potent psychedelic compound.[44] This likely explains the more pronounced paranoia, hallucinations, and nightmares reported by Ludlow, Wood, Scripture, and other nineteenth-century experimenters who ate the drug.

By 1900, American physicians, pharmacists, scientists, and writers relied on level-headed scientific inquiry to develop a reasonably accurate—though far from complete—understanding of drug cannabis and its effects. Importantly, in contrast with contemporary, nonmedical reports from Mexico and the Southwest, nobody in the US medical community appears to have observed violent impulses or permanent mental degradation in cannabis-using subjects. This body of medical knowledge not only encouraged the drug industry to oppose the inclusion of cannabis in the Harrison Act but also prompted the federal government to investigate whether American farmers could profitably cultivate drug cannabis.

Government-Grown Ganja

In the nineteenth century, practically all the drug cannabis on the American market came from England via India.[45] The only home-grown cannabis at that time was European hemp, grown for rope and canvas. Because they have been artificially selected for longer fibers, most hemp cultivars are incapable of producing drug material.[46] But even hemp material, which does not intoxicate if smoked, contains latent psychoactive cannabinoids that can be activated by treating plant parts with alcohol and ingesting them orally—a method used by Wood and others in nineteenth-century cannabis experiments.[47] The earliest documented example of exclusive drug cannabis cultivation comes from California, where Syrian immigrants grew a sizeable patch near Stockton in 1895.[48] Some Mexicans or Mexican Americans cultivated smaller plots after the turn of the century in Arizona, California, and New Mexico. But the largest producer of drug cannabis in the early-twentieth-century United States appears to have been the federal government.

Today, many first-time cannabis farmers get their growing instructions from weed-fetish magazines such as *High Times*. But in 1915 they looked to the US Department of Agriculture, which circulated the following instructions:

> Cannabis is propagated from seeds, which should be planted in the spring as soon as conditions are suitable, in well-prepared sandy or clayey loam at a depth of about an inch in rows 5 or 6 feet apart. . . . Two or three pounds of the seed per acre should give a good stand. . . . good results may be obtained with commercial fertilizers, such as are used for truck crops and potatoes . . .

when the female plants reach maturity, a sticky resin forms on the heavy, compact flower clusters, and harvesting may then be begun. . . . Drying can best be done, especially in damp weather, by the use of artificial heat, not to exceed 140°F. Returns from experimental areas indicate that yields of 400 to 500 pounds of dried tops per acre may be expected under good conditions.[49]

The USDA published these instructions in *Farmers' Bulletin* No. 663, titled "Drug Plants Under Cultivation." In it, W. W. Stockberger, "Physiologist in Charge" of the department's Drug-Plant and Poisonous-Plant Investigations, provided detailed cultivation instructions and approximate market prices for some sixty drug plants, including belladonna, lavender, ginseng, and even dandelions. According to Stockberger, the department released the pamphlet because the nation was paying other countries "large sums of money" for medicinal plants that could be grown in the United States, and because "[i]nterest in the possibility of deriving profit from the growing of drug plants is increasing yearly."[50]

But Stockberger's booklet represented more than just the government's attempt to grow a domestic drug supply. Like *Pacific Pharmacist* and some of the other medical publications circulating at the time, the *Farmers' Bulletin* series and Stockberger's specialist title were part of a developing knowledge system in the United States, one that increasingly relied on the centralized distribution of professional, scientific expertise to help solve societal problems. This expertise was organized and transmitted via professional journals, government bulletins, and specialized agencies, such as new Agricultural Extension offices. In the first decades of the twentieth century, government officials at every level routinely deferred to panels of experts when tackling a wide range of issues, from farming to flood control.[51] Cannabis's inclusion in *Farmer's Bulletin* 663 shows that, some twenty years before the plant was federally outlawed, government officials considered it as simply another subject of rational, scientific inquiry, lying squarely within the newly professionalized realms of medicine and agriculture.

True to the scientific method, Stockberger compiled his information for the USDA pamphlet from agricultural experiments on the nation's farms. One of these experiments began in 1904 in Florence County, South Carolina. On four acres of J. W. King's plantation, USDA representative Benton Young oversaw the planting of cannabis, hot peppers, opium poppies, wormseed, and several other plants said to "have valuable medicinal qualities."[52] Young, who was from Florence County, pushed for the experiment because he thought that "the alluvial soil and salubrious climate of his native State and county" could birth a new agricultural industry. The test patches would determine "the profitability or unprofitability" of that industry.[53]

Young's belief that South Carolina provided decent soil and climate for drug farms was apparently well founded. Stockberger mentioned in the 1915 bulletin that cannabis was "better suited to the warmer climates of the southern half of the United States."[54] And in 1919, writing in the recently minted journal of the American Pharmaceutical Association (APA), Stockberger reported that five states, including South Carolina, had planted approximately 115 acres of cannabis and harvested nearly sixty thousand pounds of the drug in 1918.[55] Stockberger deemed this amount "sufficient to meet market demands for the American grown drug."[56] In the same journal, APA member George P. Koch affirmed a shared interest in drug plants between agriculturalists and pharmacists when he reported that "cannabis grown by scientific methods in the United States is now extensively used by American drug manufacturers."[57] Despite its initial success, Stockberger cautioned that the American cannabis crop, like belladonna and other drug crops, was still in the "experimental stage."[58]

The USDA updated *Farmers' Bulletin* 663 in 1920, adding data from Stockberger's 1918 crop report and an additional tip for would-be cannabis farmers: "about half the seeds will produce male plants, which must be removed before their flowers mature; otherwise, the female plants will set seed, thereby diminishing their value as a drug."[59] This method produced a higher-potency drug cannabis that growers now call "sinsemilla" (pronounced "seen-se-ME-ya")—Spanish for "seedless." While the 1970s counterculture is often given credit for producing the nation's first sinsemilla crop, the updated *Farmers' Bulletin* 663 shows that the feds had already figured it out some fifty years earlier.[60]

As the USDA collected data from government-sanctioned sinsemilla farms and circulated instructions on how to grow cannabis, Southwestern authorities were arresting and harassing Mexican Americans for growing the same plant. In April 1919, "M. Cochon," a resident of Prescott, Arizona, who described himself as "Mexican," was arrested in Los Angeles

Cover of *Farmers' Bulletin* 663, rev. ed. 1920. Beginning in the late nineteenth century, the USDA's *Farmers' Bulletin* was a regularly issued informative booklet for all things agriculture. Originally published in 1915, *Farmers' Bulletin* 663 contained detailed instructions for how to grow marijuana—the first official guide to marijuana horticulture in the United States. Source: US Department of Agriculture, archive.org.

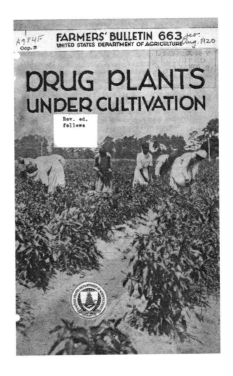

"for raising and selling the notorious marijuana weed." Prescott's *Weekly Journal-Miner* reported that "this weed is used extensively by Mexicans, and instances are known in this city . . . where those of this race . . . have had on their persons quite a supply of this 'fighting brand.'"[61] Later that year, on June 28, Sheriff John Montgomery of Maricopa County, Arizona, and a gang of deputies "wrecked a garden of a Mexican resident" near the town of Peoria. The unnamed male resident protested that "the marihuana grew as a weed in his garden and that he had not indulged in it nor sold it to his friends." The officers apparently had little evidence against the garden owner, as the *Bisbee Daily Review* reported that "whether or not he will be prosecuted could not be learned."[62] Almost a year later, on June 5, 1920, Maricopa deputies raided another garden, this one at the home of Joe Garcia in Glendale. They confiscated $1,000 worth of cannabis stored in "about 50 tobacco cans of different brands." Most of it came from a plant that "had been growing in the back yard of the Garcia home."[63]

Despite the USDA's efforts, small, illegal cannabis crops like the ones pulled up in the Southwest would not give way to large-scale legal ones, even with the sinsemilla trick. The last edition of *Farmers' Bulletin* 663 to contain cannabis instructions was published in 1927; its only new information was that the drug's market price had held steady since 1920 at around thirty cents per pound.[64] This was well below the average price for all drug plants mentioned in the report, which was around eighty-eight cents per pound.[65] While there was still some demand for medical cannabis, it was not large enough to warrant mass planting, and American farmers could make more money growing other drug plants anyway. Nevertheless, the existence of government-sanctioned ganja farms in the early twentieth century directly refutes contemporary accounts in the popular press, many of which insisted that the plant was a foreign menace.

Cannabis Confusion

For at least two decades after the turn of the century, marijuana the menace and cannabis the medicine collided in the American Southwest, turning the region into a kind of botanical borderland—a place where both identities of the plant existed simultaneously. Eventually, the ghastly reputation of cannabis that originated in Mexico was adopted by American officials and sensationalist newspapers, and over the next three decades marijuana the menace came to supersede cannabis the medicine in the popular imagination.[66] This transition was helped by the fact that, although it was readily available, the American public was unfamiliar with drug cannabis before 1920, meaning that many Americans were introduced to the plant through the marijuana narrative.[67]

Increasing restrictions on the plant and its growing reputation as a dangerous drug apparently did not prevent Mexicans and Mexican Americans from using it medicinally. For example, between 1912 and 1915, the Texas merchant firm T. Puente & Son advertised "marihuana," elderflower ("*flor de sauco*"), wild rose petals ("*rosa de castilla*"), and laurel as medicinal herbs ("*yerbas medicinales*") in *La Revista de Taos*, the Spanish-language paper of Taos, New Mexico.[68] Similarly, the *El Paso Herald* reported in 1914 that "allopathic physicians" in Mexico used cannabis "in the treatment of rheumatism" as well as "diseases of the bladder."[69]

Because cannabis was still considered to have medicinal value, some Southwestern officials and druggists were reluctant to condemn it as a dangerous weed. In 1908 the *Florida Star* reported that James Love of the

Texas Department of Agriculture "returned from a trip to the marihuana producing region of Mexico, bringing with him ten pounds of the seed of the plant which he will plant" at an "agricultural experimental station near Cuero."[70] Echoing the prevailing opinions of American medicine, Love believed "that the plant can be put to good use as a drug," that it "is known to be a cure for asthma, and it is also thought to be valuable in the treatment of tuberculosis." The Florida paper added that "marihuana" was "a far more powerful" species of "India Hemp . . . recognized in the material medica as a valuable drug." But it apparently subscribed to cannabis's ugly Mexican reputation, claiming that "[t]he marihuana weed is known as the most harmful of narcotic drugs," one that leads to "a series of insanity that frequently ends in death."[71]

Associations with marijuana and violence in the Southwest only increased as the Mexican Revolution escalated during the mid-1910s and displaced many Mexicans over the border into Texas. In 1913 a grand jury in El Paso, Texas, called for a ban on cannabis sales after a series of violent incidents allegedly caused by marijuana were reported in neighboring Juárez, Mexico.[72] Although the jury argued that "steps be immediately taken to prevent the promiscuous sale" of the plant, the city council did not deliver such a ban until June 3, 1915.[73] The ban came just two weeks after chief deputy sheriff Stanley Good told the *El Paso Herald* that "most Mexicans in this section are addicted to the [marijuana] habit" and that "marihuana . . . demands regulatory measures similar to those enforced against . . . other harmful drugs."[74] Good raved at the passage of the ban, telling the *Herald* the next day that "none better than peace officers appreciate the beneficial effects" of the ban, because "we officers have had the best opportunity to study the effects of the drug upon the human system."[75] By claiming that law officers—not physicians or scientists—were policymakers' most reliable source on drug cannabis, Good rebuffed the popular notion that only educated professionals could help solve societal problems.

Predictably, physicians and druggists disagreed with Good, as evident in their own response to the ban several days later. Although they agreed that "marihuana is a dangerous drug," representatives of the medical community wrote that "no mention is made in the new law that it may be used legitimately," adding that "nearly all of the drug stores in the city have quantities on hand for use in prescriptions."[76] No action was immediately taken to amend the law, and it is unclear whether druggists were allowed to continue selling cannabis. What is certain is that medical interest in El Paso's newest outlaw continued after the ban. In 1916, Dr. G. H. Bobertz of Detroit wrote Dr. John F. Edgar in El Paso, "inquiring into the medicinal properties . . . of the Mexican weed known as marihuana."[77] Similarly, an "F. Z. Fairman" reminded readers of the *El Paso Herald* in 1917 that "while we hear a great deal about the terrible effects of smoking marihuana . . . an extract of the plant, 'cannabis indica,' is the basis for most corn medicines."[78] But Fairman's comment also reaffirmed the popular belief that the effects of cannabis were determined by the race and class of the user: "while the smoking of Indian hemp, or hasheesh, has been affected by many artistic and literary people for the narcotic effect, the results produced by smoking marihuana by less cultivated people are murderous inclinations."[79] The medicine-menace distinction was coded into state law in 1919, when the Texas legislature passed a bill prohibiting the sale of marijuana "except upon prescription."[80]

Around the same time in Albuquerque, military officials worried about American soldiers turning to the "use of marihuana" amidst broader restrictions on alcohol in the buildup to New Mexico's voter-approved liquor ban in November 1917.[81] In response to the military's concern, the Albuquerque City Council passed an ordinance banning all sales of the plant, including those from drug "firms," on September 12.[82] The friction between medicine and menace was also evident in Arizona, where as late as 1921 Governor Thomas E. Campbell vetoed a bill that would have outlawed the "raising or selling, gift or use of marihuana."[83] While the governor "approved of the intent of the bill," he "considered the measure too drastic, since it would render impossible the use of marihuana as a medicine."[84]

While some Southwestern doctors and officials defended the plant's use as a medicine, American newspapers unintentionally bolstered the marijuana menace by confusing the effects of cannabis with those of other mind-altering plants, including opium (*Papaver somniferum*), Jimson weed (*Datura stramonium*), and locoweed (*Astragalus mollissimus*).[85] By the early twentieth century, Americans had varying degrees of experience with all three substances. Additionally, stories about hashish—a sticky concentrate of cannabis resin that was smoked or eaten in South Asia, the Middle East, North Africa, and Europe—further complicated Americans' understanding of drug cannabis. Reports of hashish use were typically filtered through longstanding European stereotypes about the "Orient," an imaginary place that encompassed most of Asia and the Middle East and was filled with oversensualized and uncivilized people—the alleged opposite of the hard-working, vice-shunning European or American.[86] However inaccurate it was, existing knowledge about opium, Jimson weed, locoweed, and hashish influenced American newspapers' coverage of drug cannabis; the marijuana menace in the United States was not simply an appropriation of Mexican ideas but was distilled from a variety of assumptions about people and plants.

Opium had a poor reputation in the United States even before the anti-vice crusades of the twentieth century. Chinese immigrants and laborers first brought the practice of smoking opium to the American West during the nineteenth century, and the Civil War (1861–1865) made thousands of morphine addicts.[87] Anti-Chinese sentiment was behind the country's first opium ban, enacted in San Francisco in 1875, as well as numerous state bans thereafter.[88] The terrible effects of opiate addiction were well known by the late nineteenth century; they took up the majority of Dr. H. H. Kane's 1881 book *Drugs That Enslave*.[89] While cannabis does not physically "enslave" users—though it can lead to psychological dependence—it can induce sleep and vivid dreams, both of which were known effects of opium. The *Daily East Oregonian* illustrated the presumed connections between cannabis, opium, and the "Orient" in a 1908 report on hashish use:

> Hashish . . . is used by the Persians, Turks and Egyptians in a manner akin to the use of opium by the Chinese . . . The drug has the power of inducing sleep and producing pleasant and fantastic dreams. Continued use of hashish renders its devotees wild and restless, and results in a complete wreck of their mental and physical constitution.[90]

The *East Oregonian* managed to distinguish between opium and cannabis, but its counterpart, the *Morning Oregonian*, was more than a little confused in 1915, after Portland police confirmed that several drugstores had sold hashish to minors. The paper correctly identified hashish as "cannabis indica" in one report, but then strangely described it as "a substitute for opium," and even as "an opiate" in others.[91] Erroneous connections between the two drug plants continued into the 1920s; in 1925, the *Bakersfield Californian* warned of "a new dope traffic" that, like the old Chinese opium trade, threatened "to create a furor in America's western states." The report went on to incorrectly claim that cannabis seeds delivered a "narcotic in greater proportions than opium in poppies."[92] In 1928, after explaining that men in India go on stabbing sprees after using "hasheesh," the *San Antonio Light* branded "marijuana" as "American hasheesh," suggesting that an Oriental menace had made its way to the United States across the southern border.[93]

While both opium and hashish were considered "Oriental" drugs, Jimson weed and locoweed were two toxic plants that shared the Southwestern landscape with cannabis. Jimson weed—*toloache* in Spanish—is a short-growing, weedy herb that produces spiny seed pods and purple flowers. It contains an alkaloid-based toxin that, when smoked or ingested, causes a number of debilitating effects, including delirium, strange behavior, intense amnesia, and death from organ paralysis.[94] A recent medical text concludes that "the overwhelming majority of those who describe the use of *Datura* find their experiences extremely mentally and physically unpleasant and not infrequently physically dangerous."[95] Locoweed, meanwhile, is a perennial legume frequently consumed by livestock. The plant contains an alkaloid toxin that affects the central nervous system and can cause anorexia, lethargy, seizures, and death in animals.[96]

Both plants look nothing like the distinct *Cannabis* genus and are far more dangerous. But descriptions of marijuana's effects at the time closely resembled those of *Datura* and *Astragalus*, and newspapers used the word "locoweed" in reference to all three plants. For example, in its 1897 report of alleged "mariguana" smuggling, the *Tombstone Prospector* called the drug "a kind of loco weed."[97] The *Weekly Herald* of Amarillo, Texas, mimicked this report in 1907 when it stated that "the marihuana weed, comonly [sic] known as the 'loco' weed, was smuggled into the penitentiary at Guadalajara [Mexico]."[98] Earlier that year, New Mexico's *Socorro Chieftain* stated that "there is every indication that the deaths of many horses near Nogales was from eating the loco weed" and that the plant in question was "the greatest danger threatening the cattle industry of the country"—a clear reference to *Astragalus*, which is indeed a major threat to livestock.[99] Cannabis, meanwhile, was not growing wild in many places in the United States at the time. Over the next several years, reporters apparently learned to differentiate between the plants, but not their effects. In a 1914 story headlined "Poisonous Weeds of Mexico Cause Death," the *El Paso Herald* reported that "marihuana" addicts "lose their minds and never recover," while "tolvache [sic]" (*Datura*) was "a kind of loco weed" that will "make a person desperately insane for life."[100] The article failed to note that both plants grew in the United States, too—the USDA even circulated cultivation instructions.[101]

A popular Mexican legend also helped mix up the plants in the minds of reporters. The story went like this: after France's Napoleon III abandoned his campaign to conquer Mexico in 1866, vengeful Mexicans used a native plant to poison Empress Carlota, wife of Maximilian, the Austrian prince whom Napoleon selected to rule Mexico. Crazed by the poisonous plant, Carlota returned to Europe and was rendered permanently insane.[102] In reports of dangerous Mexican plants in the early twentieth century, American newspapers revived this legend but apparently did not agree on which plant did the deed; "toache" (*Datura*) and "marihuana" were both named as the guilty plant in various reports.[103] The true story did not include a poisoning: Carlota did leave Mexico in 1867, but that was because France had withdrawn its troops a year earlier, leaving her and Maximilian defenseless; she returned to Europe to ask Napoleon for reinforcements. Her efforts were unsuccessful, and Maximilian was eventually captured and executed by Mexican forces under Benito Juárez. By that time it was evident that Carlota did in fact suffer from some kind of mental illness, a condition that intensified after the death of her husband but was not known to be caused by any kind of plant toxin. The *Mexican Herald* dispelled this myth in American newspapers as late as 1901.[104]

The poisoning story was pure fiction, but that did not stop the *Ogden Standard* in Utah from reviving it in September 1915.[105] Just two months earlier, several groups of Mexicans had conducted a series of deadly raids on Anglo-American communities in south Texas.[106] The *Standard* attributed the raids to "Marihuana," claiming that Mexicans lack "real nerve and courage" and would never exhibit such a "sudden burst of bravery" unless spurred on by the very same "loco-weed" that drove Carlota "hopelessly insane."[107] Like other newspapers, the *Standard* confused cannabis with locoweed, asserting that "the marihuana seems to be nothing less than the loco-weed that causes insanity to both men and beast." The article also repeatedly blends the marihuana menace with nativist fears of a Mexican takeover, claiming that the Mexican who smokes the drug believes "he can, single handed, whip the entire regular United States army," and that "with each [marihuana] cigarette the desire to take the United States and annex it to Mexico seems to become stronger."[108] As historian Isaac Campos wrote, identifying the plant as uniquely Mexican and linking it to other plants that actually caused insanity helped the American media solidify the "'Mexicanness' of marijuana and its reported tendency to produce madness."[109]

With its treasure trove of racist assumptions and nativist chest-beating, the *Ogden Standard*'s claim that the raids were the result of one big Mexican drug trip can hardly be taken seriously. But the newspaper's fear of a larger plan to take the United States was not as farfetched as it might seem. In fact, the 1915 raids were part of an organized act of resistance by Mexicans and Mexican Americans called *El Plan de San Diego* ("The Plan of San Diego"), an anti-American manifesto drawn up by radical Mexican revolutionaries in January. It called for Mexicans living in the United States, as well as Japanese, African Americans, and Native Americans, to join forces and retake the states of Arizona, California, Colorado, New Mexico, and Texas, thus forming an independent republic that could eventually be annexed to post-revolution Mexico. Followers of the plan included soldiers loyal to revolutionary general Venustiano Carranza as well as many *Tejanos*—Texans of Mexican descent—who were tired of being discriminated against in the United States. Execution of the plan was delayed until July, when adherents launched guerilla attacks against Americans on both sides of the border. Raiding continued on a sporadic basis through the spring of 1916, when an attack on a New Mexican town by Francisco "Pancho" Villa, another revolutionary general, brought the United States and Mexico to the brink of war. [110]

In all, followers of El Plan de San Diego only managed to kill twenty-one American soldiers and civilians, while the American backlash resulted in the execution of some three hundred Mexicans and Mexican Americans in south Texas.[111] There is no evidence that "marihuana" or

"Is the Mexican Nation 'Locoed' by a Peculiar Weed?" This spread in the *Ogden Standard* encapsulates many elements of Americans' growing fear and misunderstanding of cannabis in the early twentieth century. A headline with menacing typeface sits above an article that features racist commentary about Mexicans, a popular myth about the Empress Carlota, and confused statements about poisonous plants. Source: The *Ogden Standard*, September 25, 1915, Utah Digital Newspapers (https://newspapers.lib. utah.edu/).

any other drug inspired the drafting or execution of the plan, suggesting that Mexicans who fought to direct the future of two nations did in fact possess a great deal of "real nerve and courage." The *Ogden Standard*'s terrifying tale of drug-crazed Mexicans was almost entirely inaccurate, but it was nonetheless grounded in the legitimate fear of violence spilling over from revolution-wracked Mexico.

Although it stopped short of including cannabis in the Harrison Act of 1914, there is evidence that the federal government shared at least some of the *Ogden Standard*'s concerns about marijuana. On September 25, 1915, the same day the *Standard* ran its anti-Mexican piece, the Department of the Treasury advised US customs to "refuse admission" to all imported cannabis "unless it is to be used for medicinal purposes"—a response to Southwestern officials' calls to curb the marijuana trade.[112] Of course, the example of T. Puente & Son suggests that Mexican immigrants did use the

herb for medicinal purposes, but since they were unlikely to obtain cannabis through the proper channels—via prescription and a licensed druggist—officials in Washington and the Southwest could not have acknowledged such use as legitimate. Anyway, the suggestion that Mexicans or
Mexican Americans were using cannabis appropriately was likely to be
ignored in the context of the marijuana menace, the recent raids in Texas,
and the violent shadow of the Mexican Revolution.

Despite the ongoing production of hemp, the government's circulation
of cultivation instructions, and the opinions of professionals and officials
who saw drug cannabis as a medicine, the marijuana menace emerged as
the dominant cannabis narrative in the United States after the turn of the
century. This was largely due to the American media, which had blended
Mexican folklore, popular anti-vice sentiments, European ideas about the
"Orient," and the fears of white nativists into a plant portrait that was
both terrifying and appealing. In its attempts to both inform the public
and sell papers, the press exploited all of these popular views as well as
plant biology, effectively reducing several distinct plant species into one
horrifying organism: "marijuana," an "American hasheesh" that lurks in
foreign (mostly Mexican) bodies and has the murderous effects of all the
known "locoweeds." It is unknown what effect this reporting had on the
public, but it is certainly evident that early-century journalists were able
to shift the identity of cannabis from medicine to menace by connecting
the plant to popular ideas about race, class, and the threat posed by "narcotic" drugs.

"Cannabis Americana"

In the first two decades of the twentieth century, the popular press depicted
drug cannabis as a foreign substance, only occasionally admitting that
it could be grown in the United States. Progressive-Era bureaucrats and
lawmakers passed anti-cannabis laws not in response to widespread use
but largely as a preemptive strike against another potential "narcotic" fixa-
tion. But as the San Antonio Light's description of an "American hasheesh"
suggests, the "foreign" aspect of cannabis began to subside in the popular press during the 1920s and 1930s, to be replaced with hand-wringing
about more Americans using the drug and cannabis's ability to grow virtually everywhere Americans lived. These new concerns coincided with

the arrival of drug cannabis on the urban, African American jazz scene; ongoing immigration from Mexico; and an increasing number of white Americans using and trading in the weed. Having already ensconced in the public imagination the terrible attributes of marijuana—around this time newspapers began spelling it with a *j* instead of an *h*—the seemingly ubiquitous presence of the plant in the American environment became the newest weapon in the press's anti-cannabis arsenal.

In 1927, for example, the *Denver Post* reported that "marihuana grows in southern Colorado, New Mexico and Arizona," and that "[f]or many years it was used extensively by Mexicans . . . but now it is gaining favor among Americans."[113] That same year Ray Talbot, a state representative in Colorado who pushed for broader restrictions on cannabis, claimed that "it is grown in large quantities by Mexicans in their back yards."[114] A year later E. A. Hedman, a Utah detective, told the *Salt Lake Tribune* that the plant "grows prolifically in this climate."[115]

But perhaps the best example of cannabis portrayed as a foreign threat turned domestic comes from a full-page illustrated spread on marijuana in the *Denver Post* on December 30, 1928. The headline and subhead ran in bold type across the top of the page: "A Home-Grown New Drug That Drives Its Victims Mad: Raised in Any Backyard and Smoked in Cigarettes, Marihuana Is the Most Deadly Narcotic Now Fought by the U.S." The immediate call of attention to the drug plant's presence in places as mundane as the American backyard, as well as to its cigarette disguise, emphasized the discreet, deceptive nature of the threat. The article itself is an amalgam of contemporary American tropes about cannabis. The very first line reads, "Hasheesh orgies, rivalling those of the ancient Oriental days, are being staged nightly in New York's Greenwich Village." It goes on to tell of a "hardy plant" that "grows readily in the New York climate" and in vacant lots, noting that "the Mexican and Cuban elements in New York are familiar with the weed and most of the purveyors are of Latin extraction." Users experience sensations "rivaling even those produced by opium." The plant itself is referred to as the "loco weed," "Oriental hemp," and even "Cannabis Americana." The article also mentions that "[m]ari-huana smoking appeals to a certain bohemian, free-thinking, imaginative group of artists, writers, musicians, and others."[116] This observation, absent from most reports until the 1920s, marked marijuana's prevalence in the contemporary music scene and also foreshadowed the drug's place in the counterculture of the mid-twentieth century.

Images accompanying the article drove home both the nearness and the gendered nature of the threat. A photograph titled "Scene of Planting" shows what is allegedly cannabis growing amidst common brush in a vacant New York lot, while an artist's rendering of "Parties in Greenwich Village" shows flapper girls with carefree expressions dancing and lying about, presumably losing their inhibitions after a smoke. Another set of illustrations running across the middle of the page depicts a young, white, well-dressed woman picking flowers off an inaccurately drawn cannabis plant. She rolls them into a cigarette and presents a cluster of flowers for a "close-up of the weed."[117] The article reports that most cannabis dealers were men "of Latin extraction," so why did the artist draw a young, white woman picking the flowers and rolling the cigarettes? As the primary purpose of the spread is to convey the creeping nature of the marijuana threat, the illustrator probably chose to make his cannabis-preparing subject look more like someone who could be the reader's daughter, sister, or niece. Looking at the spread in all its hysterical glory, it's easy to imagine Denver parents cartoonishly spitting out a mouthful of Sunday morning coffee upon reading that their kids could so easily pluck a "deadly narcotic" from the lot down the street.[118]

Regardless of whether it achieved its desired effect, the spread reiterated earlier negative ideas about the plant and overlooked a basic element of its natural life cycle. The argument that drug cannabis relieved white women of their inhibitions and made them sexually vulnerable to drug dealers and nonwhite men became a common theme in anti-cannabis propaganda of the 1920s and 1930s, and it was connected to the drug's presence in the mixed-race jazz scene. Moreover, not all cannabis growing in vacant lots was the work of devious drug dealers—it was often simply the work of the wind or seed-eating birds, which distributed hemp as well as drug cannabis across the urban landscape.

By its ability to simply grow in close proximity to Americans, cannabis denied white, middle-class observers the familiar distance between themselves and dangerous "narcotic" drugs. While heroin and morphine could be obtained from dealers on the street corner, the substances themselves had to be imported from far-off "Oriental" lands. But not marijuana, which the *Post* asserted could be picked like strawberries. This is a crucial, if overlooked, part of why the marijuana menace narrative so easily took hold in the minds of Americans. It wasn't just that Mexicans and other disdained minorities used the drug; nature also contributed to the anti-cannabis consensus, placing the plant uncomfortably close to Americans at a time when anti-vice attitudes were not only prevalent but deemed a necessary component of the American legal system.

The Myth of the Menace and the Road to Prohibition

Did marijuana—with an *h* or a *j*—truly pose a threat to the public at the time? It is not likely, considering that sensationalism had a decisive edge over objectivity in the press during the early twentieth century, and the Southwest borderlands were awash in violence related to the Mexican Revolution. Additionally, middle- and upper-class citizens in both Mexico and the United States—the writers and readers of newspapers—held demeaning stereotypes of racial minorities and the laboring classes, people who at that time accounted for the majority of cannabis users in both countries.[119]

Recent studies considering the relationship between drug cannabis and violence indicate that a minority of users with histories of mental illness or aggression are more likely to experience increased aggression with cannabis use or withdrawal.[120] Studies performed on the general cannabis-using population have been deemed inconclusive.[121] But there are between 119 and 124 million cannabis users worldwide, and little if anything to show for cannabis-induced crime waves.[122] Violent crime actually decreased in Washington and Colorado after both states legalized adult cannabis use in 2012.[123] Cannabis users have also been shown to be far less prone to violence than alcohol or cocaine users.[124]

Other data shows that the number of negative cannabis incidents, violent or not, varies strikingly by country, possibly indicating a cultural factor in the drug experience.[125] Historian Isaac Campos argues for a cultural correlation in Mexico, writing that "it seems quite plausible that violent outbursts related to marijuana manifested themselves in nineteenth- and early-twentieth-century Mexico as a kind of 'culture-bound syndrome,' whether fueled by the realities of the insanity defense, by fears of witchcraft and poisoning by psychotomimetic drugs, or simply in a kind of feedback relationship with the widespread belief that marijuana caused madness.[126] Given the stressful nature of their day-to-day experiences, some prisoners and soldiers—the two demographics most commonly associated with the drug in Mexico—likely suffered from some kind of mental illness, which has been shown to influence the cannabis experience. In short, outside of unique cultural contexts and individuals already suffering from mental illness, there isn't much evidence supporting the notion that drug cannabis causes violence.

As they are today, violent events involving cannabis appeared to have been relatively rare upon the arrival of the so-called marijuana menace. Amidst approximately 165 mentions of "marihuana" in Southwest newspapers between 1900 and 1919, only fourteen reports, or 8.4 percent, mentioned a specific violent crime linked to cannabis.[127] This amounts to less than one violent cannabis incident per year, with some of the crimes occurring in Mexico. And not everyone who read reports of marijuana-induced violence was convinced; in 1926, for example, a Dr. W. A. Evans penned a reply to a marijuana story in the *Salt Lake Tribune*, arguing that the newspaper was "mistaken in thinking the drug is habit-forming, or that it renders its victim a public menace."[128] Evans backed up his argument with the testimony of Dr. Horatio Wood, the University of Pennsylvania botanist who took cannabis extract himself and documented his experiences as early as 1869.[129]

Of course, the occasional objection from medical professionals failed to prevent the crystallization of the menace narrative. Returning to Arizona, where in the late nineteenth century "cannabis indica" was at least partially known as a remedial herb, by 1935 "marijuana" was fully entrenched in a persistent folklore about a "lawless" Wild West. In an interview with reporter Willa Gibbs of the *Bakersfield Californian*, Maricopa County deputy Tony Orabuena described run-ins with female killer Winnie Ruth Judd, murderous cowboys, and "marijuana fiends":

> There's something sinister about a man under the influence of marijuana," he said. "You know what an eerie feeling you get when a sleepwalker lurches towards you. Those men are like that—only worse. They're absolutely insane—violently so. Their eyes are funny—kind of animalish, and seem to have red sparks in them.[130]

After the interview, Orabuena was said to have returned to Arizona, "a lawless country of marijuana fiends, drunken cowboys, and hot-blooded Spaniards."[131]

Modern scientific evidence and the spotty occurrence of marijuana-related violence in the turn-of-the-century Southwest indicate that cannabis's threat to the public was greatly exaggerated, even if some users may have been prone to violence. The 1935 testimony of an Arizona sheriff's deputy, who routinely came into contact with society's most violent and deranged outliers, is hardly a refutation of that fact. And yet over the next two decades, the classist and racist ideology of the marijuana menace—an irrational fear of a common plant and the marginalized people who used it—would spread beyond the Southwest and become the dominant narrative in the American media. It would then infect the federal bureaucracy, which would shun science and ignore objections from its own medical counsel in order to prohibit cannabis in 1937.

CHAPTER 2

Prohibition Is for the Birds

Nature, Race, and the Marihuana Tax Act

In July 1956, Sidney Silverstein and his wife were delighted to find "two leafy, tree-like plants" growing "lustily" in the backyard of their home in Long Beach, California. The couple had just purchased the property on Los Coyotes Boulevard, where the previous owner had kept an "aviary filled with parakeets." The plants were about six feet tall and the Silversteins assumed the "attractive shade trees" were weeping willows. But when Mrs. Silverstein gave a sprout from one of the plants to her sister, Lucille Price, Price's gardener identified them as "marijuana," a plant that had been federally outlawed in 1937.[1]

Concerned that their shade trees might be outlaw plants, the Silversteins called the police. Sergeant W. L. Penhollow and officer Robert P. Shaw also identified the plants as "marijuana." They claimed the two plants had some $4,000 worth of the drug hanging on their branches. "It is believed," reported the *Long Beach Press Telegram*, "that the bird seed fed to the parakeets contained some nonsterile marijuana seeds. These few seeds, passed out onto the ground in droppings from the parakeets, found a fertile spot to grow and the two marijuana plants were produced."[2]

The Silversteins' experience was actually quite common in metropolitan California during the 1950s. Two years earlier, Long Beach resident Fred Tryon and his wife tended a "luxuriant 14-foot shade bush" that also turned out to be cannabis.[3] Three months after the cops removed the Silversteins' plants, another Long Beach resident "suffered the embarrassment" of finding cannabis on her property; a neighbor saw a plant in Mrs. Barney Kane's yard and joked, "I'll bet that's marijuana." Kane called the police just to be sure. They told her it was.[4] Kane's neighbor wasn't the only one poking fun at the routine situation: "As a way to enliven the dull routine of suburban life," quipped the *Redlands Daily Facts* in 1959, "how about a little sign on the front lawn: 'Please do not walk on the marijuana.'"[5] Twelve days later,

Daily Facts columnists Bill and Frank Moore asked readers, "Are you sure you don't have a marijuana bush growing in your yard?" The writers quoted Captain Robert Graefe of the San Bernardino County sheriff's vice squad, who plainly summarized the situation: "Dope is an urban problem."[6] In all, between 1950 and 1959 there were at least twenty-four reports of cannabis popping out of the urban landscape—from gardens, yards, roadsides, and sidewalk cracks.[7]

The appearance of cannabis in cities wasn't so much an urban "problem" as it was an urban fixture. The plant had found a comfortable niche in urban ecosystems well before it was effectively outlawed by the passage of the Marihuana Tax Act in 1937.[8] Recall the *Denver Post*'s 1928 spread showing stands of cannabis growing in New York City lots. Industrial expansion during World War II and the explosive sprawl of suburbs after the war widened the footprint of cities and suburbs, creating more cannabis-friendly habitat. This occurred all over the nation, but as the preponderance of reports from California suggests, the sun-loving weed found the well-watered lawns and gardens of the Golden State to be particularly ideal. Some homeowners, including the Silversteins and Tryons, found wild cannabis to be a positive addition to their gardens—that is, until the police showed up and told them they were harboring an outlaw.[9] But not all the plants in these cases were marijuana, even if authorities like Penhollow and Graefe said so.

By the 1950s, hemp seed had been a common ingredient in American birdseed for at least fifty years; in 1937, the year Congress passed the Marihuana Tax Act, Americans bought some four million pounds of hemp birdseed.[10] In addition to their exceptional nutritional content, the oil in hemp seeds helps birds produce and maintain healthy feathers. On the ground, in outdoor cages, or in bird feeders, live cannabis seeds waited to be devoured by a variety of seed-eating urban flyers, including the house sparrow, common starling, pigeon, house finch, brown-headed cowbird, and mourning dove, as well as pet chirpers such as the canary and parakeet. Small mammals such as squirrels and chipmunks also fed on birdseed, providing another way for cannabis to spread its weedy progeny. By air or land, animals deposited seeds in their droppings. Once a female plant sprouted, it relied on the wind to bring pollen from male plants, dropped its seeds to the ground, and the cycle began anew in vacant lots, ditches, roadsides, and other open, disturbed sites across the urban and suburban landscape.

Marijuana Found on Lawn of Long Beach Home

POLICE WARNING—Have you a little marijuana plant at your home? That's what police wonder, and it is one reason these two pictures are being published. Sgt. Howard Sweet is shown with some marijuana plants found growing wild in a lawn at a west Long Beach home. The occupants at the residence didn't know what kind of plants they were but they "grew so fast we left them alone." Insp. George Doyle of the police narcotics detail says the illegal plants may be growing elsewhere over the city and gives a closeup of a leaf to identify them. Anyone finding such a plant should call the police.—(Press-Telegram photo.)

"Marijuana" grows wild on American lawns. In the 1950s dozens of bewildered residents in suburban California found cannabis growing on their property. The plants' haphazard growth and noticeable lack of flowers suggest they were nonpsychoactive hemp spread by seed-eating birds, but police mistakenly identified the plants as marijuana and ripped them up. The homeowners were rarely, if ever, charged with a crime. Source: *Long Beach Press-Telegram*, July 9, 1952, newspaperarchive.com.

Most of these seeds came from nondrug stock and could only yield tall, fibrous hemp plants, just like the ones described in contemporary reports. Thus, the plants in the yards of the Silversteins, Tryons, and Mrs. Barney Kane were likely nonpsychoactive hemp dispersed by birds or other natural means. Birdseed companies successfully lobbied Congress to create an exemption in the Tax Act for hemp seed, on the condition that the companies sterilize the seeds.[11] Again, this was unnecessary, as hemp is nonpsychoactive, but it demonstrates how the cryptic and dual nature of cannabis undermined prohibition from its inception.

Birdseed and feral hemp stands were not the only ways in which cannabis thwarted the Marihuana Tax Act. Authorities sometimes wasted manpower and resources destroying legitimate hemp crops.[12] The herb further outflanked authorities by attaching itself to white, middle-class subcultures, including youths and young adults in the suburbs and free-spirited artists, authors, and musicians in the cities. This latter group, which eventually became known as the Beat Generation, was the first to incorporate drug cannabis into a way of life that deliberately ran against the grain of mainstream American culture.

But even as it was undermined by acts of people and nature, cannabis criminalization did serve a purpose—albeit one far less noble than protecting the public from a "dangerous" drug. Prohibition functioned as a convenient way for authorities to control populations often seen as the main class of drug users and criminals and as a corrupting influence on an otherwise hardworking and morally pure society.[13] Black, brown, and poor Americans were targeted, harassed, and thrown in jail, often for simply possessing a plant that helped them get by in one way or another.[14]

Many histories of cannabis have discussed the racially charged origins of the Marihuana Tax Act.[15] Although the act is no longer in effect, cannabis prohibition endures today and still acts disproportionately against black and brown Americans. Black Americans are almost four times more likely to be arrested for cannabis-related crimes than white Americans, even though both groups use the drug at similar rates.[16] As previously mentioned, Latinos are at least twice as likely to be arrested for cannabis crimes as whites, even though they, too, use it and other illicit drugs at roughly the same rates.[17] The racist attitudes and assumptions that helped bring about the country's first federal anti-cannabis law set the stage for ongoing racial disparity in the enforcement of prohibition.

Attitudes about nature also play a role in cannabis prohibition; considering nature along with the role of race allows additional insight that could inform current debates about whether to abandon prohibition altogether. Time and again, environmental historians have demonstrated that governments ignore ecology at their own peril.[18] A fresh look at the Marihuana Tax Act hearings and subsequent enforcement efforts reveals that, in addition to basing its drug policy on questionable and sensationalized information, the US government tripped over its own ecological ignorance.

Lawmakers during the hearings had many chances to see how nature would thwart the ambitious act, whether through birds, wind, or people. Although they were aware that cannabis was a plant with certain problematic attributes—drug content, a fast growth cycle, remarkable adaptability to climate—most failed to consider how those attributes allowed cannabis to thrive within a web of relationships that had already made it an inextricable part of the American landscape. Its drug content, for instance, was attractive to humans, who had by 1937 brought it to virtually every corner of the continental United States. But in the end it wasn't knowledge, or lack thereof, that won the day in 1937; rather, it was the most dangerous drug of all—fear.

Manufacturing a Crisis

In many ways, Harry J. Anslinger is the patron saint of drug warriors the world over. Born in Pennsylvania in 1892, he did investigative work for the Pennsylvania Railroad, the War Department, as a vice-consul in Germany, and as a consul in Venezuela and the Bahamas before he was named assistant commissioner of the Federal Bureau of Prohibition in 1929. Many of his duties abroad involved the investigation of drug trafficking and other illegal rackets.[19] After a year of battling bootleggers, he was named head of the newly formed Federal Bureau of Narcotics (FBN) in 1930.[20] Anslinger's intentions were decent enough; a competent detective with a vivid, imaginative pen, his tireless work as FBN commissioner was driven by a genuine interest in protecting the public from alcohol and other harmful drugs.[21]

By upbringing and instinct, Anslinger was a staunch prohibitionist, but he could also be pragmatic. In 1929, for instance, he stated that alcohol prohibition "will never succeed through the promulgation of a mere law observance program," and as late as the mid-1930s he resisted calls for federal anti-cannabis laws, believing that "the needed legislation must be left to the states, due to the ease with which the plant can be grown in any American climate."[22] At any rate, the commissioner could hardly concern himself with cannabis at the time, because according to journalist and cannabis historian Martin Lee, Anslinger "had only three hundred G-men on his roster, hardly enough to tackle heroin and cocaine let alone a common weed."[23]

But Anslinger's pragmatism had its limits. Sensational reports of cannabis-induced violence nurtured the commissioner's imaginative, vice-crusader side, and he eventually seized the opportunity, laid out for him by the press, to manufacture a national crisis in which the FBN would be the well-funded hero.[24] Anslinger, who had been conducting research on cannabis for several years, argued that it was a "menace"—an argument based on research that was slanted toward negative depictions of the plant and neglected any contradictory evidence, such as a 1935 report by psychiatrist Walter Bromberg that dispatched the notion that cannabis caused crime.[25] Beginning around 1934, the narcotics chief embarked on a feverish propaganda campaign. He wrote editorials, gave radio talks, suggested storylines for low-budget flicks—including the oft-ridiculed *Reefer Madness* (1936)—and built up a "Gore File," his personal collection of photos and news clippings detailing grisly acts supposedly committed by people under the influence of cannabis.[26]

In the early twentieth century, the threat of the alleged "marijuana menace" was greatly exaggerated and rooted in Mexican stereotypes about cannabis users. This was still true to some degree in the early thirties, but it was also clear that Mexicans in the Southwest and blacks in the South were no longer the only groups using the drug. The "free-thinking, bohemian" city dwellers described in the 1928 *Denver Post* article speak to that. When the Great Depression hit, use of the herb by poor whites increased, and by this time a large number of white jazz club denizens had picked up the habit, too.[27] Although sensationalism persisted in the national press throughout the 1930s, newspaper stories linking marijuana to violence are too numerous to ignore. Did the weed drive the people mentioned in these reports to violence? Larry Sloman, author of the cannabis history *Reefer Madness* (1979), argues that such incidents might have been the result of an "uncharted psychic terrain":

> [I]ndividuals who were more prone to be violent for environmental or cultural reasons (i.e., lower-class people) were, in fact, the majority of users of the substance. And since marijuana was a relatively new consciousness-altering substance in American culture, the experience of getting stoned was not so thoroughly defined. . . . In the absence of that, and with a growing stream of propaganda shrilling about the crime-causing properties of the weed, a situation became ripe where to engage in criminal activities while under the weed might be to assert a self-fulfilling prophecy.[28]

This explanation seems to fit with historian Isaac Campos's observations about cannabis use in Mexico, as well as with recent data suggesting that the cannabis experience varies by culture and that the drug is more likely to produce aggressive or bizarre behavior in people suffering from mental illness.[29] Even the 1930s press sometimes admitted that the herb's effects varied; for example, in 1934 the *Denver Post* quoted Dr. R. S. McKelvey, secretary of the state board of health, who said that "the drug is not dependable in effects, and with some persons it creates sleepiness, with others dreams similar to opium, and causes others to become violent."[30] So it seems that, just as they did earlier in the century, law enforcement and the press in the 1930s held up the violent and bizarre actions of some users as universal effects of cannabis, exaggerating the menace.

Anslinger emphasized all kinds of alleged negative effects in his propaganda campaign. In addition to his insistence that the herb magically and unfailingly transformed people into Jekyll-and-Hyde-type monsters, Anslinger played on the gendered racial tensions of the Depression era, arguing that cannabis made white women susceptible to lustful black men and that it drove blacks and Mexicans to commit violent crimes.[31] Mexicans were an easy target: not only were they already associated with "marihuana," but they were also blamed for siphoning welfare funds and taking jobs from needy white Americans.[32] Bowing to these racial anxieties, President Herbert Hoover's administration deported 63,874 Mexicans between 1930 and 1933—an increase of nearly ten thousand per year over the previous administration.[33] By insisting that "marihuana" led to race mixing and turned already marginalized people into criminals, Anslinger could count on widespread support for his anti-cannabis campaign.

On the heels of the multipronged propaganda campaign and with vigorous testimony by Anslinger, Congress passed the Marihuana Tax Act in August 1937. Anslinger drafted the act in conjunction with the Department of the Treasury, and Rep. Robert L. Doughton (D-North Carolina) introduced the bill as H.R. 6385. Although the act technically allowed for the production and distribution of cannabis, anyone wanting to produce, sell, prescribe, or possess the plant had to contact the Treasury Department, purchase and fill out a license form, pay a small annual tax, and keep extensive, detailed records of nearly every operation regarding "marihuana." To do so was an incredible risk, for if a person so licensed failed in any of the required reporting they were subject to fines of up to $2,000 or a prison sentence of up to five years.[34] The law was in blatant violation of the Fifth Amendment, which protects against self-incrimination. However, because the law so often ensnared the nation's most marginalized and powerless people, the constitutionality of the Marihuana Tax Act was not challenged until 1969, when the Supreme Court struck it down. For twenty-two years until then, the FBN was free to unleash its army of drug warriors on anyone holding even the slightest bit of cannabis.

The Hearings-Impaired

The congressional hearings on the Tax Act are among the most analyzed in US drug policy history. They are a testament to the triumph of fact-free dogma in American drug policy as well as to political incompetence, as most members of Congress had not heard of cannabis and did not even bother to figure out what the act addressed before voting for it.[35] The American Medical Association (AMA) opposed the act, but that didn't stop Rep. Fred M. Vinson (D-Kentucky), a proponent of the bill and member of the committee that discussed it, from telling Congress that the bill had AMA support.[36] Importantly, many of the statements given during the hearings reflect the assumption that the government could eradicate the cannabis plant just as easily as it could jail drug users.

Unlike many newspapers that helped establish the marijuana menace in earlier decades, Anslinger and other anti-cannabis authorities were mostly aware in 1937 that they were dealing with the same plant that had a long medicinal history in the United States. Still, earlier myths about cannabis snuck into the hearings. For example, Eugene Stanley, the district attorney for Orleans Parish, Louisiana, submitted a report to Congress claiming that "cannabis . . . is sometimes mentioned in the laws as 'loco weed' because of its inebriate effect upon men and cattle."[37] Anslinger and his supporters, meanwhile, still confused hemp and drug plants, looked faithfully and uncritically on statements of law enforcement and news reports, and ignored testimony from better-informed individuals.

The makeup of the testimony demonstrates the biased nature of the hearings. Of the twenty-six statements delivered in two separate hearings during the spring and summer of 1937, only four came from medical professionals who studied the effects of cannabis on humans. Anslinger, meanwhile, was allowed three statements himself, during which he submitted racist and pseudo-scientific opinions of those who agreed with him. Various segments of his testimony asserted that "marihuana" was medically useless, posed a greater threat to the public than opium, lowered the inhibitions of women, and drove people to commit heinous crimes.[38] The racism that colored the anti-cannabis rhetoric was on full display in a letter written by the city editor of the *Daily Courier* of Alamosa, Colorado:

I wish I could show you what a small marihuana cigaret [sic] can do to one of our degenerate Spanish-speaking residents. That's why our problem is so great; the greatest percentage of our population is composed of Spanish-speaking persons, most of who are low mentally, because of social and racial conditions.[39]

Predictably, the anti-Mexican rhetoric was accompanied by tired tropes from the mythical Orient: "In Persia," Anslinger testified, "a thousand years before Christ, there was a religious and military order founded which was called the Assassins and they derived their name from the drug called hashish which is now known in this country as marihuana."[40] The "Assassins" did exist; they belonged to a distinct sect of Shi'ite Islam during the Crusades and had a knack for stealthily dispatching enemies. Of course, the Crusades did not take place in Persia and occurred well after the time of Christ, not "a thousand years before." The English word "assassin" does in fact come from *hashashiyya*, an old Arabic word meaning "hashish user," but this was a derogatory term given to the Assassins by their Sunni rivals and there is no evidence that the sect used drug cannabis.[41]

Though much of his testimony was sensational, Anslinger did include a few less hysterical and partially true statements about marijuana, including that cannabis "is dangerous to the mind and body, and particularly dangerous to the criminal type," and that it "undoubtedly gives rise to a form of addiction, which has serious social consequences."[42] To bolster many of his more outlandish statements Anslinger relied on a few friends, including Clinton Hester, assistant general counsel for the Treasury Department, and Temple University pharmacologist Dr. James C. Munch.[43] Although he appeared to have the proper credentials, Munch based most of his testimony on experiments with animals, not humans, and he made several harsh claims about the weed without evidence, including "continuous use will tend to cause the degeneration of one part of the brain," and leads to a "disintegration of personality," "extreme inertia," and "violent irritability."[44] None of these claims are backed up by modern scientific studies.[45]

Some of the exaggerative claims made by Munch and Anslinger were countered in a response to a questionnaire submitted as testimony by Dr. W. L. Treadway of the Public Health Service's Division of Mental Hygiene. Treadway stated that "[Cannabis] may be taken a relatively long time without social or emotional breakdown. Marihuana is habit-forming, although not addicting, in the same sense as alcohol might be with some people, or sugar, or coffee"—a comparison that must have horrified the Anslinger camp.[46] Despite Treadway's statement to the contrary, members of the committee continued to refer to cannabis users as "addicts" throughout the hearings.[47]

By far the most objective and reliable testimony on cannabis came from Dr. William C. Woodward, a physician and lawyer who helped draft the Harrison Narcotics Act of 1914 and represented the American Medical Association (AMA) at the Tax Act hearings. Though he admitted that many people were misusing cannabis and that this was reason enough for federal regulation, Woodward denied the certainty of some of Anslinger's claims and assailed the commissioner's camp for making such assertions without "competent primary evidence":

> We are referred to newspaper publications concerning the prevalence of marihuana addiction. We are told that the use of marihuana causes crime. . . . An informed inquiry shows that the Bureau of Prisons has no evidence on that point. You have been told that school children are great users of marihuana cigarettes. . . . Inquiry of the Children's Bureau shows that they have had no occasion to investigate it and know nothing particularly of it.[48]

Woodward made an accurate prediction when he noted that "future investigation may show that there are substantial medical uses for cannabis" and explained that its medical use was minimal at the time because the plant had denied scientists a complete understanding of its compounds and their functions. Woodward also disputed nearly every part of the proposed act, from claims that "marihuana addiction" was increasing to the unfairly high tax that would be shouldered by legitimate medical users, and even to the name of the act itself:

> I use the word "Cannabis" in preference to the word "marihuana," because Cannabis is the correct term for describing the plant and its products. The term "marihuana" is a mongrel word that has crept into this country over the Mexican border and has no general meaning, except as it relates to the use of Cannabis preparations for smoking. . . . I should certainly suggest that if any legislation is enacted, the term used be "Cannabis" and not the mongrel word "marihuana."[49]

Aware that nature would undermine any attempt to stamp out cannabis, Woodward also took aim at the act's enforceability, asking the committee to "realize the difficulty" of deploying the massive "inspection force" that "would be necessary to locate the growth of marihuana even in considerable quantities." The plant, he said, "grows wild along railroad tracks, along highways, on land belonging to the Federal Government, on land belonging to the States, on immense farms and ranches, forest land and places of that sort . . . the Federal Government could never determine where this plant was growing."[50] Ignoring Woodward's legitimate critiques of the bill and hearings, committee members insisted that the doctor opposed the bill simply because he was not consulted in the drafting of it. Woodward denied this, saying "I have drafted too many bills to be peeved about that." He continued to argue that the cannabis "menace" could be resolved by an amendment to the Harrison Act, which would tax sales of the drug without requiring a national eradication campaign.[51]

Doughton, the committee chairman, attempted to rebut Woodward's entire testimony by quoting aloud from a recent editorial in the *Washington Times* that made many of the same false claims Woodward had just refuted:

> The marihuana cigarette is one of the most insidious of all forms of dope, largely because of the failure of the public to understand its fatal qualities. The Nation is almost defenseless against it, having no Federal laws to cope with it . . . High school boys and girls buy the destructive weed without knowledge of its capacity of harm . . . This is a national problem, and it must have national attention. The fatal marihuana cigarette must be recognized as a deadly drug, and American children must be protected against it.[52]

The quotation actually proved Woodward's earlier point that "[n]ewspaper exploitation of the habit has done more to increase it than anything else."[53] But by now it was clear that the committee was not interested in any of Woodward's objections, no matter how valid. They did not expect his thorough undressing of the bill, and when faced with his fact-based critique, committee members responded not with respectful consideration but by questioning both the doctor's motives and his desire to keep Americans safe.

Committee members had already made up their minds before Dr. Woodward spoke, perhaps even before the hearings began. Members were stone-cold terrified by what they read about "marihuana" in the newspapers and what Anslinger told them at the hearings. The newspapers, it must be said, often simply parroted the opinions of law enforcement, which at the time had simplistic and often racist understandings of both crime and drug use. But in the minds of committee members, if even a fraction of what they heard about cannabis was true, the safest choice was to immediately take action via the proposed legislation. Firmly dug in with the Anslinger camp, members wanted Woodward to simply stamp the AMA's approval on the bill. There was no time to deliberate with Woodward and the AMA about how to incorporate cannabis regulation into the Harrison Act, for "marihuana" was already destroying the country. By the end of the hearings, the AMA, representing about 100,000 of some 160,000 physicians in the country, provided the lone voice of opposition to the Marihuana Tax Act.[54] Fear and ignorance triumphed in the Marihuana Tax Act hearings, in the subsequent vote, and in nearly every other federal discussion about cannabis thereafter.

Seeds of Confusion

Dr. Woodward offered plenty of reasons why a federal cannabis purge would be unenforceable. But Anslinger himself realized this back in 1931; the only difference in 1937 was that the commissioner felt more pressure to enact and enforce a federal ban. In his very first statement to the committee during the Tax Act hearings, Anslinger mentioned that Cannabis "is sometimes grown in backyards . . . is sometimes found as a residual weed, and sometimes as the result of a dissemination of birdseed."[55] These statements were much more than an admission of how difficult it would be to enforce the act; they also point to Anslinger's incorrect assumption that wild hemp plants produced a drug product. We now know that THC is barely present in wild plants, even if those plants are drug varieties. Outside of cultivation, the plant does not produce enough THC to be valuable as a drug.[56]

The use of hemp seed as bird food also complicated enforcement of prohibitory cannabis laws, as demonstrated by the case of the Silversteins and others in the 1950s. But this was occurring in many states well before federal prohibition. For example, in 1933, on his ranch near the town of Red Bluff, California, R. W. Hanna planted about one hundred acres of hemp to "provide seed for birds." Authorities cut down and burned the crop after "it was noticed that certain of the plants were being stripped of their leaves."[57] Officers apparently considered this evidence that cannabis users were stalking the field and collecting their drug of choice. But unless they are situated near the flower buds on drug-producing varieties, cannabis leaves rarely contain enough THC to be usable as a drug. So what happened to the leaves? Many cannabis growers have observed deer munching on their crops, typically before the plants reach maturity and the pungent flowers can keep the opportunistic herbivores at bay.[58] The *Woodland Daily Democrat* reported that the area where Hanna planted his hemp had been "converted into a game reserve," and given that his plants were unlikely to be drug producers, it is entirely possible that deer ate the leaves. Here was likely another example of authorities confusing an act of nature with an act of drug seekers.

Had Anslinger and other authorities known in 1937 that neither hemp nor wild cannabis produce a potent drug, they might have crafted legislation targeting cultivated drug cannabis—still a difficult task, but certainly more realistic than tracking down every rogue plant in the country. Even then, confusion might still have occurred because hemp and drug cannabis look so similar. As it was, the same plant that denied American medicine a full understanding of its therapeutic properties in the nineteenth century fooled government authorities in the twentieth century, making them believe they had to wipe out every instance of a common weed instead of one cultivated variety.

The multiple identities of cannabis showed themselves in one way or another during the Tax Act hearings. Representatives from the hemp seed oil, birdseed, and hemp fiber industries, in that order, expressed their concerns about the bill. The committee for the most part indulged them, as the final text of the act included exceptions for all industrial preparations of the plant.[59] Notably, Joseph B. Hertzfield, manager of the feed department for the Philadelphia Seed Company, implicitly refuted the idea of a "marihuana menace" in his opening statement by admitting that hemp birdseed had long been distributed across the country without any issue:

> I want to say at the outset, Mr. Chairman, that our firm is heartily in sympathy with the aims and purposes of this bill, and we have no desire to become parties to spreading this drug around the country. We have been manufacturers of feeds and mixed birdseeds for many years, and in those mixtures hempseed is a very important item.

If the committee had any interest in seriously considering Anslinger's claim that birdseed spread "marihuana," they could have stopped Hertzfield right there and clarified his belief that the drug was not spread by the hemp birdseed. After all, if there had been a dangerous drug sprouting up from birdseed for "many years," why did it just now constitute a national menace? But to do so would have put Anslinger on the defensive, a position he rarely found himself in during the hearings; as it did throughout the entire hearings, fear trumped both Congressional duty and common sense, and the proceedings went on.

If they failed to question Anslinger's claims about the source of drug cannabis, committee members displayed some sense of duty later in Hertzfield's testimony during discussion of the bill's requirement that farmers dispose of wild cannabis. Doughton, Rep. Daniel A. Reed (R-New York), and Rep. Wesley E. Disney (D-Oklahoma) repeatedly drilled Hester about the Treasury Department's plan to eradicate what Anslinger himself had said was a common weed growing in "practically all the States." Hester described the department's plan as follows:

> The person on whose land the plant was growing wild would be notified by the Treasury Department that he has this plant growing on his land, and if he did not destroy the weed, he would become a producer under the bill and subject to the tax. He would not be committing a crime if he failed to cut it and would merely have to pay a tax.[60]

This was a bad idea for many reasons. For one, it would require raising an army of federal agents to scour the nation for wild cannabis, a species that had evolved for thousands of years to thrive and reproduce in a variety of environments, including agricultural areas. For another, it would have the government intrude on private property and demand that owners remove a plant whose presence they were not responsible for—a trespass that most Americans would never accept. Finally, the department suggested a tax of twenty-five dollars per year on American farmers who failed to remove the weed. This would certainly be an egregious request in the context of an American farm industry still reeling from the worst economic collapse in national history.

Committee members instantly realized this. "You will have a revolution on your hands," Reed said, "if, as you say, this plant grows generally throughout the country and you try to charge the farmers a tax of $25." Reed added that the plan to burden farmers with marihuana removal was "the most serious question that has come up in connection with this bill." Hester responded that the twenty-five dollar tax was only a suggestion and that it was up to Congress to decide how much to tax noncompliant farmers. "Are you not going pretty far when you make a man a producer when he innocently grows wild marihuana on his land?" Disney asked. "If you do not take wild marihuana into consideration, you cannot control this at all," Hester insisted. Rank with fear, Rep. John D. Dingell (D-Michigan) claimed that if any farmers proved unwilling to "exterminate and kill the weed which kills people . . . they should be forced to eliminate the weeds." Hester maintained that "it does not seem to me to be an undue hardship to put a small occupational tax on a person who has this growing wild on his land." Anslinger defended his buddy Hester, saying that "we have never found a case where a property owner has not cooperated with us in getting rid of this destructive weed."[61]

The committee could have assailed the eradication proposal on several other fronts—it was never made clear, for example, how the government planned to carry out this massive cannabis plant-hunt across American farmland and other properties. There are no provisions in the final text of the act providing for the hiring of additional federal agents. Would the FBN expect local police to assist in this effort? Amazingly, this point was never raised for discussion. Hertzfield's testimony concluded with an agreement that the Philadelphia Seed Company and all other distributors of hemp birdseed sterilize the seeds before they went to market. "We think that takes care of the situation," Hester said. It did not.

Birdseed Busts and Other Blunders

"Nobody was more surprised than Rudolpho Laue," the *Long Beach Press Telegram* reported in April 1950, "when the birdseed he scattered for his canary grew up to become marijuana." Laue bought the birdseed at a market and scattered it among potted cactus plants in his house. He let his canary fly indoors and feast on the seeds, several of which apparently sprouted into hemp plants. The twenty-three-year-old was acquitted after he "tearfully told the court he didn't know a marijuana from a tobacco leaf."[62] Clearly, his hemp seed had either not been sterilized as required under the Tax Act, or it had somehow resisted the process; either way, nature foiled the law and taxpayer dollars were spent on Laue's mistaken arrest and trial. The Marihuana Tax Act defined "producers" as "any person who plants, cultivates, or in any way facilitates the natural growth of marihuana."[63]

Under this definition, people such as Laue, the Silversteins, and others who watered and nourished the plant could have been designated "producers" and were technically subject to fines or jail time. Of course, it was up to the courts to interpret the law, and they rarely convicted these people in cases where cultivation was deemed accidental.

Laue's inadvertent sprouts represented just a few of the thousands of essentially drugless hemp plants destroyed during the government's indiscriminate war on cannabis after 1937. A year after the Tax Act took effect, FBN agents and state narcotics officers mowed and burned a crop of thirty-two thousand hemp plants in a half-acre field near Bridger, Montana. Noting that the crop would have been worth $50,000 on the black market, they were undoubtedly pleased with their efforts—that is, until the following week, when they learned that all that time, effort, and taxpayer money had been spent destroying a fiber company's experimental hemp crop. Regretful that Montana agents had helped set back the research agenda of an unnamed "eastern fiber company," the mayor of nearby Red Lodge lamented the hemp burning "as a 'big mistake.'"[64]

Sometimes, uncultivated hemp grew in stands so thick it resisted even military-grade firepower. In August 1951 a "lush stand" of cannabis in a Denver vacant lot was deemed "enough to 'blast' every marijuana addict" in the city. Of course, even at 5,280 feet, the wild weeds wouldn't have gotten anyone close to a Mile High. But that didn't stop the Denver Police Department's Morals Bureau from enlisting GIs at nearby Rocky Mountain Arsenal in the fight against the plants. The GIs "sprayed a corner of the lot

Flamethrowers Fail to Destroy Lush Stand of Marijuana Found Here

These photos captured the spectacle of US soldiers attempting to burn a wild hemp patch, believed to be marijuana, with flamethrowers in 1951. Note the conspicuous lack of drug-producing flowers in the close-up of the plant in the middle frame. The GIs ultimately retired the flamethrowers, declaring the patch "too moist to burn." Source: *Denver Post*, August 21, 1951, Denver Public Library.

with Diesel oil and then seared it with thirty-foot jets of red fire from two flamethrowers." But the stubborn hemp could take the heat: "the fire failed to spread through the rest of the damp green weeds, and after an hour of trying the army men decided it was no use."[65] If any incident warranted reconsideration of the federal war on cannabis, this was it—here was the mighty United States military, utterly failing to destroy just one of hundreds of wild hemp stands across the country. And while flamethrower-wielding marines apparently succeeded in a similar effort in Chicago in 1957, one has to think that America's enlisted men could have been put to better use.[66]

Based on a survey of at least 150 newspaper reports in the American West from 1948 to 1967, at least twenty-six cases of "marijuana" incidents during the Tax Act era can either definitely or very likely be attributed to naturally occurring hemp.[67] Several other reports appear to indicate wild growth but lack conclusive information. This survey included a limited number of reports from a limited number of publications in a handful of states, and leans heavily on California papers.[68] Nonetheless, the survey remains instructive, suggesting that a significant percentage of police activity involving "marihuana" after the Tax Act actually involved nonpsychoactive hemp spread by birds or other natural means.

It also illustrates the effects of Congress's decision to pass a law as ambitious as the Marihuana Tax Act without investigating the assumptions that underwrote it. The result was an enforcement campaign that undermined the law's purpose, as officers wasted time and money ripping up or torching acres of hemp.

"Rope without Dope"

The United States' entrance into World War II in 1941 complicated the federal government's approach toward cannabis, if only for a short time. Hemp was a vital resource for the US military, especially the Navy, which used it for cordage. But the Axis powers quickly cut off hemp supplies from Europe, Asia, and the Philippines. In 1942, with only fourteen thousand acres of hemp in production and each battleship needing an astonishing thirty-four thousand feet of hempen rope, the USDA embarked on a campaign to stimulate hemp farming. It set an ambitious goal of three hundred thousand acres planted by 1943.[69]

To help meet this target, in 1942 the USDA released an informative short film titled "Hemp for Victory." Designed to both encourage and instruct American farmers in hemp cultivation—a practice that had all but disappeared in the United States by 1940—the film covered proper planting, harvesting, and retting techniques, highlighting machinery that would help farmers along the way. Mechanical breakers, for instance, were not available when the US hemp industry peaked in the nineteenth century, so by focusing on those and other modern machines, the film hoped to convince farmers that harvesting and preparing hemp was far easier than it had been in the past. Of course, it did not mention that, under the Marihuana Tax Act, farmers could be fined for simply having cannabis on their property. The film did note that all hemp farmers needed to obtain a license from the government. "This is hemp seed—be careful how you use it," warned the film's narrator, referring to the widely held belief among authorities that without careful management, hemp crops would turn into marijuana fields.[70]

Of course, the feds had little to worry about on that front, as it would have taken a Herculean effort from even the most dedicated marijuana user to extract the trace amounts of THC from wartime hemp plants. Federal agents had ample opportunities to acknowledge the possibility of distinct drug and fiber cannabis; the confusion on that topic was on display during the Tax Act hearings in 1937 and was never cleared up; then, a year later, Dr. Brittain Robinson of the USDA told attendees of the FBN's special Marihuana Conference that the bulk of American hemp seed was Chinese stock, and "there is a great difference between that hemp and the hemp that

Believing that hemp and marijuana came from the same plant, government scientists during World War II attempted to create an allegedly "drugless" hemp strain. Dr. H. E. Warmke's experiment claimed to show the drug potency of various hemp strains through their effect on minnows in glass beakers. Warmke then sought to cross the least potent varieties to create the ideal "rope without dope." Source: *Popular Science*, September 1943, Google books (books.google.com).

came from India."[71] Moreover, Anslinger and USDA scientists must have been aware that the French botanist Jean Baptist Lamarck found drug and fiber cannabis to be so distinct as to argue for separate species way back in 1785.[72] But in order to reap the budget windfall that came with exaggerating the marijuana menace, the FBN ignored, deflected, or dismissed any facts that complicated the assertion that hemp was marijuana. Not even the urgent context of a world war could get government agencies to examine all the evidence—or lack thereof—and adjust their position on the source of marijuana.

This explains the headline of an article in a 1943 edition of *Popular Science*, which asked, "Can We Have Rope without Dope?" Hemp was "urgently needed for military purposes," the article noted. It then parroted an Anslinger talking point: "But it also yields marijuana, a drug that makes depraved creatures out of its addicts."[73] To solve this potential "headache for law enforcement," the article reported that USDA scientist Dr. H. E. Warmke sought to breed a kind of "drug-free" hemp. But first he needed to accomplish the irrelevant: determine how much "marijuana" was in a particular hemp plant.

To do this, Warmke devised a strange and problematic experiment: he extracted "marijuana" from individual hemp plants and placed four different concentrations of the extract—very strong, strong, medium, and weak—in its own water beaker with two minnows. Apparently, scientists had previously found that high concentrations of cannabis extract would kill certain species of small fish, such as minnows or goldfish (as far as I can tell, modern science has not confirmed this, but this procedure is notably absent from later cannabis studies).[74] Thus, Warmke determined the potency of a certain plant by how many fish were killed by its extract. He then crossbred the least potent varieties with the hope of creating a "drugless" hemp strain. The *Popular Science* article asserted that "actual breeding has definitely resulted in improvement" and that Warmke "seems close to his goal."[75] But Warmke never performed a control test with extracts from actual marijuana plants, so his "very strong" extracts might not have been all that strong.[76] Plus, USDA scientists evidently did not consider that most marijuana smokers weren't going to show up at a hemp field with acetone extraction kits and start making tinctures. If anything, they would try to smoke the hemp flowers. Perhaps Warmke should have ditched the beakers and simply tested the effects of hemp joints instead, although that would have risked turning him or his subjects into "depraved creatures." At any rate, we now know that the federal government was exaggerating the possibility of hemp being used as marijuana.

Ultimately, American farmers—predominantly in the Midwest—upped their hemp acreage to seventy-five thousand in 1943, providing plenty of rope for the Navy. Predictably, there was no mass plundering of hemp fields by animalistic drug seekers. Like the ineffectual burning of wild hemp stands, Warmke's bizarre wartime hemp experiments showcased the federal government's utter confusion about cannabis and demonstrated the bureaucracy's tendency to waste taxpayer dollars on the hemp-is-marijuana goose chase.

But the harmful effects of federal cannabis policy in the twentieth century are not counted solely in wasted taxpayer dollars. Rather, the heaviest cost is tallied in the hundreds of lives unnecessarily disrupted or ruined by policy created and enforced by people whose assumptions about cannabis vastly outweighed their knowledge about it.

Stung

It should come as no surprise that two of the first three people arrested under the Tax Act were of Mexican origin. A survey of more than eighty marijuana case files in Colorado's US District Court docket from 1938 to 1952 reveals that nearly all the defendants in these cases had Hispanic surnames.[77] The first person arrested under the Tax Act in California was a Latino, thirty-eight-year-old ranch hand Harry Jara, who was charged with cultivation and sale.[78] Despite the fact that Mexicans and Mexican Americans were not the only people using drug cannabis at the time, a September 1937 report in the *Denver Post* made no secret of who would be targeted under the new law: "Certain areas of the Rocky mountain states where there is a concentration of laborers from outside the United States have been troubled for years in trying to curb the use of the narcotic weed."[79] With Anslinger in attendance, Judge J. Foster Symes handed down the first two sentences under the new law to two Denverites: Samuel Caldwell, a fifty-eight-year-old small-time dealer, received four years in Leavenworth penitentiary, while Moses Baca, twenty-six, got eighteen months in prison for possession.[80] If the "marijuana menace" wasn't real, the punishments for trading in the drug after 1937 certainly were. And while authorities were quick to target Mexican Americans as growers or users, sometimes they went too far.

Leo Acosta was a World War II veteran who fought in the Pacific theater; he also had a brother, Malo Acosta, who was involved in the marijuana trade.[81] On March 18, 1948, Leo Acosta was drinking a beer at the Diamond Café in Denver when he was approached by Leroy Lockett, an acquaintance who, unbeknownst to Acosta, was also an undercover officer. Pointing out a man in dark glasses in the café, Lockett said the man refused to sell him weed because Lockett owed him money. After initially refusing, Acosta eventually took fifteen dollars from Lockett and met the man in dark glasses at Julian Sito's pool hall, where he swapped the cash for a tin of cannabis.

Upon returning to Lockett, Acosta refused payment for the transaction but was still arrested. He later told a probation officer, "I just did this for Lockett because I thought he was a friend of mine," adding that he had "never done anything like this before."[82] Before his case, Acosta sent a request to the jury claiming that "the offenses here charged were conceived and planned by officers or employees of the government." It was rejected, and on May 14, 1948, the US Navy veteran and new father was sentenced to two years at Leavenworth.[83] Apparently, in the eyes of the court, Acosta's insistence that he had been set up, his lack of past involvement in the trade, and his honorable military service were not enough to separate him from his family's Mexican origins or his brother's cannabis dealings.

Harshing the Mellow

As more white Americans began using and dealing in cannabis after 1937, and names like Sam Caldwell, Thomas Hill, Alexander Evans, Joe Bacino, and Clarence Sells began appearing in arrest reports, authorities could no longer afford to only target Mexicans in their marijuana manhunts.[84] And though there were some people involved in criminal organizations who sold harder drugs as well as cannabis, there were also many Americans of all ethnicities and backgrounds who were subjected to unnecessarily harsh punishments under prohibition, especially after courts began doling out the mandatory minimum sentences made possible by the 1951 Boggs Act.

Advanced by Rep. Hale Boggs (D-Louisiana), and supported by Harry Anslinger, the Boggs Act was designed to help curb an uptick in hard drug addiction among American youth, but it also dealt a blow to the separation of powers. Under the act, federal judges no longer had the option to put defendants guilty of a second drug offense on probation, suspend their sentences, or grant them parole. Their authority curtailed, judges reacted to the law with chagrin, but their complaints largely fell on deaf ears—the nation's anti-drug fever was too high.[85] As with the Marihuana Tax Act, which required cannabis violators to incriminate themselves by filling out a tax form, the Boggs Act weakened lauded constitutional protections in order to strengthen the war on drugs.

To many officials and authorities, cannabis was the "gateway drug" that whetted youths' appetites for the harder stuff.[86] With the Boggs Act, which made all cannabis offenses felonies, Congress literally tried to nip harder drug addiction in the bud. In November 1957, Dawn Swanson was arrested for growing three plants in her Pasadena home. On December 18, she received the astonishingly harsh sentence of five years to *life* in prison. Swanson had a felony burglary conviction on her record, and apparently growing the three plants was two strikes too many for the judge, who decided to lock her away at only twenty-seven years of age.[87] The number of possession arrests during the era of the Boggs and Marihuana Tax Acts speaks to the ability of those laws to keep police departments funded and busy; for example, authorities in California alone arrested nearly 538 people per year for cannabis possession between 1948 and 1952.[88]

But just as ripping up stands of wild hemp did little to contain natural cannabis growth, arresting hundreds of people and doling out harsh sentences for marijuana offenses did relatively little to curb the growth, use, or sale of the plant. Even with all the enforcement activity, by the 1950s the herb was in such great supply that dealers typically sold joints for a dollar.[89] In fact, while the use of drug cannabis had been mostly confined to poor minorities, transients, and the jazz scene during the 1920s and 1930s, by the mid-1950s a new cannabis subculture had developed among middle- and even upper-class white Americans. "A lot of nice people, rich people, smoke marijuana," quipped thirty-two-year-old Andrew Livesay, a "$95-a-week printer," after he was arrested for growing forty-five plants in Denver in 1951.[90]

In California, where there was great concern over marijuana use among teenagers, authorities began profiling cannabis users based on appearance instead of race. "Show me a crowd of young people," said John Misterly, the supervising inspector for the California State Bureau of Narcotics in 1954, "and I'll pick out the marijuana users by their haircuts and their mannerisms—the way they slouch and can't look you in the eye." In addition, Misterly advised that a teen on reefers will "[b]e evasive about acquaintances and whereabouts, act like a smart alec," and "have little pride in his personal appearance but will want clothes of extreme styling." He or she will "show little interest in books or sports" and the boys will sport Elvis-like "ducktail haircuts." Of course, many of Misterly's "warning signs" constituted normal teenage behavior; if parents took him seriously, nearly every teenage bedroom in the Golden State would be turned upside down in a frenzied search for reefers. But this was the 1950s, after all, a time when an older generation of Americans was having trouble coming to terms with a suburban youth culture invigorated by rock and roll and the promises of post-war prosperity.

A Different Beat

While teenagers experimented in the suburbs, groups of young, middle-class artists, musicians, and poets residing in American cities represented another new class of cannabis enthusiasts. A restless minority fed up with mainstream culture, this free-thinking creative class believed that the society built by the likes of Anslinger and Misterly assaulted individualism and preached a heavy doctrine of conformity. Frustrated with the nation's hard rejection of philosophic pursuits, they likely began experimenting with drugs like cannabis in the privacy of a jazz club or at a poetry reading. As Martin Lee notes, it was these middle-class minds that began to popularize drug cannabis in the United States:

> As cultural expatriates, the Beats linked cannabis to a nascent groundswell of nonconformity that would develop into a mass rebellion in the years ahead. They were the key transmission belt for the spread of marijuana into mainstream America. A trickle of white, middle-class pot smokers, once confined to jazz clubs, would become a nationwide torrent during the social tumult loosely known as "the Sixties."[91]

The Beats searched for new experiences, new ways of understanding reality, so it makes sense that as part of their search they would pick up one of the cheapest and most widely available drugs. Many illegal purveyors of cannabis looked at the weed and saw either dollar signs or a good time. But cannabis appealed to the Beat Generation for more complicated reasons. As the famous Beat poet and cannabis activist Allen Ginsberg explained, the drug allowed people like him to "explore consciousness," to slow down and experience the depth of things—especially music and art.[92]

The desire to slow down and appreciate nonmaterial aspects of life was indeed out of place in 1950s America, where the idea that one could buy happiness pushed life into a frenzied pace. Factories, those unstoppable manufacturing maws of the military-industrial complex, churned out an endless stream of consumer goods—automobiles, refrigerators, can openers, televisions—and cunning advertisers made sure those goods found their way into American homes by inventing new sets of wants and needs for an entire generation. The variety and accumulation of possessions came to represent, in the words of then vice president Richard Nixon, "what freedom means to us."[93]

In reality, Nixon's "us" was far less inclusive than he implied. The political and economic system that supported the vice president's definition of "freedom" also helped shackle women to the home, weakened workers' ability to fight exploitative companies, and denied African Americans access to homes, colleges, jobs, and other fruits of postwar prosperity.[94] Young people were unfree in a more intellectual but no less real way, as schools and popular culture pressured them into joining the ranks of productive society and ostracized those who questioned the system or yearned for a more meaningful existence. As the contemporary social critic Paul Goodman explained, the national "organized system"—the one that Nixon touted as exemplary of freedom—with "its role playing, its competitiveness, its canned culture, its public relations, and its avoidance of risk and self-exposure" brought "death to the spirit, and any rebellious group will naturally raise a contrasting banner."[95] The Beats were perhaps the most influential of those rebellious groups, having "resigned from the organized system of production and sales and its culture."[96] Whatever their flaws, Goodman wrote, the Beats' "peacefulness is genuine" and their "tolerance of differences is admirable."[97] Rejecting standard elements of the dominant culture such as Cold War nationalism, social segregation, and the pursuit of material possessions, the Beats acted out their own definition of freedom, which included art, literature, sexuality, and cannabis.

In *The Botany of Desire*, journalist and plant aficionado Michael Pollan observes that the shift in consciousness induced by drug plants may "function as a kind of cultural mutagen" that leads to new ideas, many of which may be "useless or worse," but some of which "inevitably turn out to be the germs of new insights and metaphors."[98] America's cannabis-influenced jazz and counterculture movements are evidence for Pollan's claim, showing that the plant's weedy habit was not the only way it defied prohibition; in THC, it also possessed a mind-altering chemical of considerable appeal, especially to those interested in getting beyond what they considered to be a mundane American state of mind in the 1950s.

Indomitable Weed

From birds to beatniks, cannabis had plenty of natural appeal that allowed it to skirt the Marihuana Tax Act and propagate itself across the United States—especially in sunny, open, or urban regions of the American West. As the death knell of cannabis prohibition gets louder in the twenty-first century and a great mistake of the past is corrected—as it was with alcohol prohibition—the somewhat comical experiences of the Silversteins, the unfortunate Montana hemp field, and the failure of flame-throwing GIs serve to illustrate what many legalization advocates have tried to point out: cannabis prohibition is a futile policy. We must also remember the more serious stories of people like Acosta and Swanson, just two of the thousands whose lives were either ruined or profoundly disrupted in the enforcement of that futile policy.

One final example from Beaumont, Texas, in 1958 perfectly encapsulates the indomitable nature of cannabis and provides a fitting metaphor for the US government's determination to oust it from the American landscape. In February, noting that "rookie cops knew little about the weed," Assistant Police Chief Willie Bauer acquired some cannabis seed and planted a patch on his lawn. When the plants were nearly eleven feet tall, he harvested some for the police school, cut the rest down, and burned them. Sprouts came back, and he pulled them up. They came back again; he pulled them up. When the sprouts appeared a third time, Bauer doused his garden in oil and set it on fire. The sprouts just kept coming. "For several days," an article on the incident reported, "Bauer spent most of his spare time trying to mow faster than the plants grew," until he eventually came up with a final solution: he ordered a concrete slab laid over his garden and built a shed on top of it. The article does not say where Bauer obtained the seeds; he may have sown hardy hemp instead of drug cannabis. The Associated Press noted that the episode left Bauer "recovering from considerable stoop labor, calloused hands and a pocketbook dent."[99]

In its attempts to eradicate cannabis, the US government has been playing the role of Willie Bauer for nearly a century. No matter how much the government rips, burns, jails, spends, or lies, the cannabis sprouts just keep coming. Indeed, so far the best solution has been to lay a concrete sheet of silence over the entire subject, using research restrictions and absolutist drug categorizations to limit the influence of history, science, medicine, and the American people themselves.

The Congressional committee that discussed the Marihuana Tax Act might have turned from this path in 1937 had they just considered a few simple facts—ones rooted not in criminology, prejudice, or even medicine, but in ecology. Cannabis grows fast and well in a multitude of climates and environments. Its flowers are easily pollinated by the wind and its seeds are easily distributed by a host of small, fast creatures, be they furry or feathered. The plants that produce drugs look exactly like the plants that do not, and furthermore, the non-drug-bearing plants have a long history of practical use in the United States. Cannabis thrives in human landscapes and offers people a pleasing intoxication that encourages them to cultivate the plant. Against this formidable arsenal of evolutionary defenses, honed over tens of thousands of years, an ill-informed crusade overseen by a clumsy human bureaucracy stood no chance. But as it was, authorities who supported and enforced anti-cannabis policies of the mid-twentieth century committed themselves to the path of Willie Bauer—the plant had to be destroyed at all costs, even if it meant setting your own lawn on fire.

CHAPTER 3

Workers' Weed

Cannabis and Labor in the Rural West

After more than a decade of toil on the beet farms and railroads of Colorado, by June 1946 Manuel Hernandez had achieved the American Dream. On the surface, Hernandez did not exactly appear to be living that dream; he lived with his wife and ten children on a forty-acre beet farm a few miles west of Mead, a small farming community north of Denver. But the forty-two-year-old Mexican immigrant owned two cars and an apartment building in the Colorado capital, which was plenty more than any other tenant beet farmer could boast.[1] Indeed, it was beet-thinning season, and had the sugar-bearing crop accounted for most of his hefty income, Hernandez would have been out in the fields with his wife and children. However, his landlord reported that Hernandez himself hadn't worked in the last year, even though there was a "continual parade of new and expensive cars" rolling up and down the farm's dusty driveway.[2]

Hernandez told his landlord that the traffic was simply customers "buying eggs."[3] But it would only take one tramp through a three-quarter-acre cornfield on his farm to realize that Hernandez's latest business had nothing to do with eggs or sugar beets, but with another agricultural product—cannabis. Growing amidst the young corn stalks were between seven and fifteen thousand specimens of the weedy, psychoactive herb, which was not only easier to cultivate than sugar beets but also far more valuable.[4] Hernandez sold the drug wholesale to dealers in Denver and apparently made some sales in the city himself. Money from these illegal transactions paid for his two cars and the apartment building, things he wouldn't have been able to afford as either a field laborer or a tenant farmer. Perhaps Hernandez planned to one day give up the marijuana trade and use the money to retire with his family, but he showed no signs of slowing down. What neither Hernandez nor his family knew was that more than a decade of success in the marijuana trade was about to catch up with him.

A. M. Bangs, district supervisor for the Federal Bureau of Narcotics, shows off the nearly one hundred pounds of marijuana authorities seized from Manuel Hernandez's farm. Source: *Rocky Mountain News*, June 13, 1946, Denver Public Library.

His product caught the attention of Denver authorities, who learned his name by grilling one of his customers in the city. On June 11, 1946, undercover agent Henry Pratt paid Hernandez an unlisted sum for seven ounces of pot in Denver and then arrested him. The next day, agents had Hernandez take them to his farm, where they confiscated "more than fifty pounds of dried marijuana" and pulled up at least seven thousand plants from the cornfield.[5] The value of Hernandez's crop was estimated to be $40,000 or $60,000, depending on which newspaper one picked up the next morning.[6] In August Hernandez pled guilty to charges of sale and cultivation of cannabis, in violation of the Marihuana Tax Act of 1937, and was sentenced to eighteen months in prison.[7]

In the end, Hernandez made the same mistake that many in the illegal drug trade make when the money is rolling in—he failed to quit while he was ahead. But there is much more to his story than a weed grower who got busted. Like many other Mexican and Mexican American workers in the first half of the twentieth century, Hernandez endured grueling manual

In the summer of 1946, former beet field worker Manuel Hernandez, alias Jose Rodriguez, grew between seven and fifteen thousand marijuana plants on his farm near Mead, Colorado. Hernandez was a major supplier of Denver's marijuana market until authorities raided his farm in June 1946. Hernandez was ultimately sentenced to eighteen months in prison. Source: *Rocky Mountain News*, June 13, 1946, Denver Public Library.

labor, meager wages, seasonal employment, and the other challenges that stemmed from being part of a society where most people saw him as little more than a career laborer. For many like him, money from illegal cannabis crops helped offset the meager wages and intermittent nature of agricultural work. Unlike white suburban teenagers or beatniks in the cities, workers of Mexican descent used the herb as a traditional medicine, an escape from lives of oppression and toil, and as a vehicle for income generation and social advancement. But the decision to grow cannabis also came with tremendous risk, especially after the plant was federally outlawed. If growing or using cannabis allowed some laborers to reclaim some control over their daily lives and destinies, it could just as easily cost them what freedom they had—yet another example of the curious dualities surrounding the cannabis plant.

Hernandez's story also sheds light on the rural geography of cannabis during the first half of the twentieth century. Beyond the assorted metropolitan plots described in the previous chapter, a patchwork of illegal cannabis plots grew on farms and ranches. These rural plantings further demonstrate that humans were expanding the plant's habitat across the West at the same time that cannabis prohibition became state and federal policy. Hernandez and other rural growers planted cannabis in between corn and other crops, in personal gardens, along irrigation ditches, or in remote sections of the farms and ranches they worked on. In doing so, they made marijuana part of the agricultural development of the West. Unlike concrete-corralled spaces in cities and suburbs, these sprawling tracts of well-watered agricultural land allowed for some of the largest illegal cannabis crops in the country. Moreover, as illustrated by Hernandez's dealers in Denver, the rural and urban landscapes of cannabis were fundamentally linked by the same producer-consumer roles that governed interactions between farms and cities across the country.[8]

Cases like Hernandez's, however, with thousands of plants, were rare in the Tax Act era. Unlike in later decades, the total marijuana crop in the first half of the twentieth century was too small to meet anything beyond local demand or produce any significant environmental effects. But by planting cannabis alongside other crops and in remote sections of rural America, Mexican and Mexican American growers set a precedent for future pot-growing generations from the second half of the twentieth century through the present. While hippies and back-to-the-landers often get credit for launching the homegrown weed industry, Mexican and Mexican American laborers were its true pioneers.[9]

They may seem out of place in today's cannabis culture, awash in groovy counterculture imagery and Rastafarian fashion, but the Mexican workers discussed in this chapter were part of a larger working-class tradition of using, producing, and trading in mind-altering drugs. Just as nicotine and alcohol did for urban white men working in factories or on construction sites, THC offered Latino men working on farms and ranches a respite from the considerable stress they endured on a daily basis. And like the illegal production and sale of alcohol and loose cigarettes, the growth and sale of cannabis helped many impoverished people make ends meet, and sometimes more. Stories of Latino bootleggers peddling cannabis during alcohol prohibition show that these outlaw enterprises were sometimes pursued in tandem. As they did in the working-class alcohol experience, gender roles also figured prominently in the cannabis trade. The wives and children of alcoholic workers suffered from financial hardship due to their husband's or father's drinking habit, and the spouses and children of cannabis growers were left without husbands, fathers, and providers when these men were arrested and sentenced to multiyear terms in prison.

Recognizing cannabis as another working-class drug undercuts popular mythology about marijuana as the drug of idealistic middle-class students, lazy stoners, or juvenile delinquents. Indeed, the symbolism and stereotypes attached to marijuana during the 1950s and 1960s eclipsed earlier and opposing identities of the plant, including its use by hard-working Mexicans and Mexican Americans. Their stories remind us that Americans have used and found value in cannabis for many reasons over time, including some that were more noble than we might expect.

Beet Field Buds

In the American West after the turn of the twentieth century, thousands of Mexicans and Mexican Americans found work as field hands, or *betabeleros*, for the sugar beet industry. As they shepherded the beet crop from sprout to sugar vessel, their dirty, calloused hands made the wealth that underlay booming agricultural economies in California, Colorado, Montana, and other states. But workers saw little of that wealth themselves. As members of a permanent underclass with little hope of graduating from contract labor and farm tenancy to property ownership and the middle class, Mexican workers turned to a variety of strategies to survive and support their families. After beet season, many workers sought jobs on railroads or in construction. Like generations of working-class people before them, *betabeleros* also modified the landscape to their benefit, planting vegetable gardens, furnishing and improving shacks or other basic housing, and sometimes growing cannabis, either for personal use or sale.[10]

Much like the other booms in the American West, the region's sugar beet boom and its dependence on Mexican labor sprang from the timely intersection of multiple events, actions, and attitudes.[11] First, the expansion of irrigation projects in the arid West after 1900 put millions of additional acres under cultivation, laying the groundwork for the region's sugar industry. The Spanish-American War in 1898 interrupted foreign sugar supplies, opening the door for domestic sugar. By that time, refining technology had greatly improved, finally allowing for the profitable extraction of beet sugar. Harvesting beets, however, was still too involved to be done mechanically, and since many white Americans considered themselves above "common labor," it fell to a succession of poor, work-seeking immigrants to ply the beet fields of the West.[12] Chinese, Japanese, and German-Russian immigrants, in that order, were among the largest groups of beet laborers from the 1880s to the 1920s.[13]

However, these labor pools dried up when German-Russian or Japanese workers transitioned to farm ownership or because of discriminatory immigration policies—such as the Chinese Exclusion Act of 1882, restrictions on German immigration in 1917, and restrictions on Japanese immigration in 1924.[14] By 1930, due to a combination of labor shortage in the sugar beet industry, more lenient immigration policies toward Mexicans, and economic and political upheaval in Texas and Mexico, *betabeleros* accounted for the majority of beet field workers in the American West.[15]

To secure a steady labor supply, recruiters for sugar companies routinely traveled to Texas or Mexico to solicit beet labor contracts with Mexican or Mexican American families. In these arrangements the company sometimes paid for transportation to and from the fields and required beet farmers to provide basic housing, where families were often allowed to keep livestock and gardens.[16] Some of these gardens became sites of cannabis cultivation, as one observant Californian remembered in a 1938 letter to the *Oakland Tribune*:

> Some 30 years ago, while residing in the sugar factory town of Chino, I learned some facts about marijuana and its effects. A large number of Mexicans were employed there in the beet fields and on the railroads . . . One night a popular constable was stabbed to death by a Mexican whom he was trying to arrest. His assailant was never caught. Subsequent to this murder I discovered that some Mexicans were growing marijuana in their yards. They were putting the product up in small tobacco sacks and retailing it to their countrymen at 25 cents a sack.[17]

The workers around Chino were hardly the only ones growing cannabis. If the letter writer's memory can be trusted, his observations took place around 1908; in the decades that followed, many similar reports of cannabis cultivation appear in newspapers across the sugar beet–growing West. During the 1920s, in Montana's Yellowstone River Valley, "Mexican beet workers" had "brought with them the marijuana, which grows well in their gardens."[18] In 1931 a group of those workers lined irrigation ditches near Forsyth with cannabis, storing their harvest in an "abandoned shack."[19] The *Billings Gazette* reported that "the presence of marijuana" among the valley's beet workers was such that the sheriff vowed to "get farmers to add a clause in their contracts with laborers which will specify that the laborer forfeit his contract money should marijuana be found growing on land contracted by him."[20] In 1935 authorities "confiscated about 500 pounds of marijuana which was growing in the gardens of Mexicans" in Wyoming's Bighorn Basin, another beet-farming hot spot.[21] Significantly, not all of these reports came from beet-farming areas; some came from other places where Mexicans, Mexican Americans, or Hispanos were known to have worked and built communities, including the "Pajarito and San Jose Districts" of Albuquerque, New Mexico, the "outskirts" of Wasco, California (and elsewhere in California's Central Valley), and the Arkansas River and San Luis Valleys in Colorado.[22]

The author of the 1938 letter to the *Oakland Tribune* was clearly focused on cannabis's supposed role in the murder of the constable, as well as in several other murders that "had occurred among these laborers" at the time of his observations.[23] Of course, we know that it was common in this era for "newspapermen"—as the writer of this letter described himself—to obsess over marijuana as a cause of violence in Mexican communities. But the prevailing focus on violence in this and other reports obscures an important and unanswered question: Why were these laborers growing cannabis and "retailing it to their countrymen?"

A simple answer may be "to make a few extra bucks"—but that still doesn't explain why there was a market for the drug. The strenuous nature of these laborers' work regimens offers a possible explanation. Beet field workers in particular acquired a "host of physical ailments," including "carpal tunnel syndrome, tendonitis, back strain, sore muscles, knife cuts, allergies, asthma, heatstroke, sunburns, skin cancers, and illnesses resulting from exposure to pesticides."[24] A 1923 report by the US Department of Labor detailed the effects of beet labor on children, but some of the report's findings could easily apply to adults as well. One is the weakening of the serratus anterior—a muscle that connects the shoulder blades to the rib cage—caused by the constant extension of the arms during long periods of "steady stooping in the kneeling and crouching position."[25] As the serratus anterior weakens, other muscles in the back are forced to compensate, which may have been the source of back pain in some workers.[26]

As a medicinal and even recreational substance, cannabis could have alleviated some of these conditions. It would have been most effective

Sugar beet and cannabis growth in the American West, c. 1900–1945. The map on the left shows reported instances of cannabis cultivation in the American West between 1900 and 1950, while the map on the right shows the regional concentration of sugar beet farms in 1944. Bounded areas demonstrate overlap between major beet-producing areas and reports of cannabis cultivation. Source: Sugar beet map from US Department of Agriculture, Census of Agriculture Historical Archive, Cornell University (http://usda.mannlib.cornell.edu/usda/AgCensusImages/ AgCensusImages/1945/02/08/1206/Table-21.pdf); cannabis map created by author using custom Google Maps.

in treating the general aches and pains of a hard day's fieldwork, as THC helps tense muscles unwind and floods the brain with mood-lifting and pain-blocking dopamine.[27] The anti-inflammatory properties of another cannabinoid, cannabidiol (CBD), helps reduce sinewy tissue swollen by tendonitis and relieves joints stiff from hours of repetitive bending, picking, and hoeing.[28] Of course, the highly subjective nature of the cannabis experience, as well as the substance's nefarious reputation in Mexican culture, meant that some laborers found cannabis treatments useful, others did not, and still others avoided it altogether.

Mereciano Vigil, a beet worker in Colorado's Arkansas Valley, was one who found cannabis useful. Arrested in 1937 for possession near Las Animas, he told the police that using the drug "kept him from getting tired" during long, intense days of beet harvesting.[29] Sometimes people caught with illegal drugs make up excuses on the spot. This likely applied to the case of a "C. Sota" in 1925, who was nabbed trying to smuggle small sacks of cannabis across the US-Mexico border in his armpits—he told police that he carried the sacks under his arms to relieve his "rheumatism."[30] But cannabis historian Chris Duvall notes that the herb has historically been "dispersed alongside labour underclasses because the drug enhances the ability of workers to endure lives of physically demanding but mentally dulling tasks."[31] This historical perspective, along with the known therapeutic properties of cannabinoids, lends a good deal of credibility to Vigil's statement.

Though it comes from a newspaper clipping of fewer than one hundred words, Vigil's story is exceptionally valuable because it provides evidence for a phenomenon—the therapeutic use of cannabis among Mexican beet workers—that was likely quite common but is nonetheless scarcely documented. There may be a number of explanations for this. The language barrier may have prevented Spanish-speakers from explaining their behavior on their arrest, and even if they could speak English, there may have been little certainty that explaining would help their situation. On the other side, authorities and newspapers were so swept up in racist stereotypes of Mexicans and ideas about "Reefer Madness" that many may not have considered that some workers used cannabis medicinally. Most police and reporters had neither the incentive nor the desire to rationalize growth or use of cannabis, and most of the people arrested for such crimes either lacked the will or ability to explain themselves.

While it is rare to come across contemporary reports of beet workers explicitly using cannabis as a medicine, there is enough diversity in the reports to suggest that workers used the herb for more than just profit or recreation. For example, after the 1928 beet harvest near Billings, Montana, a Mexican worker referred to only as "Gerrero" (probably a misspelling of "Guerrero") informed the cops who found "several stalks" of cannabis in his cabin that "his friend" had a "pain in his stomach and drink[s] marijuana."[32] The relatively small amount of pot involved, as well as modern medical evidence for cannabis as a treatment for gastrointestinal problems, suggests that this is another instance of a beet worker using the herb medicinally.[33]

In 1958 Joe Castro, a fifty-three-year-old laborer from Colorado Springs, was acquitted on charges of possession and cultivation of cannabis after he and his wife testified that they mixed the herb with olive oil as a treatment for her rheumatism.[34] Richard Grove, a curator at the Taylor Museum of the Colorado Springs Fine Arts Center, helped the couple's case by testifying that "Mexicans have used marijuana to heal rheumatism for hundreds of years."[35] The documented association between laborers—especially beet workers—and cannabis, the known therapeutic benefits of cannabinoids, and these sparse but informative reports of medicinal use by workers suggest that many Mexican and Mexican Americans who labored in the American West during the first half of the twentieth century grew or used cannabis as a remedial substance.

While it may have proven to be a therapeutic adjunct to a life of hard labor, the drug plant also helped treat another stressful condition these workers faced—chronic poverty. Contracts with growers and sugar companies did offer destitute Mexican and Mexican American families jobs, housing, and steady wages, but these contracts were brokered within the same context of white American racial anxiety that inspired the restrictive immigration acts of the late nineteenth and early twentieth centuries. Most American farmers and companies welcomed Mexicans for their temporary labor, not for their potential as citizens or neighbors. Advocates of keeping the southern border open to Mexican laborers routinely offered the explanation that, as a racially inferior and backwards people, Mexicans were perfectly suited to agricultural labor and posed no threat to white American society.[36] The prevalence of these beliefs among politicians, sugar company executives, and beet growers indicated that unlike their Japanese and German-Russian predecessors, *betabeleros* would not be afforded many opportunities to transition from labor to farm ownership.[37]

Nor could beet workers expect to climb the economic ladder by scrimping and saving. Wages for beet workers in the 1920s were higher compared to those for other agricultural workers but still amounted to a meager income. Before the Jones-Costigan Act of 1934 prohibited child labor, a family of four that was particularly adept at beet tending could make as much as $1,200 per six-month season.[38] Since beet workers' employment contracts expired after the harvest, many sought additional employment throughout the year, perhaps on railroad or construction crews. Others returned to Mexico. To determine how much an off-season job might bring in, let's take the example of a construction worker. A carpenter in Denver in 1927/28 earned about $50 per forty-hour workweek. If a beet worker, assuming he had the skills, found twenty weeks of carpentry work—nearly the entire beet off-season—he could earn about $1,000. So it appears that working construction or a similar supplementary job might bring beet-working families an additional $500 to $1,000.[39] In 1925 the average American household still brought in between $2,500 and $3,000 more than a *betabelero* family would in that scenario.[40] Thus, even if many were provided with free housing—which was often scarcely more than shacks—it is difficult to argue that Mexican beet laborers in the first part of the twentieth century lived even moderately comfortable lives.[41]

Given these circumstances, it is easy to see why many laborers chose to grow and sell cannabis. For one thing, it gave workers an autonomy that they didn't have in the beet fields or in construction and railroad work. The weedy herb grew fast and well in the open, irrigated landscapes of agriculture or in workers' gardens, and it only took about a half-dozen plants to produce a pound of the drug, which by 1933 could be sold for around eighty-five dollars.[42] At that rate, the harvest from fewer than one hundred plants could more than double the income that an entire family earned in a season of beet work. To workers paid a pittance, holed up in ramshackle housing, and stuck in an annual cycle of back-breaking toil and seasonal unemployment, cannabis—like every forbidden fruit—was certainly tempting.

For a time, the herb wasn't the only illegal drug that working-class Latinos could turn to in an oppressive economy. During Prohibition (1920–1933), some Mexican cannabis growers moonlighted as moonshiners. In 1923, Tom Medideno, Ercuiano Jiminez, and Porfirio Casas and his wife were arrested in Wasco, California, after officers discovered their liquor still and an adjacent grove of tall cannabis.[43] In 1928 in Salt Lake City, officers took a cask of wine, some whiskey, weapons, and fifteen large cans of marijuana from John Parren and Ventolo Lopez.[44] Later that year, federal prohibition officers raided a small moonshine operation run by two Mexican beet workers in Billings, Montana; in addition to fifteen and a half pints of booze, officers confiscated a box of cannabis buds.[45]

Even with alcohol prices skyrocketing during prohibition, some outlaws saw a better opportunity in the cannabis trade. For instance, after Valdo Santos was arrested with five pounds of the herb in New Orleans in 1924, he opined that the marijuana business "beats bootlegging because the fines are smaller and I sell it for thirty-five cents a cigarette."[46] Probably because it viewed the herb as a possible replacement for alcohol, Montana's *Billings Gazette* referred to marijuana as the "New 'Booze.'"[47] While some bootleggers offered cannabis along with alcohol, it does not appear that the two illicit industries became further entangled, and there was no significant cannabis trade amongst the powerful liquor mobs that dominated Los Angeles and other big cities during the 1920s. This was likely because cannabis was nowhere near as popular as liquor and, at least in the West, was still predominantly the crop of working-class Mexicans or Mexican Americans—and not just beet workers, either.

Ranchers, Farmers, and the (Illegal) American Dream

Beet farms and fields were not the only places where drug cannabis could be found in the first half of the twentieth century. Small, hand-tilled garden plots may have been ideal places to grow cannabis for personal or even community use, but the sprawling landscapes of ranches and farms allowed for bigger crops and bigger profits. Corn patches and irrigation ditches on many of these properties provided perfect cover for cannabis.

So it is hardly surprising to see that out of a sampling of sixty reported instances of cannabis cultivation in the West from 1920 to 1950, a third took place on farms or ranches.[48] Additionally, of the reports that identified a grower, nearly all had Hispanic surnames and were not the legal owners of the property, again reflecting the affiliation between a marginalized people and the weed of ill repute. This sampling is small when compared to the larger population of Mexicans and Mexican Americans employed on farms or ranches during this period, but it only reflects plants that *were reported* or growers *who were caught*. As the ongoing failure of cannabis prohibition indicates, growers have for the better part of a century proved as stubborn as the weedy plant they grow—when one grower gets arrested, it does not take long for another to take his or her place. We can reasonably assume that there were many more instances of cannabis cultivation than were reported.

Few newspaper reports from this sampling offer clear reasons why these farmers or ranchers grew the plant. But the value authorities placed on the crop often provided reason enough. Five thousand dollars would go a long way for most people in any decade, but during the Great Depression it would have gone even further. That was the estimated value of Ynes and Adolfo Simental's cannabis crop in July 1933, right before police burned it up. The West Sacramento Land Company had agreed to let the Simentals farm the land a few miles south of Broderick, California, if they first cleared away the brush. Hoping to squeeze even more value out of the opportunity, the brothers hid their illicit crop "behind other plants" on their farm. Adolfo, who had previously been locked up for selling "marijuana cigarettes," would have been arrested with Ynes for growing the weed, but he was already sitting in jail—his wife had had him arrested earlier that day for failing to provide for her and their four foster children.[49] Adolfo may not have failed in that endeavor had the duo's $5,000 worth of cannabis made it to market. The brothers avoided prison only by agreeing to return with their families to Mexico.[50]

A smattering of accounts from around the West tell similar stories about marginalized people planting cannabis in unassuming parts of the agricultural landscape.[51] Few, however, compare to the story of Melitone Garcia, the fifty-three-year-old "alien" whom federal drug agents crowned the "Marijuana King of America." Over the course of three weeks during the winter of 1940to 1941, agents led by John H. Van Treel of the Federal Bureau of Narcotics purchased $4,000 worth of marijuana from dealers in Denver. They eventually traced most of it back to a motherlode on Garcia's farm five miles outside of Fort Collins. Posing as a would-be grower, Van Treel gained Garcia's trust and learned the elaborate workings of his ring: Garcia had a small army of pot pushers in the Mile High City, some of whom operated a "hashish parlor"—a lounge where his customers could buy and smoke his product. In order to conceal the location of his farm, he would blindfold his clients—"men and women" who "were well known in Denver"—and drive them to a quarry near Windsor where he would complete the transaction. Van Treel said Garcia "told him there was a fortune to be made in the sale of the weed in Colorado, where its use had reached almost unbelievable proportions."[52] True to Garcia's proclamation, as well as to the nature of the illegal American marijuana industry, it wasn't long after authorities dethroned Garcia that Manuel Hernandez became Colorado's new cannabis king.

The stories of working-class Latinos growing and using cannabis in the first half of the twentieth century yield at least two important insights for the broader history of cannabis in the United States, and the American West more specifically. First, the conditions that allowed these workers to grow their illicit weed—such as large cornfields or irrigation ditches—did not exist in the West before the advent of large-scale irrigation projects in the twentieth century. Cannabis may have been illegal, but it was nonetheless embedded in the same complex agricultural economy as the workers who grew it, the sugar beets and other crops those workers tended, and the farmers and companies that profited from the workers' labor. Today, most westerners are cognizant of irrigation's fundamental role in their communities' past, present, and future. Scholars who study the sugar beet industry readily acknowledge irrigation infrastructure as one of the primary reasons for the industry's success in the region. But it is unlikely that either scholars or the average westerner have considered that, without the massive, continual investment in the manipulation of the West's scarce water supplies, the domestic marijuana industry that the region is now famous for would also not have been possible. This realization should prompt public officials and citizens in California, Colorado, and other pot-friendly states in the arid West to think more about how best to balance the water needs of the cannabis industry with those of cities and other agricultural endeavors across the region.

The stories in this chapter also make it clear that the illegal cannabis trade in the United States developed not just to serve the habits of hippies and other strictly recreational users, but because, long before the counterculture took shape, the plant helped meet certain needs of a marginalized and exploited people. Whether it was used as a medicine, an escape from everyday drudgery, or to earn supplemental income, cannabis offered tangible benefits to working-class Mexicans and Mexican Americans, many of whom simply could not attain those benefits by other means. Of course, cannabis use likely produced dependence in some laborers or exacerbated the problems of others who suffered from mental illness. Mexicans and Mexican Americans who grew or used cannabis also appear to have been a minority within the larger Latino community. But by and large, working-class Latinos who used or planted cannabis in the rural West simply applied their traditional knowledge of a plant to help improve their lives in a new and often hostile environment.

CHAPTER 4

Seeding the Nation

Cannabis and the Counterculture, 1960–1980

In the midst of the tumultuous 1960s, as an entire generation sought to rehash what it meant to be American, one mysterious individual took it upon himself to put a new face on an old national legend. Like a long, slender shadow, he appeared only at dawn and dusk, emerging from a stand of trees or from a diner in some sleepy town. He walked to a spot along a roadside or field, dipped his hand into the mail sack slung over his shoulder, and flung a fistful of seeds to the ground. Having left his green thumbprint on another patch of rural America, he adjusted his black derby hat and headed out of town. Eventually, he'd hitch a ride in a passing truck and rumble off to his next hiding place, next set of dishes to wash, next round of seeds to sow. Once safe and alone—or in the right company, perhaps—he drew botanical treasure maps guiding others to his funky flower patches. A countercultural Johnny Appleseed, the traveling hippie known as "Johnny Pot" did this dawn after dawn, dusk after dusk, from Oregon to Ohio, Kansas to Idaho.[1]

His real name is not known, but he was more legend anyhow. By October 1968, Johnny Pot had built quite a reputation, at least if federal drug agents are to be believed. Never once "relieved" of his supply of cannabis seeds, Johnny embodied the counterculture's relationship with the plant: rustic, hip, fun—throw some seeds in the ground, let them grow, have a toke and a laugh, and keep on living. While many modern growers would likely identify with Johnny's rebel spirit, some might cringe at his crude form of agriculture: it involved no clones from a mother plant, no carefully concocted soil mixtures, no lights, trellises, or pesticides. They would have also balked at the Associated Press article covering Johnny's exploits, which claimed that his "task of planting" was "relatively easy," and that "[m]arijuana seeds . . . need almost no cultivating."[2] But in the 1960s this was mostly true. For people like Johnny Pot and his followers, there was indeed very

The exploits of Johnny Pot, a hippie Johnny Appleseed who sowed cannabis seeds across the country, appeared in newspaper reports in the late 1960s, and even inspired a Broadway musical—"The Ballad of Johnny Pot"—which earned a poor review in the *New York Times* in 1971. Source: New York Public Library Digital Collections.

little science to growing cannabis, and it wasn't about making money. It was more about having fun while sticking it to the man—giving the finger to an American culture infected with greed, hollow consumerism, conformity, and the suppression of creative and sexual expression.[3] Johnny Pot and the counterculture's other cannabis aficionados did more than simply frustrate authorities; they directly challenged the dominant understanding of cannabis in ways that produced important social, political, environmental, and cultural consequences.

Socially, the hippie movement brought the herb to an unprecedented level of popularity, especially among young adults and college students. As they experimented with cannabis, young people began to realize that, not only was smoking pot fun and rebellious, but it was also not driving them insane and making them commit murder or other crimes (except, of course, the crime of using cannabis). By championing the plant as part of an alternative lifestyle that emphasized peace, love, personal expression, and a oneness with nature, the counterculture shattered the popular consensus of the marijuana menace.[4] Seeing the plant as something more than just another dangerous drug gave rise to a renewed discussion about its medical qualities, as demonstrated when the Supreme Court granted medical cannabis rights to Robert Randall, a college professor with glaucoma, in 1975. As it was in the early twentieth century, the identity of the plant was again thrown into question, and in an era marked by civil rights movements, labor strife, and antiwar protests, many young Americans began to see cannabis as yet another thing that government and mainstream culture got wrong. In this way, pot smoking was transformed from a petty individual vice into a powerful collective symbol for hippies, back-to-the-landers, and other cultural rebels.

Of course, the herbal habit of the counterculture generated quite a bit of resistance, and not just from law enforcement. The movement's view of cannabis as a useful part of a more harmonious relationship with nature clashed with the belief of more traditional Americans that many parts of nature—especially drug plants like cannabis—needed to be controlled in order to have a productive, functioning society. Thus, the roots of the social conflict over cannabis between the counterculture and mainstream America lay not only in opposing political ideologies but also in opposing understandings of nature. During the 1960s and 1970s, this conflict was apparent in many neighborhoods, college campuses, and other places where the two understandings existed in close proximity.

Politically, the new population of mostly young, white middle-class cannabis users presented a problem for authorities. Gripped by widespread assumptions about race and criminality, most middle- and upper-class white Americans barely noticed as droves of blacks, Latinos, and even poor whites were arrested for cannabis violations before 1960. But as historian Matthew Lassiter explains, authorities created a class of "impossible criminals" after 1960 by arresting thousands of white middle-class youths for those same violations.[5] In their parents' eyes, and increasingly in the eyes of judges, these were otherwise law-abiding kids who had a singular lapse in judgment or were victims of a larger drug racket run by nonwhites. As a result, new federal drug regulations downgraded drug possession from a felony to a misdemeanor, and state legislatures increasingly considered easing penalties for possession and raising penalties for drug production and sale. Oregon became the first state to decriminalize cannabis possession in 1973 and was joined by ten others by 1980.[6]

The counterculture also changed the politics of prohibition. In 1969 the Supreme Court ruled the Marihuana Tax Act unconstitutional in *Leary v. United States*. However, drug regulation in the United States and beyond got a complete overhaul with the passage of the Comprehensive Drug Abuse Prevention and Control Act (CDAPCA) in 1970 and the creation of the Drug Enforcement Administration (DEA) in 1973. Under the CDAPCA, cannabis was placed in the same "schedule," or category, as heroin, which meant that the herb was officially recognized as a highly dangerous, addictive substance with no proper medical use. In the meantime, the decidedly anti-hippie Nixon administration commissioned the largest federal study on cannabis to date in an attempt to prove that the weed deserved this harsh categorization. But the final report of the Shafer Commission, released in 1972, shocked the president, as it found no justification for cannabis prohibition and called for "a more rational discussion of marijuana policy."[7]

Environmentally speaking, the plant itself benefited greatly from the back-to-the-land movement of the 1970s, but that movement also set the stage for an illegal cannabis industry that would contribute to environmental destruction. Embracing the same kind of rustic idealism that fueled the commune movement during the sixties, counterculturalists fled the cities seeking a simpler life off the grid. In doing so, they introduced drug cannabis to parts of the nation the plant had never seen before, most notably the rugged hill country of northern California and southern Oregon. Cannabis growers in this remote region soon found that the climate, geography, and struggling local economy produced a favorable environment for their illicit industry, and it wasn't long before their cash crop brought them right back into the same capitalist economy they tried to escape.[9] It also wasn't long before authorities figured this out and began staging raids, initiating a decades-long game of cat and mouse that degraded the region's environment, tore at its social fabric, and ultimately failed to uproot the cannabis industry.

Perhaps the most important consequence of the activities of Johnny Pot and other countercultural cannabis enthusiasts was the reimagination of the plant on a large scale. In 1960, most people did not believe cannabis to be anything other than a deplorable, dangerous vice. By 1980, however, perceptions of the plant had multiplied considerably: it was still seen as a vice, but now it was also considered by many to be a symbol of protest, a fun pastime, a creative tool, a medicine, or a valuable agricultural product that could revive an entire regional economy. The cultural seeds sown by Johnny Pot and others had sprouted into a whole new crop of identities and uses for the plant, and it sank its roots even deeper into the rich soil of American life.

Naturally Opposed

The social conflict over cannabis in the 1960s and 1970s was mostly a generational conflict, and it hinged on two different understandings of nature. Labeling entire generations, assigning them distinct attributes or attitudes, is an inherently problematic way of conceptualizing the past; while it may seem easy enough to generalize about a particular generation, many people do not fit so neatly within a given age bracket, and this way of grouping people inevitably overlooks those who went against the grain. However, comparing the strongest cultural currents of one generation to those of another can still be enlightening. For instance, while some members of the so-called Greatest Generation—those who became adults in the 1930s and 1940s—undoubtedly smoked pot, most saw cannabis as another part of nature that needed to be subdued and controlled. Meanwhile, their children—the so-called baby boomers, who came of age in the 1960s and 1970s—for the most part saw the herb as a valuable part of a more open, reciprocal relationship with nature.

Many members of the baby boomer generation grew up starved of an authentic connection to nature. The surge in industrial production during World War II continued after the war, when factories switched from making planes, ships, and bullets to churning out refrigerators, microwave ovens, and vacuum cleaners. Meanwhile, agriculture was entirely transformed during the 1940s by the advent of synthetic pesticides and fertilizers.[10] As a result, children in the 1950s grew up in a nation saturated with manufactured products, many of which were designed to quicken or simplify day-to-day tasks such as cooking and cleaning. The mass production of fridges, toys, coffeemakers, automobiles, even homes and food, led to the mass creation of jobs to produce, sell, manage, and distribute these products. Middle-class Americans increasingly worked on assembly lines, as advertising or real estate agents, as store clerks and managers, or as drivers ferrying loads of products cross-country on newly built interstate highways. These jobs, all centered around the mass production and sale of stuff, greatly expanded the middle class and gave Americans the money they needed to buy more stuff. Indeed, advertisers pitched the perfect life as being just the right combination of "stuff."[11]

Institutional discrimination in housing and employment, as well as educational segregation, meant that the fruits of postwar prosperity were disproportionately distributed to white Americans.[12] Most men in this new, white middle class worked in the city and came home to the suburbs, where hundreds of quaint, identical houses were built to serve as both the sanctuary of the working man and the well-kept nest of his housewife. Here, the industrial output of postwar America piled up in garages, living rooms, kitchens, and attics—that is, until the goods became worn out, outgrown, broken, or out of style, in which case they were replaced by newer, shinier versions.[13] But the suburbs were more than a giant storage shed for America's stuff—they were also safe breeding grounds where children could be raised behind picket fences, far from the bad influences of the vice- and poverty-stricken cities.

For many baby boomers growing up in the 1950s, technology and manufacturing at once gave them the world and cut them off from it. Almost every part of their lives that seemed natural, from the food they ate to the grass they played on, had been artificially produced or modified in some way. Even their experiences in so-called wilderness, at summer camps or family visits to national parks, were idealized forays into carefully managed ecosystems.[14] Moreover, in a society that increasingly valued someone for the amount of mass-produced products he or she could help make and consume, there was little room for exploring one's individuality. Raised without a unique, authentic connection to nature, and with the simple expectation that they would one day get jobs or husbands of their own, it is little wonder that as adults, many baby boomers would utterly reject the numbing cycle of produce-consume in search of a less restrained, more deeply satisfying life.

Their parents, however, saw things quite differently. This was a generation that grew up in the painful era of the Great Depression and Dust Bowl and took part in the massive national sacrifice of World War II. To those who had lived through such hard times, the abundance of postwar America was both a welcome reprieve and a just reward. Moreover, consumption became their patriotic duty in the era of the Cold War, as Americans increasingly saw the booming postwar economy as proof that their capitalist system was far better than anything the communist Soviets could come up with.[15] Most importantly, middle-class parents now had the means to provide for their kids the secure, comfortable childhood that so many of their own generation never got to enjoy.

Nature was mostly a closed case to this generation. After all, they had witnessed the passage of federal land protections after the Dust Bowl, the work of the Civilian Conservation Corps, and the construction of dams and other massive reclamation projects in the arid West—all of which served to protect, conserve, and ensure the bountiful production of hundreds of thousands of American acres. Like the generations before them, the Americans who came of age in the late 1930s and 1940s often drew a sharp divide between humans and nature, believing that nature had to be both tamed and preserved for the benefit of civilization.[16] There were, of course, clashes between those who would tame nature and those who would preserve it. Ecologist Aldo Leopold's 1949 conservation treatise, *A Sand County Almanac*, drew attention to environmental degradation and inspired many Americans to reconsider how their individual actions affected local ecosystems. In 1955, a coalition of conservation-minded groups defeated the Bureau of Reclamation's proposed dam in Colorado's Dinosaur National Monument, bringing an end to an era in which dams received near-universal praise. Still, by the 1960s, few were complaining as publicly funded park systems, dams, irrigation projects, chemically assisted agriculture, and roads seemed to have subdued nature and made it available for consumption in public lands, reservoirs, supermarkets, or on scenic drives.[17]

While members of the Greatest Generation and its predecessors were content with this orderly view of nature, their children came to see it as overly simplistic and detrimental to both the environment and people. As they grew older, they began to take note of some of the problems inherent in the orderly society their parents had helped create. Every river, it seemed, had to have a dam; forests and grasslands were being pulverized to make way for strip malls, shopping centers, and subdivisions; agricultural chemicals were seeping into the environment and harming wildlife, as biologist Rachel Carson demonstrated in her 1962 book *Silent Spring*.[18]

This all did not sit well with a generation that now increasingly sought ways to break out of the stifling, conformist bubble it was raised in. Many of these young adults—especially those who grew up near cosmopolitan cities such as New York and San Francisco—were heavily influenced by the long beards and unhinged style of the artistic, free-thinking beatniks.[19] They were also inspired by the ongoing civil rights movement, which demonstrated both the moral failure of the current social order and the power of collective protest, and by Native American culture, which they saw as far more respectful of the balance between humans and nature.[20] The shocking brutality of the Vietnam War, meanwhile, sparked hundreds of protests on university campuses and further undermined this generation's trust in the American establishment. Dissatisfied with the mainstream press, the counterculture breathlessly championed its causes in the pages of its own underground publications, including the *Berkeley Barb* and *Los Angeles Free Press* in California, the *East Village Other* in New York City, and the *Straight Creek Journal* in Denver.[21]

In this new cultural amalgam, an alternative way of living, rooted in the strong utopian tradition of the United States, began to take shape.[22] Instead of an individualistic society in which people worked to out-purchase one another, counterculturalists took up the mantle of earlier American utopian thinking and imagined a pluralistic society in which residents of small communities worked the land for everyone's benefit. Nobody in the Boomer Generation seemed to agree on a blueprint for how to achieve such a society, but however these communities were imagined, the key to creating them lay in changing the human relationship with nature. By bending nature to its will, the earlier generation was able to harvest millions of products and billions of dollars from the environment, making life a bit easier and more enjoyable. But the problem, counterculturalists believed, was that these products and the money that paid for them became substitutes for genuine human connection.

The counterculture's search for new experiences was not limited to participation in campus social movements, the underground press, or communes. Adherents also sought a deeper connection with themselves. This led them to explore different levels of consciousness by ingesting powerful psychedelic drugs, most commonly lysergic acid diethylamide—LSD or "acid"—and psychedelic mushrooms. These non-habit-forming drugs put a strange, colorful, and entertaining lens on the world and were just as likely to produce insight and introspection as they were to produce nightmarish trips, making them popular among a culture that mostly rejected harder, more addictive drugs such as cocaine or heroin.[23]

But far and away the most common drug used by the counterculture was cannabis, or "grass," as it was popularly known. If the movement was a fleet, its flagship would have undoubtedly flown a banner sporting the serrated leaves of the cannabis plant, for a number of reasons. For one, as a plant that produces a mind-altering drug, it sat squarely at the intersection of three natural entities the counterculture sought to bring closer together—bodies, minds, and the environment. For another, as Johnny Pot demonstrated, it could be grown pretty much anywhere, with relative ease, meaning that basically everyone had access to it. Finally, cannabis was the bogeyman of the federal government, and nothing demonstrated one's flagrant opposition to the established order more than lighting up some grass. In sum, even on their wildest acid trip, the hippies could not have designed a more fitting drug plant for their movement.

Of course, not everyone in the counterculture smoked grass or did other drugs. Nevertheless, a former director of the National Institute of Mental Health estimated in 1969 that the number of cannabis users was somewhere between eight and twelve million.[24] While there were few reliable estimates of the number of cannabis users before 1970, there is no evidence that the amount of users before 1960 came anywhere close to a million, much less eight million.[25] In 1960, marijuana arrests accounted for 27 percent of all drug arrests in California; in 1968 they accounted for 58 percent.[26] Although the herb had already been used in the country for decades, it is safe to say that the counterculture formally introduced a new generation of Americans—whatever we'd like to label them—to Mary Jane.

Unsurprisingly, university campuses in the sixties were hot spots for cannabis use. A survey of students at Colorado College in 1968 revealed that 41 percent had smoked pot and 67 percent favored its legalization.[27] Even conservative Montana was not immune; the *Helena Independent*, quoting the student newspaper at the University of Montana, reported in 1966 that between two and three hundred students "were buying, selling, and smoking marijuana on and off campus."[28] The student newspaper claimed that "three main groups . . . were bringing the drug from Denver and the West Coast . . . and selling it."[29] By 1970, a nationwide Gallup poll of college students reported that 42 percent of responders said they had smoked pot.[30]

During the Summer of Love in 1967, about one hundred thousand young people, many of them university students, gathered in San Francisco's Haight-Ashbury neighborhood in an open and emphatic declaration of their alternative lifestyle, which emphasized peace, creative expression, and a shared obligation to one another. Plenty of grass was smoked there, but it was an incident in far-off Montana during that same summer that perhaps most clearly demonstrated the opposing understandings of nature at the heart of the national conflict over cannabis.

Montana was no San Francisco—in fact, the conservative state was outright hostile toward the counterculture. In 1967, for example, the editorial board of the *Helena Independent* considered a group of young men who had recently "staged a panty raid" at Eastern Montana College to be role models for the rest of America's university students. Stealing female students' underwear, the board argued, was "a better escape from this meaningless world than marijuana and LSD." Not only that, but a panty raid was a demonstration of true masculinity, as opposed to the "lispy, limp-wristed swishes who write dirty words on signs and spit obscenities at cops and soldiers."[31] Another *Independent* editorial in December contrasted the patriotism of the 1940s with the "unbelievably vile demonstrations" of the 1960s: "Twenty-six years ago . . . young men huddled in damp foxholes, afraid to light a smoke and wishing they had a shave, in contrast to the bearded creeps puffing marijuana in today's hippie pads."[32] In a November 1967 letter to the editor of the *Billings Gazette*, Bozeman resident Patricia O'Connell wrote that two local young men should be forbidden to open up a "psychedelic shop" because it would attract "a large unsavory clientele" to main street. "Bozeman considers itself a safe, friendly, clean, wholesome town to which any Montana family can send its young people to college without misgivings," O'Connell wrote. The shop "would therefore not meet with the approval of the majority of Bozeman voters."[33] Though she considered friendliness to be one of the town's assets, the virtue apparently need not apply to "hippies and the illegal users of marijuana."

But whether they liked it or not, by July 1967—smack in the middle of the Summer of Love—O'Connell and other Montanans were indeed living amongst "illegal users of marijuana." On July 22, in a raid that capped a yearlong investigation, police arrested Sidney Kurland, a thirty-four-year-old art professor at Montana State University, along with Norman Strung, a thirty-four-year-old local magazine editor, Strung's wife Priscilla, and seven others. Police confiscated two and a half pounds of cannabis—a large amount for a small Montana town, even during the sixties—and six of those arrested were charged with "disposing of narcotics to a minor."[34]

The presence of pot in their community shocked conservative Bozeman residents, and follow-up articles in the *Billings Gazette* vividly outlined the ensuing controversy. First, Kurland denied any association with the drug; police had woken him up in the middle of the night to search his home but found no trace of cannabis. *Gazette* reporter Dick Gilluly then wrote a column informing Bozeman citizens about grass, noting that penalties for pot "are regarded as absurdly severe by those who know about the drug," which he referred to as "the mildest" of psychedelic substances. A week later, in a news story that explained why the recent pot arrests produced such a local ruckus, Gilluly articulated the view of nature espoused by most Bozeman residents:

> Bozeman is clean and pleasant appearing. Rugged blue mountains to the south and east seem almost literally to shine in the clear and unpolluted air. Tree-lined residential streets are well-maintained, and the MSU campus stretches beautifully landscaped across a gentle slope on the southeast.[35]

In this description, one of civilization's most orderly institutions—the university—is necessarily surrounded by perfectly ordered nature. The "rugged" nature of the mountains does not intrude, but still serves civilization by creating a pleasing backdrop. The implication here is clear: whether in town or miles beyond it, nature existed to serve humanity. As long as wild and ordered nature was kept in its proper place, all was well.

In general, most members of the counterculture rejected the idea that nature—including human nature—could (or should) be tamed. To the hippies and other young rebels in Bozeman, people, mountains, landscaped campuses, and cannabis were all parts of the same nature, and it was nobody's place, not even the law's, to restrain any of it. But to conservatives, it was the law that kept nature, human as well as nonhuman, in its place.

Whether it was federal land-use rules in the wilderness or local ordinances in town, laws brought order to the landscape and were to be respected.

This was certainly the opinion of Bozeman resident Mason Melvin, who in Gilluly's report drew a strange comparison between laws against marijuana and traffic laws: "Maybe it's not rational to have a law that people must drive on the right side of the road," he said, "but if people drove on the left when they felt like it, it would be a mess." Meanwhile, local rancher Harvey Griffin, who had been recently ousted from the university's executive board, blamed the pot fiasco on the arrival of "Charlie Brown Artman, California 'hippie' and avowed LSD user, on the campus last fall." "Anything is possible from the MSU art department," Griffin scoffed, referring to the embattled Kurland.[36]

To conservative residents, drug cannabis and the people who brought it into Bozeman were like other weeds—wild invaders disrupting the natural and social order of their community. But that belief did not hold up in this particular case, because several of those arrested were in fact local kids, "'clean cut' products of the way of life so revered."[37] Clearly, Bozeman residents' black-and-white understanding of nature, both human and non-human, blinded them to the diversity within their own community. This was also evident when some of the defendants in the MSU case considered arguing in court that cannabis was not as harmful as widely believed; one of their lawyers quickly advised against it, saying the argument would go nowhere in law-and-order Montana. As Gilluly wrote, "residents of Bozeman have no sympathy for such subtleties."[38]

If they were among the most blatant about it, Bozeman residents were hardly the only Americans to reject the counterculture and its groovy weed. In 1967, a year after San Francisco attorney James White submitted an initiative in Sacramento to legalize and regulate cannabis in California, columnist Russell Baker mocked the cause, and the general air of protest in the sixties, in Pasadena's *Independent*: "Many people spend more time dissenting than working. We have dissenters actively defending marijuana, Communism, extramarital sex, Mao Tse-tung, rioting . . . draft-dodging," he wrote; "Is there no one in this entire country with the courage to stand up and defend air pollution?"[39] In 1968, Richard Bradley, a juvenile probation officer in Sequim, Washington, told the *Port Angeles Evening News* that "raw marijuana is coming into Seattle at the rate of 100 pounds a day" and blamed hippies for introducing the drug. Bradley said there were "approximately 23 hippies living in the area and [he] thinks there will be an invasion of them this summer. He stressed their demoralizing influence on some of the local youth. . . . He hopes the community will make it known collectively they are not wanted."[40] Facing staunch resistance in town, many in the counterculture simply decided to leave.

Living on the Earth

While the counterculture's alternative vision for society clashed with mainstream America in cities and on college campuses, some young people in the movement searched for refuge in the countryside. By the late 1960s the commune movement was attempting to show Americans that utopia wasn't just a pipe dream. As demonstrated by its relationship with cannabis, the generation that came of age in the sixties believed that trying to live *with* nature instead of trying to control or perfect it would allow people to live more happily with one another. This opinion was not shared by all those who opted for communal living in the 1960s. There were many urban communes and communes founded for other purposes. But the desire to find the true place of humans within nature was nonetheless a deep-seated motivation for many who chose to leave behind work, school, and family in order to test their utopian dreams on the American landscape.[41]

It is difficult to generalize about the sixties communes, since there were so many and each reflected the particular values of their diverse inhabitants. The late political scientist Jeff Lustig probably nailed it when he wrote that "[t]he idea at its heart is obligation—to others, to a shared purpose, or sometimes to a larger religious or political ideal."[42] If nothing else, it can also be said that many were deliberately founded in remote places amidst breathtaking scenery. Some of the more famous communes included Drop City, founded in 1965 east of Trinidad, Colorado; the Hog Farm, established the same year on (surprise) a hog farm overlooking California's San Fernando Valley; Morning Star Ranch, founded in 1966 in Sonoma County, California; and New Buffalo, founded near Taos, New Mexico, in 1967.[43] While many of the most influential communes were founded in the West, hundreds of these small, ramshackle communities cropped up all over the nation in the 1960s.

Most commune dwellers came from cities and were part of a generation raised with many modern conveniences, so they faced a steep learning
curve out on the land. Creating a functional community where everyone
had decent shelter and a reliable food supply was hard work, and as a result
the euphoria wore off for many commune residents after a few months. In
fact, most residents were transients, spending a few weeks or months in
one community and moving on to the next. Some of the roamers took their
valuable skills with them when they left, a problematic setback for a community. Others—unwilling to do much work and partaking in as many free
meals and as much booze and drugs as they could before moving on to the
next place—treated the whole movement like one giant party. Those who
stayed rarely encountered the kind of hardworking, cooperative, and committed individuals needed to keep the community afloat. And despite the
desire of many residents to get away from the trappings of currency, money
was still needed to pay land taxes, buy farming equipment and building
materials, and make other essential purchases. Some communes withered
and disappeared under these realities, while others found ways to manage
their populations and make money. New Buffalo, for example, acquired a
decent herd of dairy cattle and sold milk in Taos.[44]

Despite voluntary poverty, a high turnover rate among residents, and
a general lack of experience, the most dedicated commune dwellers soon
developed some tricks of the trade. While living on the Wheeler's Ranch
commune in Sonoma County, California, former *Los Angeles Free Press*
writer Alicia Bay Laurel produced a comprehensive compilation of these
tips, to which she later gave the simple title *Living on the Earth*. The book
was published in 1970 and met with exceptional acclaim and fanfare,
even earning a favorable review in the "square" *New York Times*.[45] In the
introduction, Bay Laurel—who changed her surname from her parents'
Kaufman to the name of her favorite tree—perfectly articulated the counterculture's view of nature and how it was supposed to help society. "This
book," she wrote, "is for those who would rather chop wood than work
behind a desk so they can pay PG&E [Pacific Gas & Electric]. . . . When
we depend less on industrially produced consumer goods, we can live in
quiet places. Our bodies become vigorous; we discover the serenity of
living with the rhythms of the earth. We cease oppressing one another."[46]

Written entirely in flowing, cursive handwriting and illustrated with simple line drawings and diagrams, *Living on the Earth* features step-by-step instructions for virtually every task required to make a living off the land, including bread making, maintaining a wood-burning stove, making soap from animal fat, building rudimentary houses and other structures, fashioning one's own clothing, and even giving birth. It also includes detailed instructions on how to grow, harvest, and store drug cannabis, as well as a recipe for "stoney-butter"—marijuana-infused butter that adds a kick to "any confection recipe."[47]

While grass was about as common as beards on the communes, very few of these communities engaged in the commercial production of cannabis, largely because commune dwellers rejected any kind of for-profit industry. Growing might also attract unwanted attention from thieves or authorities. However, as suggested by Bay Laurel's instructions, some communes did grow small amounts of cannabis. Libre, a commune named after the Spanish word for "free," was founded as a nonprofit "school" in Colorado's Huerfano Valley in 1968.[48] Former Libre resident Roberta Price wrote about cannabis cultivation in her memoir, *Huerfano*, and the cover features a photo of its young, barefooted author embracing several bushy stalks of freshly harvested grass:

> Like the Lakota and other Plains tribes, who used every part of the buffalo, and like the Makah and other Northwestern peoples, who never let any part of a whale go to waste, we use every part of the marijuana plants we harvest. What to do with the stems and seeds is the biggest challenge and takes the most ingenuity.[49]

Price then provides her own "stoney-butter" recipe—except she calls it "funny butter" for its giggly effect.

Price's comparison of the Libre ganja harvest to Native Americans' use of buffalo and whales was not random. It reflects the counterculture's admiration of Native American culture, especially its relationship with nature—Indians were "the original hippies," as residents of New Buffalo called them.[50] Traditional Native American structures such as kivas and teepees were erected on some communes, and gardens held the staple Indian crop arrangement of corn, beans, and squash. For their part, many Native Americans saw the counterculture's attempted emulation as naïve and disingenuous, as most tribes were forced to abandon their old ways of living as they adapted to the economic realities of twentieth-century America. Still, some in the counterculture managed to build genuine relationships with Indians around a shared vision of living in greater harmony with nature; hippies even stood alongside Native Americans in some of the demonstrations of the American Indian Movement during the 1970s. Indians sometimes traded with commune residents and served as advisors.[51]

Libre was certainly not the only commune that experimented with cannabis growth. By 1967, Marc Weisberg had established a hippie colony about twenty-five miles east of Chico, California, in Butte Creek Canyon. About a dozen residents killed their own game and grew cannabis there until their sanctuary was raided by Butte County sheriff's deputies.[52] Thirty miles west of Spokane, Washington, hippies grew cannabis on Huw Williams's commune, Tolstoy Farm.[53] Still, most of the grass smoked on communes and elsewhere was grown in Mexico and smuggled into the United States.[54] Although it was far from ubiquitous, cannabis cultivation on the communes fit neatly into the new landscape their residents tried to create—a landscape of cooperative sustainable living, bolstered by innovation and defiance.

Like the cannabis plots of Mexican workers in the 1930s and 1940s, the communes of the 1960s were part of what historian J. B. Jackson called the "vernacular landscape"—the patchwork of personal gardens, hand-built homes, sheds, greenhouses, and anything else that people put on the land without official approval. Elements of the vernacular landscape exist outside of zoning laws, building codes, or landscaping crews. Johnny Pot, who sowed random cannabis patches, was a steward of the vernacular landscape, as were the commune residents, who built their own homes, planted their own gardens, and dug their own irrigation ditches. By contrast, the "political" landscape includes things like roads, power lines, squares or plazas, courthouses, lawns, sidewalks, parks—things that are publicly maintained and reflect the popular notion that orderly nature makes for orderly society. The political landscape strives "to impose or preserve a unity and order on the land," while the vernacular landscape lacks structure and uniformity because it reflects the everyday needs of individuals.[55]

The vernacular and political landscapes often occupy the same space— think of the "hippie pads" and illegal cannabis patches within well-ordered cities—but the political one is typically more "visible," more "distinct from its surroundings."[56] Tree-lined streets and a well-manicured campus, for example, were (and remain) distinct markers of the political landscape in Bozeman. Citizens there and elsewhere look to this landscape to produce "law-abiding citizens," among other things.[57] In the 1960s, as the example of Bozeman shows, most of the nation's older generations touted the political landscape as the proper model for civilization.

But the younger generation increasingly saw that landscape as a place where other citizens' rights were denied, where the individual was persecuted, and where young men could be sent off on a whim to be slaughtered in a brutal and unnecessary fight. So, as suggested by the outbreak of communal living during the 1960s, many young Americans chose the vernacular landscape instead—they intentionally violated building codes, zoning ordinances, draft orders, drug laws, and other elements of the political landscape. Their relationship with cannabis came about because the plant was, and had long been, an outcast herb, part of the vernacular verdure. More than a simple disagreement over drug use, the social conflict over cannabis in the 1960s and 1970s reflected the opposing ways in which different generations viewed humanity's proper relationship with nature.

White Is the New Green

With so many young members of the white middle class "turned on" to grass in the 1960s, authorities had a problem. Cannabis violations had been felonies since 1951, when the Boggs Act imposed mandatory minimum penalties for all drug violations. These penalties were further increased by the Narcotic Control Act in 1956, so that by 1960 first-time possessors of cannabis in most states faced a mandatory minimum of two years in prison and a fine of up to $20,000.[58] But then the counterculture popularized cannabis, and thousands of young people started getting popped for pot. While it was generally acceptable among whites to lock up Mexicans and blacks for using or distributing drugs, the arrests of so many white, middle-class youths led many suburban parents to call for a revision of the nation's drug laws.[59]

By the mid-1960s courtrooms were also better attuned to the social climate surrounding weed. Believing many young defendants to be otherwise law-abiding citizens who either made a poor decision or were victimized by a drug dealer, judges were reluctant to enforce the harshest penalties, especially for first-time offenders.[60] In 1967 a judge in the Los Angeles juvenile department was fired for openly "favoring legal use of marijuana by adults" and telling a newspaper that the drug was "no more of a public danger" than alcohol.[61] By that time, the prosecution rate for cannabis defendants in California had fallen by about half, dropping from 93 percent in 1960 to 48 percent in 1967.[62] Meanwhile, Harry Anslinger retired from the Federal Bureau of Narcotics in 1962, leaving federal prohibition without its most fiery crusader (Anslinger had characteristically pushed for the harsher penalties enacted under the Boggs and Narcotic Control Acts). Watching marijuana, his botanical archnemesis, become the nation's most popular illicit substance in the years after his retirement must have given Anslinger convulsions.

Equally disturbing to Harry would have been the Supreme Court's ruling in 1969 that his Marihuana Tax Act was unconstitutional. In *Leary v. United States*, the court sided with former Harvard psychology professor Timothy Leary, one of the nation's most prominent advocates of psychedelic drugs. Leary was arrested in 1965 at the US-Mexico border for possessing a small amount of cannabis and convicted under the Tax Act in 1966. In court he argued that the act violated his Fifth Amendment protection against self-incrimination. The nation's highest court agreed, ruling that if Leary had attempted to obtain an order form, as the law required, he would have identified himself "as a member of a 'selective group inherently suspect of criminal activities.'"[63] Just like that, Anslinger's baby was killed off after thirty-two years, and Leary's thirty-year sentence was wiped out.

The Tax Act wasn't the only legal casualty of the counterculture. From the late sixties through the mid-seventies, anti-cannabis laws were contested in several states, and penalties were lessened in some. In 1967 friends of Melkon Melkonian, a school principal fired after one of his educators was arrested for selling cannabis, formed an impromptu group in San Francisco for the legalization of the drug.[64] A year later, as part of its national campaign to legalize and regulate the adult use of cannabis, the American Civil Liberties Union (ACLU) began its challenge of Washington state's marijuana laws; in 1969 state lawmakers removed cannabis from stricter narcotics laws, changing the penalty for first-time possession from a minimum of five years in prison to a fine and a maximum of six months in jail.[65] In 1970, a young lawyer named Keith Stroup founded the National Organization for the Reform of Marijuana Laws (NORML) in Washington, DC.[66] In its first few years of operation, NORML cobbled together support from across the political spectrum—including Gordon Brownell, a Republican lawyer and defector from the anti-drug Nixon administration—to lobby for the decriminalization and legalization of cannabis.[67]

It wasn't until the mid-seventies, however, that these efforts began to pay off in more statehouses across the country. Oregon decriminalized cannabis possession in July 1973, limiting the penalty for possessing up to one ounce to a $100 fine.[68] Although a bill to legalize cannabis in Colorado failed in 1973, the legislature passed a bill in 1975 that brought punishment for possession of up to one ounce in line with Oregon's law.[69] California passed a nearly identical law a month later.[70] Those three joined Alaska and Maine as states that had decriminalized possession by July 1975.[71] By the end of the decade, Nebraska, Minnesota, Mississippi, Ohio, North Carolina, and New York had all decriminalized cannabis possession, bringing the total number of states to eleven.[72]

The New Politics of Prohibition

The federal government also backed off the harsh penalties for drug possession during the 1970s, but new legislation reinstituted cannabis prohibition after the dissolution of the Marihuana Tax Act. As previously mentioned, the CDAPCA of 1970, commonly referred to as the Controlled Substances Act, restructured federal drug control around the prevention of interstate drug trafficking. While the act limited the penalties for possession of any drug, including cannabis, to a misdemeanor, the CDAPCA's scheduling, or categorization, of drugs placed the herb in Schedule I—the category reserved for the most dangerous, highly addictive drugs that had no accepted medical use.[73]

This categorization was immediately challenged on two fronts, one official and one grassroots. First, in an attempt to prove once and for all that cannabis was harmful, the Nixon administration commissioned the largest-ever federal study of the drug. The National Commission on Marihuana and Drug Abuse was to report on, among other things, "the nature and scope of use, the effects of the drug, the relationship of marihuana use to other behavior and the efficacy of existing law."[74] Former Pennsylvania governor Raymond

Shafer (R) chaired the thirteen-member commission, which included two psychiatrists and the pharmacology department chair at the University of Michigan. Regarding the effects of cannabis, the Shafer Commission, as it came to be known, found that "there is little proven danger of physical or psychological harm from the experimental or intermittent use of the natural preparations of cannabis . . . The risk of harm lies instead in the heavy, long-term use of the drug, particularly of the most potent preparations."[75] In its final report, released in 1972 and numbering more than one thousand pages, the Shafer Commission recommended that cannabis be decriminalized, concluding that "the existing social and legal policy is out of proportion to the individual and social harm engendered by the use of the drug."[76] In a policy addendum, it also recommended "increased support of studies which evaluate the efficacy of marihuana in the treatment of physical impairments and disease."[77]

The final report of the Shafer Commission was the most rational federal statement about cannabis since the La Guardia Report in 1944, which came to similar conclusions and sent Harry Anslinger into a rage. President Nixon, however, proved to be just as much of a cannabis curmudgeon as the retired narcotics commissioner. In 1972 Nixon declared drug abuse to be "public enemy number one" and specifically requested "a goddamn strong statement about marijuana" from the Shafer Commission.[78] Because its findings were politically inconvenient, the president flatly rejected the commission's proposals without ever reading its report.

The counterculture's legacy loomed large in the continuation of cannabis prohibition during the reformation of federal drug policy in the 1970s. After all, Nixon's stubborn refusal to read the Shafer Commission's report came not out of hatred for the plant itself but out of disdain for those who used it—the same crowd who had protested the war, burned draft cards, sided with African Americans during the tumultuous civil rights movement, and in general caused the federal government a great deal of anxiety during the late sixties and early seventies. Nixon hated hippies about as much as Anslinger hated jazz musicians. As it turned out, the new political recipe for prohibition called for the same hefty portions of denial and vindictiveness as the original.

Although the Shafer Commission did not produce the findings he wanted, Nixon could have both respected the facts *and* pursued his tough-on-drugs agenda. He could have pushed Congress to reschedule and decriminalize cannabis, while at the same time authorizing new trials to further investigate both the helpful and harmful effects of the drug. This would have been a hard pill for hardline conservatives in his party to swallow, but it might have taken the potency out of cannabis as a countercultural symbol. If the feds had revised their pot policy, the antiestablishment crowd would no longer be able to point to the weed as an example of federal dishonesty. The herb would have lost its hip, outlaw appeal, and its popularity may have suffered. Changing the policy also would have saved millions of dollars in taxpayer money and kept a substantial number of those taxpayers out of jail. Meanwhile, Nixon could have redirected resources to suppressing the use and traffic of cocaine, heroin, morphine, and other more debilitating drugs, allowing him to keep his tough-on-drugs promise to the so-called "Silent Majority"—the base of conservative voters that elected him.

Nixon, of course, did none of those things. Carrying on with his anti-drug agenda, in 1973 Nixon created the Drug Enforcement Administration (DEA), the replacement for the old FBN. The next year, he established the National Institute on Drug Abuse (NIDA), which remains the federal focal point for drug research in America. NIDA has a reputation for disproportionately funding studies designed to highlight the harmful effects of cannabis, while rejecting or suppressing studies designed to test the plant's medical applications. The institute's approach contradicts the Shafer Commission's recommendation; the fact that such bias exists in an institution that serves as one of the primary funding sources for cannabis research partly explains the current lack of well-funded, comprehensive studies on medical cannabis.[79] Thanks to Congress and the Nixon administration, federal drug policy in America was clearly and constitutionally defined by the CDAPCA, enforced by the DEA, and backed with research from NIDA. Despite subsequent modifications under different presidential administrations, these three elements provided a legislative and institutional framework for the war on drugs that endures today.

Professor Randall's Prescription

In 1975, about a year after Nixon resigned in the midst of the Watergate scandal, the counterculture's mass experimentation with cannabis again bore political fruit—this time it would help reestablish cannabis as a legitimate medicine. Despite the Shafer Commission's report, the herb had remained classified as having "no currently accepted medical use." But a 1976 decision by a superior court in the nation's capital would put an important asterisk next to that clause.

Robert Randall, a college professor from Washington, DC, had long suffered from glaucoma, a degenerative condition in which fluid collects and builds up pressure in the eyeball, injuring the optic nerve. It eventually results in blindness. In 1973 a friend handed him a joint, and after a puff or two Randall found that his vision improved. He also found that he could grow his own medication, raising "six beautiful marijuana plants" on his sundeck. But the police came in 1975, ripped up his plants, and arrested him. Randall was charged with a misdemeanor but chose to fight the charge in court on the grounds of "medical necessity."

Randall found the evidence that would make him the first legal medical cannabis patient in the United States since 1937: in a NIDA report of a study designed to help cops identify stoned people by looking at their eyes, UCLA ophthalmologist Robert Hepler found in 1971 that smoking cannabis did more than dilate pupils and cause redness—it also lowered users' intraocular pressure. Hepler even went on to treat several glaucoma patients with the herb. Once again, federally funded research aimed at supporting prohibition only weakened the case for it.[80]

In December 1975, Randall underwent a series of medical tests run by Dr. Hepler at UCLA's Jules Stein Eye Institute. With NIDA supplying the joints, the tests showed conclusively that smoking cannabis was the only known treatment capable of lowering Randall's intraocular pressure to a safe range. Interestingly, oral ingestion of the THC pill Marinol failed to reduce the pressure, suggesting that THC was not the only therapeutic compound in cannabis smoke. Randall's personal physician, Dr. Ben Fine, concurred with Hepler's assessment that Randall would go blind without cannabis. This was all the evidence a superior court judge needed, and Randall was acquitted in 1976. Afterward, he filed a petition requesting that the government provide him with his medicine. The government agreed, but only to controlled, medically supervised consumption. So for fourteen months, Randall used cannabis provided by Dr. John C. Merritt of Howard University in Washington, DC, who kept strict tabs on Randall's intraocular pressure and general health. Merritt concluded that Randall's cannabis use continued to stabilize his intraocular pressure, thereby "preventing further damage" to his optical nerve. Even though another physician was willing to monitor Randall's continued use of cannabis, the feds abruptly cut off the professor's supply in 1978.[81]

Randall sued the feds again, and again he won; this time, an out-of-court settlement guaranteed that the government would fill Randall's pot prescription. It was poor-quality bud grown on the government's experimental farm at the University of Mississippi, but it worked for Randall. After decades of smoking legal, federally furnished joints, he never went blind. Once his own medical supply was secure, Randall dedicated himself to helping others obtain clinical cannabis, including sufferers of not only glaucoma but also multiple sclerosis, chronic pain, and AIDS.[82] Not one to shy away from touting the medical benefits of the herb, he even recounted his experience in a chapter in *Cannabis in Medical Practice*, a 1997 book edited by registered nurse Mary Lynn Mathre. Randall died of complications related to AIDS in 2001, but his legacy lived on in the form of the federal government's Compassionate Investigational New Drug Program, which provided between fifteen and thirty-four patients with medical cannabis from 1978 to 1992.[83]

Thanks to the broader influence of the counterculture, which had introduced a new generation of Americans to cannabis, Randall was able to break four decades of official silence on the medical use of the plant. It is important to mention that cannabis is not widely considered to be an effective treatment for glaucoma today—it does lower intraocular pressure, but a person must smoke every three to four hours to keep it down. This basically requires the patient be stoned all day, which, as the American Glaucoma Society points out, means that many patients would not be "functioning at maximum mental capacity."[84] Of course, some patients will function better under the influence than others, but based on recent research it seems that eye drops, pills, and surgery provide more effective treatment.[85]

By turning to science to verify his own experience with the drug, Randall forcefully restarted an official conversation about medical cannabis that endures today and has helped thousands of people find effective, alternative treatments for a variety of conditions. The genie was out of the bottle, but the federal government would spend the next four decades—and counting—trying to awkwardly shove it back in. The awkwardness persists: a

DEA publication from 2014, for instance, trashes the raw plant and defends its nonmedical classification, while listing in the same publication several FDA-approved medicines derived from it. The message in the publication is clear: the federal bureaucracy, not popular belief or actual experience, determines what is or isn't a medicine.[86]

Grass Goes Back to the Land

While Randall received his medicine from the government's experimental cannabis farm, the rest of the nation's pot smokers in the 1970s relied mostly on imported herb from Mexico. In 1975, one narcotics officer from Tucson, Arizona—a city then referred to as "the marijuana capital of the country"—estimated that between 50 and 70 percent of cannabis smoked in America came from Mexico.[87] Other estimates place it as high as 90 percent, with imports from Jamaica and Colombia accounting for most of the remainder.[88]

But thanks to a growing population of countercultural runaways, the United States would soon have its own cannabis-producing hot spot. By the late 1960s, as the Vietnam War dragged on and hippies found their traditional urban neighborhoods under assault by street gangs and organized crime, more and more members of the counterculture became convinced that salvation, not just for themselves but for the entire nation, could only be attained by returning en masse to the land.[89] In 1967, for example, near the end of the Summer of Love, a hippie newsletter lamented that "some of the most 'beautiful' people in the San Francisco hippie community are moving elsewhere."[90] Some headed for existing communes, while others traveled to remote locations to build their own homesteads and begin a new, more natural and independent life.

The previously mentioned mass movement of young people to communes, homesteads, and other remote places during the late 1960s and 1970s is collectively known as the back-to-the-land movement.[91] Communes represented a distinct piece of this movement, as their devotees were focused specifically on achieving social harmony through the sharing of obligations and resources. But even though many ended up living cooperatively or near one another on homesteads, not all back-to-the-landers were committed to communal living. Most were simply looking for a remote sanctuary where they could build their own houses, grow their own food, and raise their

own children without anyone telling them to clean up or get a job. As one
back-to-the-lander remembered:

> What we wanted to do was eventually carve out niches, which were convivial
> for people, of an alternative lifestyle that we were convinced would serve as
> laboratories of the next civilization that would supplant the existing discred-
> ited American civilization.[92]

Carving out those niches proved harder than many of these young people
imagined. Like commune residents, most back-to-the-landers were ex–city
dwellers who had little practical experience on the land. But by 1970 they
had plenty of help. Not only was Laurel's *Living on the Earth* published that
year, but in 1968 countercultural media mogul Stewart Brand began publishing the *Whole Earth Catalog*, a popular magazine featuring do-it-yourself
columns, environmentally focused product reviews, designs for sustainable
housing, and other advice on how to live a more eco-friendly life.[93] Between
Brand's catalog and Laurel's rustic guidebook, idealistic young adults had a
rather detailed set of blueprints for making their utopian vision a reality.
The only thing left to decide was where to go.

Many back-to-the-landers from San Francisco, Portland, and other West
Coast cities made their way to northern California and southern Oregon,
where a mild climate and rugged, remote landscapes made it possible to live
an isolated life outdoors. The region was a countercultural magnet, pulling
young people out of their urban enclaves and into Humboldt, Mendocino,
Trinity, Shasta, and Siskiyou Counties in California, and Josephine and
Jackson Counties in Oregon.[94] Some of these emigrants congregated in
existing communities, such as the small town of Takilma in Josephine
County, Oregon.[95] Others merely sought a quiet homestead, and land was
plentiful in timber country, where logging companies often sold cutover
land to migrating counterculturalists on the cheap.[96] To these newcomers,
the forested hillsides on either side of the Oregon-California border represented a new beginning, a place where they could live both off the land and
off the grid.[97]

By 1973, a typical group of these back-to-the-landers lived on about a
dozen homesteads near the tiny town of Briceland in Humboldt County,
California. Most were young couples in their twenties or thirties who
hoped to make a quiet life amidst the tangled woods. They cleared brush,

built houses, and planted vegetable gardens.[98] But while they sought to live almost entirely from the land around them, even the most resourceful and experienced homesteaders needed money for land taxes, not to mention building materials, vehicle parts, stoves, storage tanks, and other items.

The homesteaders near Briceland were generally unwilling to take traditional jobs, but even if they had been, the local economy did not have much to offer. By the early 1970s the timber industry, which had been the backbone of the northern California economy for decades, was in its death throes. And as one experienced homesteader told the *Eureka Times Standard*, the land near Briceland was "problem country for farming"—it was simply too rugged and too steep, and the soil was not as rich as it was farther north, in the deltas of the Eel and Mad Rivers.[99] With traditional employment and truck farming largely out of the question, the back-to-the-landers could turn to making homemade crafts or other items to sell at local markets. But since that was one of the only profitable activities, the local markets became "pretty much glutted for most of that stuff," the homesteader explained.[100]

There was another option for homesteaders, and though it was far riskier than craft making or truck farming, it was virtually guaranteed to bring in cash. Not long after they moved to Humboldt County, back-to-the-landers discovered that the same environmental factors that brought them there—a mild climate and a rugged, mostly uninhabited landscape—also made for a nice place to grow cannabis. The Eel and Mad River watersheds offered hundreds of creeks and streams that could be diverted for irrigation, and vast tracts of dense forest offered excellent cover for the illegal crop. Growers also wouldn't have to go very far to make a sale, as their peers in the region's countercultural communities provided a ready market; deputies in nearby Mendocino County only made six arrests for cannabis use or possession between 1936 and 1966, but by July 1967 they had made twenty-nine such arrests in just nine months.[101] Northern California's climate and topography, as well as its resident population of pot smokers, made the region a dreamscape for the cannabis farmer during the 1970s. Had Johnny Pot ever wanted to settle down, it's a good bet he'd have made his home in Humboldt County.

Bill Drake and the First Growers' Guides

But unlike Johnny Pot and other earlier growers, by the mid-1970s Americans no longer simply planted cannabis near a ditch or on a vacant lot and hoped for the best. Rather, they found plenty of guidance in a budding literature on cannabis cultivation. One of the earliest of these publications was Bill Drake's *The Cultivator's Handbook of Marijuana*, first published in 1970. Drake, then a world-traveler in his late twenties with a degree in anthropology, later wrote on his blog that he first learned the secrets to marijuana farming "in Mexico in the 1960s." After his travels, which also included visits to Morocco and Colombia and a stint in Chad with the Peace Corps, Drake settled near Eugene, Oregon. He grew a few marijuana plants but ducked out of the industry after seeing many of his friends busted. Discouraged, he soon decided that if he couldn't grow weed, he would write about it.[102] Drake would go on to write "cultivator's handbooks" for other controversial plants, including tobacco and coca, but as his first, *The Cultivator's Handbook of Marijuana* set the precedent for today's ultra-detailed, intensely scientific marijuana manuals.

True to the era that produced it, *The Cultivator's Handbook* presents a typewritten trove of serious scientific data alongside rustic, quirky, and lighthearted imagery. As readers take in soil temperature and water-use charts, an annotated list of potential nutrient deficiencies, explanations

THE CULTIVATOR'S HANDBOOK OF MARIJUANA

By Bill Drake
Illustrated by Terry Rutledge
Calligraphy by Jim Drake
First Edition (Revised)

In 1970, Bill Drake, a former anthropology student in Eugene, Oregon, published *The Cultivator's Handbook of Marijuana*, the first book-length work on marijuana horticulture in the United States. Drake was nearly arrested by California deputies on his way to sell the first five hundred copies in San Francisco. Photo by Bill Drake.

of the various types of light and "photoperiodicity," and detailed fertilizer instructions, they are repeatedly joined by a companion—a bearded, Jesus-looking hippie farmer, drawn by illustrator Terry Rutledge. Other illustrations include a whistling garden worm and anthropomorphic suns. Poems in Chinese calligraphy adorn many of the pages; this was apparently a nod to the ancient Chinese, who were among the first civilizations to find use for the cannabis plant.[103]

Drake's book includes chapters on marijuana's environmental requirements, seeds and germination, lighting and growth patterns, harvesting, and even hybridization. Unlike today, with most marijuana produced indoors, in 1970 indoor growing was more of a hobbyist's pursuit; still, Drake included model numbers of appropriate lights and other instructions tailored to indoor cultivation. The writing is mostly straightforward, scientific, and instructional, punctuated by refreshing frankness, such as when Drake notes that "[t]here's an awful lot of pure bullshit associated" with the challenge of growing high-potency cannabis. "Many people believe," he continues, "that drug potency has something to do with climate, soil, harvesting technique and the like. The real dope, as far as a scientific explanation is concerned, is that drug potency in cannabis sativa is directly related to the genetic properties of the plant." This is one of many myths Drake aimed to debunk with his inaugural guide to funky flower farming. Among others were the myth that more nitrogen is better (a nitrogen overdose will kill a young plant or a stunt resin production in an older one, he warns); that "cannabis doesn't need much water" (it needs a lot of water but not constantly wet soil, he clarifies); or that marijuana needs high heat and humidity to thrive (temps over 75° Fahrenheit are not necessary, Drake writes, and high humidity "can cause an accumulation of plant poisons which will kill it in short order.")[104]

Perhaps more interesting than anything in Drake's first book, though, is the story of how it got published. As Drake notes on his blog, *Panacea Chronicles*, writing a book about weed in the 1970s wasn't nearly as risky as growing or smoking it, but that didn't mean he was left to peacefully publish his guide. At first, things went rather smoothly. He wrote the book on a typewriter in his apartment in Eugene, where local college students sometimes paid him to write their research papers. Friends at the *Eugene Augur*, a local counterculture newspaper, helped Drake print the first five hundred copies. He loaded the books into a friend's truck and they headed off to San Francisco to see if bookstores would be interested. Then, just after midnight in northern California, a Shasta County deputy pulled them over and inspected their load of books. Miraculously, even though Drake and his friend had been smoking pot in the truck and were carrying a shipment of books on how to grow the Schedule I substance, a Shasta County sheriff's deputy gave them a verbal warning and let them drive off.[105]

Bookstores in San Francisco, that epicenter of the American counter-culture, snapped up *The Cultivator's Handbook* like candy, with customers lining up to buy copies before Drake even left the building. Famed counter-cultural poet Lawrence Ferlinghetti, owner of City Lights bookstore, bought one hundred books and referred Drake to Stewart Brand, who was just starting *The Whole Earth Catalog* and sold goods to homesteaders and com-munes out of his truck. Brand's assistant bought Drake's remaining 250 cop-ies and urged him to print thousands more. But soon after Drake returned to Oregon, he found himself tailed by suspicious black cars and his phone lines tapped; his book and traffic stop had aroused the suspicion of J. Edgar Hoover's FBI, which immediately dispatched G-men to monitor him.[106]

Under the FBI's threat of conspiracy charges, no publisher in Oregon would touch Drake's manuscript until he received help from the unlikeliest of men: Dave Holman, an anti-hippie, anti-drug, pro-Constitution, conser-vative newspaper publisher in the small coastal town of Florence, Oregon. Betting that Holman would side with him on the feds' attempts to suppress his First Amendment rights, Drake paid Holman a visit. But first he led his FBI trailers on a wild goose chase meant to fool them into thinking he was growing pot out in the Oregon woods; he even brought along trimmers and a duffle bag with oregano dust and traces of other cooking herbs to confuse them.[107]

Drake's gamble paid off, and then some. When he finally reached Holman's building—with the FBI still in tow—and pitched his book, Holman agreed to print it, then turned an angry, ex-marine scowl toward the agents parked outside. The conservative firebrand called up an acquaintance at the Oregon FBI headquarters and, as Drake remembers it, told the agent, "I'm printing this guy's goddamn book, and I better not see any of your agents anywhere near my shop or his house or I'm going to tear you and your agency a new asshole." As unlikely as it was, an anti-pot, hardline conservative in a tiny

Oregon town published the nation's first guide to growing marijuana, right after he chewed out the FBI.[108]

Other cannabis enthusiasts followed in Drake's footsteps. In 1974, former pot smuggler Thomas Forcade founded *High Times* magazine in New York City. Some four million Americans read Forcade's publication, which published articles on "gourmet ganja growers," black-market marijuana prices, and cannabis-friendly celebrities.[109] Also in 1974 a pair of New Yorkers, Mel Frank and Ed Rosenthal, published their own short guide to cannabis farming. The duo continued to research and experiment with the herb after they moved to California in 1975. In 1978 they published the much longer and more comprehensive *Marijuana Grower's Guide*.[110] Oregon native George Van Patten, writing under the pseudonym Jorge Cervantes, followed with his own self-published guide to indoor growing in 1983.[111]

These were the first American publications exclusively dedicated to cannabis growing, and the first ones to thoroughly address the topic since the USDA's *Farmers' Bulletin* 663 in 1915. Unsurprisingly, they were also considerably more detailed and comprehensive. In the 1920s, for example, the *Bulletin*'s hottest tip was that removing male plants produced a higher quality drug crop. By the mid-1970s, that was common knowledge among the authors of book-length growers' guides and *High Times* articles, who routinely delved into far more intricate topics such as light deprivation (which encourages earlier flowering), proper pruning, and precise soil mixtures.[112]

These publications gave a boost to the nascent US cannabis industry that cannot be overstated. For the first time ever, American cannabis growers had an intellectual link to one another, a forum where they could share and preserve an informal body of horticultural knowledge that had been growing in secret for decades. Drake, Frank, Rosenthal, and others conveniently packaged and published this knowledge in easy-to-read guidebooks, which further undermined cannabis prohibition by offering anyone who could read a crash course in raising the illegal herb. Tomato, corn, and turnip farmers had long enjoyed practical advice from the USDA and Agricultural Extension services; now, the nation's cannabis farmers had their own agricultural support network, with Drake et al. serving as enthusiastic extension agents.

Home Grown on the Homestead

Whether they were raising twelve plants or twelve hundred, most of the back-to-the-land growers in northern California acquired seeds from a local distributor. This might be someone who took a cache of seeds into the countryside, a hippie who had recently returned from Pakistan, Afghanistan, or Mexico, or even an army veteran who returned with seeds from Southeast Asia.[113] Unlike today, most of these backwoods growers had no idea what kind of grass they were growing; dope was dope, and even though every grower had his or her own method of raising it, the growing season was not unlike most other crops. Seeds from the previous year's harvest went into the ground in late April or early May, and most crops were mature by late August, although some growers harvested as late as October.[114]

Some growers diverted water from nearby streams for irrigation, and other experienced growers figured out that cannabis produced more THC during a drought, so they cut their plants' water supply in the last two weeks before harvest.[115] Growers cut down the mature plants when they were ready, removed the flower-laden branches, and hung them in a shed or another dry enclosure. Once dry, the flowers were removed from the branches and placed in paper bags to cure, a process that took anywhere from several days to more than a week, depending on the condition of the plants and the preferences of the grower. When cured, growers trimmed the excess leaves around the flowers and packed the buds into bags for distribution.[116] The first small crops were initially consumed locally, but by the mid-1970s the sheriff's office reported that "most Humboldt County marijuana [was] sold in the Bay Area."[117]

Humboldt County authorities started busting people for cultivation as early as 1968.[118] Enough people were growing by the early 1970s that deputies began using aircraft to spot larger cannabis fields; this prompted most growers to raise no more than a few dozen plants and keep them out of conspicuous open spaces.[119] Nevertheless, there was the occasional bumper crop. In October 1970, for example, growers near the small town of Weitchpec in northern Humboldt County produced a whopping 233 pounds of cannabis.[120] In early August 1973, deputies pulled up 267 plants from "six small fields" and "two homemade greenhouses" in northwestern Humboldt

County near Fieldbrook.[121] Another huge raid in September 1976 netted 2,500 plants from "small hill farms" near Salmon Creek in the southern part of the county.[122] As indicated by the timing of these major busts—August, September, October—deputies often moved in during harvest time.

The Briceland Bust

The deputies who raided the cannabis farms near Fieldbrook in August 1973 never found the farmers, but they redeemed themselves later that month when they nabbed nine suspects in a massive raid on the homesteads near Briceland.[123] Unlike smaller raids, the big bust and its aftermath—from the community's response to the burning of the plants to the subsequent court proceedings—received wall-to-wall coverage in the local press, demonstrating how quickly cannabis growing in northern California had transitioned from a small "cottage industry" to big business. Indeed, it happened so fast that the growers themselves didn't even realize it, arguing that the thousands of plants they grew were simply part of their efforts to have "peace and quiet."[124] The heavy-handed tactics used by the Humboldt County deputies during the raid foreshadowed the military-style campaigns that would be launched against growers in ensuing decades, as the cat-and-mouse struggle between cops and growers mushroomed into a kind of guerilla warfare.

It's not clear why the pot growers around Briceland decided to grow so many plants in 1973. Maybe they were tired of living in near-perpetual poverty or racked up too much debt, or maybe they simply got greedy. In any case, by early August, while county deputies scratched their heads over the weed farms by Fieldbrook, some three thousand cannabis plants were nearing maturity on ten separate homesteads in the Briceland area. The plants were "irrigated and fertilized," and some were growing "on terraces cut into hillsides" while others matured in hothouses.[125] By the end of the month the crop would be ready for harvest. Humboldt deputies later estimated that each plant would yield about a pound of marijuana, and each pound would fetch between $50 and $100 on the black market. That would place the value of the whole three-thousand-plant crop at $150,000, but for reasons that remain unclear, later estimates from the same sheriff's deputies were considerably lower, at around $15,000 or $20,000.[126]

Either way, the homesteaders' crop would turn a significant profit. But while they tried to focus on their upcoming payday, many became preoccupied with the loud drone of an airplane—a sound heard with unsettling regularity in those last few weeks before harvest.[127] Their fears were confirmed on August 21, when twenty-five deputies stormed the homesteads. With guns drawn and only a single warrant, they kicked in doors, smashed windows, trampled vegetable gardens, pulled up the unharvested plants, and clapped nine homesteaders—five men and four women—in handcuffs. The rest fled into the brush. Two days later, all nine homesteaders were charged with possession, cultivation, and possession for sale of marijuana.[128]

With the growers in jail, deputies may have thought the matter was on its way to being settled. As it turned out, the arrests only marked the beginning of a series of post-bust difficulties for the Humboldt Sheriff's Department. First, to avoid inviting scavengers, deputies tried to burn all of the plants while they were still green; this produced a ridiculous series of events reminiscent of the army's failed attempts to burn a Denver hemp patch some twenty years earlier. The Humboldt deputies dumped diesel fuel on the weeds, but they quickly ran out of fuel and had to borrow more from the US Coast Guard. The plants still wouldn't catch, prompting Deputy Mel Ames to crack that the weeds were "tougher than them damn hippies." If he had it his way, Ames said, he would airmail the whole crop into the Pacific Ocean. Another deputy, evidently bored, "danced through the smoke, imitating a high hippie." The deputies eventually figured out that they needed to feed the plants piecemeal into the fire, but then they realized that neither they nor the closest residents had a pitchfork or a rake. One deputy left to see if he could find the proper tools, but at 9 p.m. he still wasn't back. By that time, the pile of cannabis still hadn't burned down, and news reporters sent to cover the burning had already adjourned to a local bar. The next day, *Times-Standard* city editor Harold Kitching explained that decision, writing that if the reporters "had to smell the marijuana burning, they might as well do it in someplace where it's warmer and where they could get some of the stuff the prohibition agents used to dump down the gutter."[129]

As if dealing with indestructible plants and sarcastic reporters wasn't enough, the sheriff's department got additional grief in the form of some 180 protesters who gathered in nearby Garberville three days after the raids. The protesters accused Sheriff Gene Cox of unnecessary property destruction, raiding ten locations with only one warrant, and of general "hippie harassment."[130] For his part, Cox managed to come up with two more warrants after the raids and said the other properties were legally searched on "probable cause." Moreover, he said he actually went easy on the growers: "Legally, we could have confiscated all their tools, vehicles, hoses, water pumps, anything which was connected with the cultivation," he told the *Times-Standard*. "We didn't do so because we aren't interested in giving people a hard time."[131] Cox apparently did not consider that his actions may indeed cause some of the homesteaders to do "hard time." Still, the sheriff's decision not to confiscate the growers' gardening equipment was generous, and was perhaps motivated by politics; he had to enforce the law, but in this case, in this community, he decided not to enforce it to the letter, likely with the intention of minimizing public backlash. If that was his calculation, though, the Garberville protest showed he was wrong.

It still wasn't over for Cox. Two days later, the sheriff again came under fire at a county budget meeting where he requested more deputies. Ted Kogon, part owner of Evergreen Natural Foods in Garberville, brought signed statements and photographs from homesteaders that confirmed deputies' threatening and destructive actions during the raids. Kogon waved the statements and photos in Cox's face, declaring that "if you're considering budget requests, you ought to consider the way the men will be used." The county supervisors, not wanting to be seen endorsing illegal activity, tentatively approved Cox's request for seven additional deputies.[132]

Things quieted down a bit after that. Neither Kogon nor the homesteaders, now free on bail, could make good on threats of legal action against the sheriff's department. But investigations and court proceedings continued over the next two years, and ultimately showed that only one of the nine homesteaders arrested was actually guilty of a marijuana offense. Two had their charges dismissed at a preliminary hearing, and on September 3, 1975, a California superior court ordered felony charges dropped for six others. The court found that, other than the fact that they were on the properties during the raids, there was no evidence they had broken any laws. The remaining homesteader was given the chance to have his charges dropped if he completed a rehab program.[133] The Humboldt County Sheriff's Department probably hoped that the seizure of so many plants and the arrests of nine alleged growers would discourage pot growing in the area. But at the end of the entire episode, people were still growing lots of marijuana in Humboldt.

Although Sheriff Cox said he wanted to avoid "giving people a hard time," that was about the only thing his department accomplished by raiding all those homesteads in August 1973.

On the other side, even though the courts eventually sided with the homesteaders, it can hardly be said in hindsight that their decision to grow three thousand plants was a good one. Far from bringing in enough cash to live the quiet, out-of-the-way life they desired, growing so many plants only brought them broken windows, trampled food, and two years' worth of legal proceedings and court fees. And yet, with mouths to feed, land taxes to pay, and the price of cannabis at $100 per pound, an immense opportunity was staring them right in the face. After the collapse of the timber industry, nothing else growing in northern California could bring in that kind of cash. And if growing three thousand plants was a reckless decision in 1973, it pales in comparison to the ambitions of growers who would move into the area over the ensuing decades.

Post-Countercultural Cannabis

For residents of northern California and southern Oregon, the three thousand plants seized in the Briceland raid of 1973 were the tip of a giant green iceberg. The counterculture brought cannabis into this rugged part of the country hoping that it would be a casual accompaniment to life in the woods, one that would occasionally provide some extra cash for the homestead. But the movement had already made the plant too popular, and thus too valuable, for it to remain part of a small-scale "cottage industry."[134] In a little more than a decade, the small skirmishes unfolding between local cops and hippies would evolve into a guerrilla war between federal and state law enforcement and a new generation of large-scale, big-money growers who would do whatever it took to get their crop to market.

By the end of the 1970s, the counterculture had ushered cannabis across social, political, and environmental boundaries. Once confined to jazz clubs, inner-city bohemian dens, and working-class Mexican communities, the herb now found favor among thousands of young members of the white middle class. They smoked cannabis as part of a broader search for new experiences and new ways to navigate a social landscape that was becoming increasingly dysfunctional during the 1960s. These cultural revisionists found that cannabis fit neatly within their vision of a more harmonious relationship between people and nature; such an open-minded approach to the plant allowed people such as Robert Randall and others to rediscover its medical potential, an important intellectual frontier that had been closed since 1937.

The weed's popularity among so many white, middle-class young people fundamentally altered how all levels of American government approached drug use. The counterculture managed to win legal victories for grass in the 1970s, getting eleven states and even the federal government to decriminalize possession. These gains would quickly be unraveled by subsequent administrations, but they nonetheless laid important political groundwork for future legalization campaigns. By scouring the globe for hardier varieties of drug cannabis and planting the herb in the hills of northern California and southern Oregon, hippies and back-to-the-landers helped the plant expand both its genetic diversity and its territory in North America. By 1980 cannabis growing in the United States had gone from the haphazard seed-scattering of Johnny Pot and other hippies to a high-stakes backwoods industry that kept entire communities afloat, even as it dragged them into the destructive whirlwind of the drug war.

The counterculture's popularity was ebbing by the end of the 1970s, and the stage was set for a strong backlash from conservatives and prohibitionists. The federal government used the prohibitionist trifecta created by the Nixon administration—the Controlled Substances Act, the DEA, and NIDA—to put the squeeze on domestic growers and discredit anyone who argued for legalization. In response, growers moved their crops indoors or onto public lands, and pro-pot citizens made a hard grassroots push for access to medical cannabis.

CHAPTER 5

Black Market Blues

Capitalized Cannabis and the Environment, 1980–1996

After they bashed in the front door of an East Oakland warehouse in January 1991, police were at once impressed by what they saw and distressed by what they smelled. "The smell of marijuana was overwhelming," officer Ralph Nuno recounted. A twenty-five-year-old man, Michael McCune, had converted a ten-by-fifteen-foot room into an indoor farm lined "wall-to-wall and floor-to-ceiling" with fifty-three cannabis plants. The grow lights suspended from the ceiling were attached to a motor that rotated them around the room, simulating the changing angles of sunlight. The lights operated on a timer and were also attached to a pulley system that allowed them to be raised as the plants grew taller. Authorities also said McCune had unspecified "growth enhancers"—most likely nutrient booster mixes—throughout the room. Nuno admitted McCune's system was "sophisticated"; other weed growers might have called it "dope."[1]

It was the grow room's sophistication, however, that ultimately got McCune busted. Police noticed that his electricity usage had quadrupled over the past few months. It didn't help McCune that he was also wanted for burglary and vandalism. He told police that the plants were for his "personal use" and that they were his "first-ever" crop. Nuno and the other officers didn't believe a word of it.[2] McCune's operation isn't just an example of the agricultural ingenuity of modern cannabis growers; it's an example of an underground industry that was in transition during the late 1980s and early 1990s.

For more than sixty-five years, cultivation of drug cannabis had a negligible effect on the American environment. This began to change after 1980 for several reasons. First, like other valuable crops, the cannabis gene pool diversified after it became popular.[3] In the 1970s, new varieties of marijuana came from Vietnam and Central Asia. Through experimentation and a growing base of how-to literature, growers learned to hybridize these varieties and produce a crop that was more potent, and thus more valuable.[4]

When the Mexican government, with sponsorship from the US government, began spraying cannabis fields with a toxic herbicide, American pot smokers flew into a panic, and homegrown cannabis became more appealing just as more people were figuring out how to grow it. A massive black-market industry developed in some of the nation's most remote regions, and the cannabis-growing population shifted from easygoing hippies to an ambitious crowd of profit-hungry outlaw farmers. Finally, in the early 1980s, federal and state authorities intensified efforts to wipe out the domestic cannabis industry, driving growers off the land and into homes, basements, and warehouses, where fossil fuel–powered operations like McCune's flourished.

Paraquat Panic

Between 1969 and 1974, US forces helped destroy more than five hundred thousand cannabis plants in Vietnam, largely using herbicidal chemicals that often missed their mark and damaged trees, crops, and animals.[5] Then in 1975, determined to cut off the marijuana supply from Mexico, the Ford administration began collaborating with Luis Echeverría's Mexican government to spray Mexican cannabis fields with paraquat, a toxic herbicide used for general weed control that could kill a pot plant within a day.[6] From 1975 to 1978, the US government gave Mexico $30 million per year toward "indirect support" of the spraying program, most of which went toward the purchase and maintenance of aircraft.[7]

The American public was mostly ignorant of the program until 1978, when articles in *High Times* and *Time* magazines catapulted paraquat into the national consciousness.[8] Suddenly, most of the fifteen million pot smokers in America became very worried about the safety of their stash.[9] At the time it was widely known that paraquat, if inhaled or ingested in its pure form, caused a slow and incurable suffocation; what smokers wanted to know was whether it had that same effect once ignited and inhaled in a joint, pipe, or bong. Keith Stroup of NORML got wind of the paraquat program by 1977 and eventually gathered enough information to mount a legal challenge, but a political scandal involving Stroup and President Jimmy Carter's drug advisor, Peter Bourne, ultimately derailed the effort.[10]

Pot smokers, meanwhile, were still left in the dark as to just what it was they were smoking.

NIDA didn't help ease the paranoia when it warned in early 1978 that "smoking marijuana containing paraquat presents the greatest potential hazard" and that "a heavy smoker (one to three joints a day, every day) could possibly have measurable lung damage after several months."[11] Two months later the *Straight Creek Journal*, Denver's weekly countercultural paper, kept the anxiety level high by reporting that Dr. David Smith, a physician at the Haight-Ashbury Free Clinic in San Francisco, had treated three young men—all habitual weed smokers—for "suspected paraquat toxicity." A research firm in Palo Alto confirmed that samples of the men's weed stash were "contaminated with paraquat."[12] The same firm estimated that, of the fourteen hundred cannabis samples it analyzed, 23 percent contained the chemical. The *Journal* gave pot-smoking readers step-by-step instructions, vetted by the Palo Alto firm, to test their own stash for the herbicide, and anxious smokers across the country sent in samples to other labs.[13] The Mexican government, meanwhile, blamed the whole controversy on American pro-cannabis groups. Late in May 1978, Mexico's deputy attorney general, Samuel Alba-Leyva, told the *New York Times* that "there hasn't been a single proven case of paraquat poisoning from marijuana," and that "the whole campaign has been orchestrated by groups favoring legalization of marijuana."[14]

Although he had his own government and anti-drug campaign to protect, Alba-Leyva was probably right. Despite the dire warnings of *High Times*, the *Straight Creek Journal*, and even NORML, the paraquat scare turned out to be mostly hype. One later review of the joint Mexican-American paraquat program estimated that between six hundred and twelve hundred American cannabis users had been exposed to the chemical between 1975 and 1979, but there were no credible cases of poisoning reported. Furthermore, the spraying affected only a tiny portion of the Mexican crop, and most contaminated plants were ditched by the growers before they even made it to market.[15] Studies have since revealed that cannabis laced with paraquat poses no real threat to the smoker, as plant combustion fundamentally alters the herbicide and renders it harmless during inhalation.[16] Federal support for spraying drug fields with paraquat was suspended in 1978 but reinstated in 1981 under the Reagan administration.[17] For once, it was the pro-cannabis press—not the federal government or the mainstream press—that had irresponsibly sensationalized a cannabis issue. But the most important consequence of the paraquat program was that it made domestic cannabis more attractive within the national marijuana market.[18] Suddenly, homegrown weed, which had for years been considered inferior to the imported stuff, could be marketed as au naturel.

Cash Crop in the State of Jefferson

The domestic cannabis industry in northwest California and southwest Oregon was the legacy of the back-to-the-land movement, but hippies only partly explain why the region became the heartland of American pot production in the 1980s. As it turned out, cannabis farming was a perfect match for a remote, sparsely populated region whose rugged landscape produced a long history of outlaw activity and a strong culture of frontier individualism. During prohibition, for instance, the area was a haven for bootlegging with its vast expanses of dense forests, rolling hills, and jagged, craggy mountains. Living in isolation from the largest populations of their respective states, the region's residents have often felt disconnected from and underrepresented in Sacramento and Salem.

This sense of alienation and regional solidarity produced many efforts to make the region into its own state. They began as early as 1852, when residents in gold-mining communities on either side of the California-Oregon border proposed the creation of the state of Shasta.[19] Perhaps the most famous attempt occurred in 1941, on the eve of the United States' entrance into World War II. Frustrated residents along the border blockaded roads and handed out pamphlets announcing their intention to create the "State of Jefferson," which would have consisted of Curry County in Oregon and Del Norte, Modoc, Siskiyou, and Trinity Counties in California. Would-be Jeffersonians justified their secession movement by arguing that their respective state governments had shortchanged them on support for road development, schools, and other public services. They elected their own representatives and established the new state's capital in the Siskiyou County town of Yreka. But in late 1941, just as the movement hit peak momentum, the Japanese bombed Pearl Harbor, and the ensuing wave of patriotism turned many Jeffersonians away from their local cause.[20]

The boundaries of the so-called State of Jefferson have never been consistently defined, but over time they have included as many as eleven counties in northern California and six counties in southwest Oregon. While it has sometimes taken concrete form in the plans of restless separatists, the State of Jefferson has always been more of an idea, a shared sense of regional orientation and identity, than an actual place.[21] But it is nonetheless an appropriate label for the areas of southwest Oregon and northwest California that developed a burgeoning cannabis industry in the 1980s. Beginning with a host of scattered growers in the late 1970s, cannabis became yet another distinctive marker of the region's rugged individualism—it was the number one cash crop in the State of Jefferson.

Cannabis production wasn't all that popular in southwest Oregon until after the state decriminalized possession in 1973; after that, growers in the remote region saw an opportunity to fill the baggies of many smokers, not just in Oregon but also in neighboring California.[22] The centers of production were Jackson and Josephine Counties.[23] By 1978, authorities estimated the crop value there to be around $7 million, acknowledging that "a considerable amount of pot is grown on a small scale by amateurs in backyards, basements (with grow lights) and in isolated patches on public and private lands."[24] By 1981, conservative estimates of the cannabis crop in Jackson County alone approached $10 million.[25]

"Marijuana culture was just everywhere," remembers Richard Reames, fifty-seven, a grower who lived in the area during the cannabis boom of the early eighties. "It was just ingrained. And they talked to each other—if they trusted each other." Reames said he learned how to grow in those days by reading botanist Robert Connell Clarke's *Marijuana Botany*, published in 1981. "It was like a bible," he said.[26]

The local growing population evidently took a great deal of pride in its work. By the late seventies growers had their products sampled by cannabis connoisseurs at Josephine County's annual Doper's Fest, and by the mid-eighties some were even branding their product with "Grown in Oregon" labels.[27] The quality of southern Oregon bud even impressed local authorities, including Josephine County undersheriff Jim Carlton. "If other agricultural developments had kept pace," Carlton told a reporter in 1983, "we'd be growing 500-pound watermelons now."[28] Contrary to what Bill

Drake wrote in his *Cultivator's Handbook*, growers in Jackson and Josephine Counties attributed their high-quality herb to the climate, with its long stretches of hot weather in the summer and mild springs and falls.[29]

Of course, northern California had its own thriving grass industry at the time, and many local residents welcomed the cash flowing in from the illicit crop raised in the surrounding hills.[30] Cannabis farmers were spread all throughout northern California, but Humboldt and Mendocino Counties were consistently large cultivation centers. By the mid-1980s, authorities estimated the value of cannabis plants seized in annual raids to be between $300 and $400 million.[31]

Even though they sought profit from an illegal enterprise, the first wave of cannabis growers in the region also sought to fit in with local communities. Elizabeth Watson, a sociologist at Humboldt State University who has lived in the hills near Arcata, California, since the mid-1980s, said many were content to make a living as quietly as possible, and being good neighbors helped keep them out of trouble.[32] Growers also earned the favor of locals by donating money to local schools, fire departments, and other municipal services, as well as environmental and civil rights organizations.[33]

They might have been neighborly, but not all of these growers practiced sustainable cultivation methods. For instance, the inaugural report from the state of California's Campaign Against Marijuana Planting (CAMP) in 1983 notes that 85 percent of growers encountered in fourteen northern California counties used chemical fertilizers, while just 5 percent used organic fertilizers and 2 percent used none. Seventy-five percent used chemical rodenticides, which can be fatal to local wildlife. Growers also littered the woods with fertilizer bags, plastic growing containers, and other garbage, and left open fertilizer bags on the ground or in streams.[34] Over-fertilized streams produce excessive amounts of algae that suck up all the oxygen, making them toxic environments for other forms of aquatic life. These practices were regularly documented by later CAMP reports.[35]

The local pollution of grow sites documented by CAMP represents the beginning of unsustainable cannabis cultivation in the United States. Never before had the herb been cultivated on such a large scale, with farms so heavily concentrated in one region; nor did growers have access to so many artificial pesticides and fertilizers, many of them designed for mainstream agriculture and home gardening.[36] It is impossible to determine the cumulative effect of some growers' negligent practices, but based on the scale of cultivation in the region, they likely amounted to a significant number of negative local impacts across a landscape already scarred and denuded by decades of careless logging.

The cannabis boom in the State of Jefferson wasn't just a product of the countercultural presence, tainted foreign supplies, or relaxed possession laws in Oregon. It was also fueled by the continued publication of instructional journals and books on cannabis growing as well as by the rediscovery of an important horticultural technique. One of the most common problems with homegrown weed was that it often contained too many seeds, which are nonpsychoactive and produce a harsh smoke. Moreover, female cannabis plants only produce the psychoactive resin until they are pollinated; when that happens, the plant focuses its energy on seed production.[37] Sometime in the mid-1970s hippies in the State of Jefferson—whether it was Oregon or California is a subject of debate—learned that removing male plants from cannabis crops encourages the female plants to produce bigger, more potent flowers.[38] Of course, the USDA knew about this technique in 1915, and it was likely first developed in India centuries before British observers noted it there during the nineteenth century.[39] In the mid-seventies, traveling hippies may have observed the technique in India and, as Bill Drake's story shows, they definitely observed it in Latin America, explaining the rise of the term "sinsemilla."

As growers in California and Oregon began experimenting with sinsemilla crops, many had their experiences and advice printed in *Sinsemilla Tips*, a magazine started in 1980 by Tom Alexander, a former pot grower in Corvallis, Oregon. Like Bill Drake, Alexander began his marijuana publishing career after a run-in with the cops—in 1979 Corvallis officers busted his 1,324-plant crop, started selling it on the side, and were later arrested by the Oregon State Police. Meanwhile, Alexander found a technical error in the search warrant used to seize his crop and got his charges dropped. Still miffed at the authorities who busted him and then tried to profit from his work, Alexander composed the first edition of *Sinsemilla Tips* by kerosene lamp and typewriter in 1980.[40] Among the advice Alexander offered in that first issue was "how to tell the males from the females, exactly how to set up a drip-irrigation system," and "when to transplant the seedlings."[41] He printed one thousand copies, and growers immediately gobbled them up. Soon, Alexander was delivering *Sinsemilla Tips* up and down the West Coast, from Seattle to San Francisco. In the fall of 1980 he secured a national distributor, and by 1985 the magazine had a press run of ten thousand copies. The West Coast complement to *High Times*, Alexander's magazine included grower-authored articles and how-to guides for both outdoor and indoor cultivation, as well as cannabis-related political commentary, cartoons, and advice on how to deal with law enforcement.[42] Portland NORML described the content of *Sinsemilla Tips* as "original, astute, and consistently more adult than that of *High Times*."[43]

Like Drake's *Cultivator's Handbook*, Alexander's pot publication attracted federal drug enforcers. By the mid-1980s law enforcement began targeting garden supply shops and other businesses that, whether knowingly or not, routinely sold lights and other equipment to marijuana farmers. Once he got out of pot growing, Alexander started Full Moon Farm Products, a company that sold bat guano and other gardening products; of course, cannabis growers made up a primary, if discreet, market for Alexander's goods. In 1989 the DEA confiscated Full Moon Farm's entire inventory as part of "Operation Green Merchant," a campaign to shut down suppliers of the marijuana industry.[44] Alexander was never charged with a crime, but the DEA was already putting many of the shops that advertised in *Sinsemilla Tips* out of business, so Alexander shuttered the publication and focused his efforts on a new magazine he began publishing in 1988. The new journal, the *Growing Edge*, made no mention of cannabis but supplied advice and product recommendations for indoor vegetable gardening, most of which could be applied to marijuana.[45]

While growers thumbed through *Sinsemilla Tips* for advice to improve their crop, law enforcement struggled to comprehend the "new" seedless trend in marijuana. Because sinsemilla is more potent, authorities often mistook it for a completely new variety of cannabis. In 1980, for example, Steve Helsley, the director of Operation Sinsemilla in California, told the *Oakland Tribune* that "sinsemilla is a variety of marijuana five times stronger than that from Mexico or Colombia."[46] In 1981, the *Mail Tribune* in Medford, Oregon, described sinsemilla as "an exotic hybrid specie of marijuana that contain 10 times the amount of THC . . . than is found in the usual types of marijuana."[47] Like the 1930s belief that fiber plants produced drugs, the misunderstanding of sinsemilla in the 1980s demonstrates how cannabis continually confused authorities.

The Gipper v. Ganja

While the State of Jefferson raked in millions from its illicit cash crop, the federal war on drugs got an unprecedented boost when former B-movie actor and California conservative Ronald Reagan, nicknamed "The Gipper," won the presidency in 1980. In addition to his personable charm and sense of humor, Reagan would be remembered for presiding over the end of the Cold War; implementing a "trickle-down" theory of economics; a full-frontal assault on organized labor; and a scandal in which his administration sold arms to the Iranian government in exchange for freeing American hostages, then used the money to back a right-wing coup in Nicaragua.[48] During his two terms as president, he also became known for a staggering number of factual gaffes, with one of the first coming in a 1980 campaign speech: "Leading medical researchers," Reagan said, "are coming to the conclusion that marijuana, pot, grass—whatever you wanna call it—is probably the most dangerous drug in the United States, and we haven't begun to find out all of the ill effects."[49]

It is not quite clear what he meant by "leading medical researchers." Perhaps he was referring to the biased work of NIDA, which in 1974 claimed that results from a study in which rhesus monkeys were asphyxiated with cannabis smoke offered sound evidence that cannabis caused brain damage.[50] Like Nixon before him, Reagan had clearly not read the Shafer report. But he got a shot to reevaluate his opinion on cannabis during the second year of his presidency. In 1982 the National Academy of Sciences (NAS) released a comprehensive review of cannabis titled *An Analysis of Marijuana Policy*. The NAS report generally agreed with the Shafer commission's findings. Although it noted that "heavy use by anyone or any use by growing children should be discouraged," it drew the following conclusion:

> [C]urrent policies directed at controlling the supply of marijuana should be seriously reconsidered. The demonstrated ineffectiveness of control of use through prohibition of supply and the high costs of implementing such a policy make it very unlikely that any kind of partial prohibition policy will be effective in reducing marijuana use significantly below present levels.[51]

The report was published in June. It appeared to have little effect on the president. "Drugs are bad," Reagan explained in a national address in October. "And we're going after them. As I've said before, we've taken down the surrender flag and run up the battle flag. And we're going to win the war on drugs."[52] While he ignored the recommendations of serious scientists, Reagan took advice from his drug policy advisor, Carlton Turner. Remarkably enough, Turner was an ex-cannabis farmer, of sorts. The biochemist once grew and researched the plant at the government's experimental farm at the University of Mississippi.[53] Despite this, Turner made it no secret that he hated cannabis users—he made all kinds of bizarre claims about the weed, once saying that it turned people into homosexuals.[54] Although he had within his reach a report from an entire committee of pharmacists, sociologists, psychologists, and other clinical professionals, the president's number one advisor on drug policy was a man who thought weed turned people gay. Casting aside a wealth of credible evidence against its effectiveness, the Reagan administration ratcheted up the war on drugs.

In 1984 Reagan signed the Comprehensive Crime Control Act, which raised federal penalties for drug possession, cultivation, and sales, and granted police the right to seize the property of people suspected of drug crimes.[55] As journalist Martin Lee points out, "Accused rapists, murderers, and kidnappers—unlike marijuana suspects—did not have their assets confiscated without a trial."[56] Meanwhile, a pair of Supreme Court decisions weakened two key Bill of Rights protections, thereby aiding authorities in their campaign against drug offenders. In *Illinois v. Gates* (1983), a case involving cannabis traffickers, the court loosened the Fourth Amendment's protection against unreasonable search and seizures.[57] Then, in *United States v. 89 Firearms* in 1984, the court ruled that asset forfeiture did not constitute double jeopardy, as prohibited by the Sixth Amendment.[58]

The Reagans continued to sound the drug alarm bell throughout the Gipper's two terms; First Lady Nancy Reagan launched her famous, youth-focused "Just Say No" campaign, while the president himself inaugurated the invasive practice of employee drug screenings by peeing in a cup himself in 1986.[59] But while the Reagan administration toughened federal drug laws and deployed the eager agents of the DEA to enforce them, it was a campaign originating in Reagan's home state of California that would ultimately prove to be the most troublesome for American cannabis growers in the 1980s and beyond.

Gone CAMPing

In 1980, two California officials blew the whistle on covert attempts by the state and federal government to use high-altitude surveillance planes in the war on weed. Gilbert Fraga, a Humboldt County rancher and chief of the Water Resources Division of the Water Quality Control Board, and Carl H. Strandberg, member of the Alameda County Water District Board, told the *Oakland Tribune* that they interpreted infrared photographs from U-2 spy planes to aid a federally backed campaign to identify cannabis farms.[60]

Developed after World War II to spy on the Soviets, the U-2 plane was a high-altitude, military reconnaissance aircraft that could obtain high-resolution photographs of the ground while staying out of sight. By the 1980s NASA used the planes in California "for checks on water pollution, timber crops, and earthquake faults." In the photos, taken from sixty-eight thousand feet, cannabis plants had "a bright-red hue." Fraga claimed that, based on the kind of equipment in the area, the photos could also reveal places where growers were preparing to put plants in the ground.[61]

Helsley, the state chief of narcotics enforcement, denied the charge that law enforcement was using the photos to obtain search warrants for suspected grow sites. But Fraga said that was only because judges, especially in the Emerald Triangle, were hesitant to accept the photos as evidence because of a potential clash with a 1974 state amendment that guaranteed Californians the right to privacy.[62] Helsley did admit that he considered using the technology as the director of the Sinsemilla Eradication Project, a program that used a two-year, $144,400 federal grant to "attack marijuana gardens" in Del Norte, Humboldt, Mendocino, and Lake Counties.[63] Helsley may have considered the use of U-2 planes to be impractical in 1980, but the state embraced the technology with open arms after California's newest pot eradication program began three years later.

In 1982, riding the rising tide of movement conservatism that swept Reagan into the White House, law-and-order Republican George Deukmejian was elected governor of California. Deukmejian's anti-cannabis stance was no secret to constituents; in his previous post as attorney general, he presided over a number of large-scale raids and even invited the press to the Emerald

Triangle to watch him take part in one.[64] The next year, Deukmejian established the Campaign Against Marijuana Planting (CAMP), an interagency program that brought local and federal law enforcement together in a coordinated assault on cannabis farmers. It remains active today.[65]

By its own assessment, CAMP's first season was a resounding success. Officers from a fourteen agencies, both state and federal, raided 524 grow sites and pulled up 64,579 plants from fourteen northern California counties at a cost of more than $1.6 million. Authorities made seventy-eight arrests. CAMP relied on standard aircraft to detect grows, though the U-2 surveillance flights were much anticipated; however, CAMP reported that the U-2 "flights provided no operational information and that aspect of the program will require further analysis before inclusion in future CAMP programs." Nonetheless, judging by the number of sites raided, standard aircraft seemed to do a fine job.[66]

The "success" of the inaugural 1983 campaign convinced sheriffs from twenty-three other California counties to join CAMP. Predictably, the expanded territory brought in more plants and led to more arrests. In 1984 the campaign pulled up 158,493 plants and cuffed 218 people. By the end of the decade, CAMP had uprooted nearly a million cannabis plants from more than four thousand grow sites and arrested more than twelve hundred people. All of that cost taxpayers $16.5 million.[67] During the 1985 to 1987 campaigns, more than one hundred state and federal agencies participated in the program, making it one of the largest law enforcement task forces in US history.

If it seems like CAMP officers in the California woods had it easier than their colleagues back in the cities, they did not. To growers, officers were an invading army coming to steal their livelihoods, and they would defend their plants at all costs. Many armed themselves, not only in anticipation of a raid but also to protect their crops from thieves or wild animals. Officers seized nearly nine hundred firearms in the 1984 and 1985 seasons alone.[68] Growers developed a special contempt for "CAMPers," as they often called them, and became adept at making it difficult, even dangerous, for officers to approach their crops. Reports for the 1983 to 1989 campaigns include many instances of growers cursing, threatening, and even shooting at officers; there is even one report of a grower shooting a CAMP helicopter so many times it was rendered inoperable.[69] Growers also left guard dogs and

CAMP

FINAL REPORT
1986

The Campaign Against Marijuana Planting, which began in 1983 and continues through the present, is a coordinated effort between state and federal authorities to wipe out illegal marijuana farming in California. Although it always fell short of that goal, each year CAMP removed millions of plants and made dozens, sometimes hundreds of arrests. This cover photo from the program's 1986 report shows a large marijuana plant held by handcuffed hands—captioned on the next page as "'Primo Bud' in custody." It is not known whether the hands belonged to an officer or a grow suspect. Source: Campaign Against Marijuana Planting, Humboldt Interdisciplinary Institute for Marijuana Research.

rigged their gardens with booby traps, including shotgun shells on rat traps, transparent wire lined with fishing hooks, and pits lined with sharpened nails.[70] The phrase "war on drugs" may have been a metaphor elsewhere during the 1980s, but CAMP officers in California had to take it literally. Remarkably, while local authorities did end up killing one Butte County grower in 1985, there is no evidence that CAMP officers killed anyone.[71]

Although they gave themselves credit for eradicating up to 92 percent of the annual crop in participating counties, the authors of CAMP reports repeatedly noted that it was impossible to know just how much cannabis was being grown in California during a given year.[72] Despite that lack of data, the program was consistently credited with eradicating a major chunk of the cannabis statewide during the 1980s. CAMP's peak year came in 1991, when the program accounted for 56 percent of all the cannabis eradicated in the state.[73]

These all might seem like impressive numbers—certainly CAMP thought so—until one considers that by its own estimates, the per-plant price of cannabis rose by nearly $1,000 from 1983 to 1989, and hiked up an additional $4,400 by 1994.[74] While the price spike could be partly attributed to the decrease in supply, other factors, including the increasing quality of sinsemilla and the increased risk that came with growing marijuana in the

CAMP era, may have also contributed. Moreover, regardless of how much domestic marijuana it took off the black market, CAMP could not claim to have diminished its availability in California or elsewhere. The high prices ensured that there would still be Californians willing to grow, while authorities in southern Oregon noted that growers there were still producing enough marijuana to supply the whole region, as they were largely not subjected to the same blitzkrieg unleashed on their counterparts just over the border.[75]

It may have put a dent in California's annual cannabis crop, but CAMP cost taxpayers more than just money—many lost their peace of mind. In 1983, tired of all the disturbances that came with living in a quasi-military zone, ten residents from Humboldt and Trinity Counties petitioned in federal district court to have the raids temporarily stopped "on the ground that their constitutional right to privacy was violated by the authorities' use of U-2 spy planes," as well as roadblocks, detention, and "widespread display of firearms." After the residents were denied a temporary injunction, they filed a suit "seeking $10 million in punitive damages, as well as unspecified general damages for alleged violations of civil rights, including the right to privacy."[76] The suits filed by the ten northern California residents represent just one of many documented incidents in which drug war shock troops terrorized American citizens—all in the name of protecting them from drugs.[77]

California and Oregon received national attention, but they weren't the only battlefields of the 1980s drug war. While CAMPers raided in California, the DEA gave Colorado authorities $40,000 annually to pay for overtime and training for officers, as well as aerial surveillance on plots of cannabis. In 1985 authorities removed 15,375 plants "from Colorado farm fields, forests, hillsides, and river banks."[78] But, just as with all prior efforts, these campaigns did not make a meaningful dent in the Colorado cannabis crop; indeed, the agent in charge of the Denver office of the DEA "conceded that the business of growing pot has become more attractive since successful eradication programs have curtailed the supply and driven up prices." The DEA also found its estimates of the US domestic weed industry to be far off the mark—it seized more of the drug in 1984 than was thought to exist in 1981.[79]

Moreover, like the pot-growing farm workers of earlier decades, cannabis growers on the eastern side of Colorado's Rocky Mountains continued to benefit from large-scale, irrigated agriculture. Sheriffs from agricultural areas reported that "marijuana growers prefer cornfields . . . because corn requires plenty of water . . . and corn's 8- to 10-foot height camouflages the shorter pot plants." Meanwhile, growers in the western part of the state, lacking the irrigated cornfields of the east, rigged up "water supplies from drainage culverts and small reservoirs."[80] When they subtly planted cannabis in between neat rows of corn or redirected water from a state-sponsored reservoir, cannabis growers in 1980s Colorado blurred the lines between the official and vernacular landscape, hoping it would help them beat the law.[81] Despite the best efforts of state and federal authorities, some fourteen years after the oft-stoned John Denver wrote his iconic ballad of the Rockies, there was still enough marijuana in Colorado to get anyone "Rocky Mountain High."[82]

But for many weed growers in the 1980s, it wasn't just about selling people drugs; it was about making a living in an era where conservative policies privileged corporate agribusiness and the cocaine addicts on Wall Street, siphoning wealth from the rest of the economy.[83] As Congress and the Reagan administration increasingly favored farm policies that rewarded large agribusiness producers, some farmers in the Midwest turned to planting cannabis.[84] In Colorado, Dave Carter, communications director for the Rocky Mountain Farmers Union, noted that "there's probably a couple farmers with some pot growing between the corn rows—any way to make some money these days." Carter joked that the government should outlaw wheat, corn, and cattle, implicitly criticizing the policies that sank the value of farm products: "Maybe that way, we could get a good price for them," he cracked.[85]

With all the money, machinery, and manpower they poured into the Drug War during the 1980s—and all the uprooted plants and arrests they had to show for it—state and federal authorities must have thought that time was running out on the nation's cannabis growers. As early as 1983, Sheriff C. W. Smith of Jackson County, Oregon, certainly thought so. "What these growers don't realize," he told Medford's *Mail Tribune*, "is that time is on our side. Jackson County won't become known as the marijuana growing capital of the Pacific Northwest if I can help it."[86]

He could not.

Paraquat, Part II

Noise, privacy violations, and excessive brandishing of weapons were not the only problems that local residents had with anti-cannabis enforcement in the 1980s. Early in the decade the Reagan administration revived the controversial tactic of spraying pot crops with paraquat—but this time it was the US government purchasing the chemical and spraying it on public lands. In August 1983, in response to a recent paraquat campaign in Georgia's Chattahoochee National Forest, the editors of the *Mail Tribune* in Medford, Oregon, penned a scathing indictment of the federal government's tactics. The editorial called the domestic paraquat program "reckless, criminal, and unacceptable," arguing that recent statements from the DEA and other federal officials confirmed that the government did not care whether cannabis smokers were poisoned by the deadly toxin. "Using paraquat in this manner is not an attack on pot. It is an attack on people who use pot," the paper asserted. "This spray program kills more than pot—it kills faith in government."[87]

The editorial noted that local Georgians vociferously opposed the paraquat program and convinced a federal judge to order the DEA to stop the spraying. Meanwhile, NORML and a coalition of three environmental groups—the National Coalition Against the Misuse of Pesticides, the Sierra Club, and Friends of the Earth—filed for an injunction against the DEA, arguing that the agency violated the National Environmental Policy Act of 1969 by failing to produce an environmental impact statement before it began spraying.[88] In 1983, a federal district judge agreed and put the paraquat program on hold until the government produced the required review of environmental impact.[89] The DEA furnished such a review in 1984, but instead of pushing the issue, the agency decided to abandon its paraquat campaign on federal lands.[90]

That did not mean the feds were finished using the herbicide. In 1985, the DEA quietly revived the practice of spraying cannabis with paraquat. This time the program targeted cannabis grows on nonfederal lands, which included state-owned, private, and Indian lands. It even sought to eliminate "naturally occurring cannabis, or wild hemp," despite the DEA admission that "the quality of the [wild] cannabis, in terms of the level of psychoactive ingredient, is correspondingly poor."[91] Why the agency continued to devote resources to destroying cannabis that was unlikely to be harvested by even the most desperate stoner is anyone's guess.

The DEA published a separate environmental impact statement (EIS) on its nonfederal lands campaign in May 1985, which was slyly written to advocate for "a full range of manual, mechanical, and herbicidal cannabis eradication methods."[92] Of course, the DEA was already engaged in "manual" and "mechanical" removal of cannabis all over the country; the report's true purpose was to justify its herbicidal program.

On page three of the EIS, a map of drug cannabis production in the United States outlined the impossibly huge task that confronted federal drug agents. Cultivation was most heavily concentrated in the West—primarily in California, Oregon, and Washington—the South, and the Midwest. There was not one state that did not see at least a small amount of cultivation; this is unsurprising, given the tremendous popularity and value of the plant at the time.[93]

The DEA purported to consider a "range of alternatives" to cannabis eradication, including "legalization/regulation of cannabis."[94] These "alternatives" were screened by "an interagency group consisting of representatives" from all the federal agencies that would be cooperating in the eradication campaign. Of course, being part of a federal bureaucracy that had a major investment in cannabis prohibition, none of the representatives seriously considered the legalization option, so that was one of the first "alternatives" tossed out in the screening process.[95]

In its discussion of "alternative" eradication methods, the EIS also outlined the DEA's extensive mechanical and chemical arsenal already used against cannabis: portable power tools, hoes, axes, machetes, weed eaters, chainsaws, mowers, reapers, and "bush hogs with high speed rotary blades" rounded out the mechanical weaponry, while the chemicals included paraquat, 2,4-D, and glyphosate. If this all seems a little excessive, we might remember authorities' history of failure in its attempts to destroy the vigorous, weedy plant; at least the DEA had the good sense not to use flamethrowers in the 1980s. Paraquat was noted as the DEA's chemical of choice "for mature cannabis plants . . . because its speed of effectiveness minimizes the possibility that cultivators could harvest treated cannabis."[96] Again, all of this was lip service to potential opponents—the DEA would have preferred to spray whatever chemicals it wanted wherever it wanted to, with zero concern for the health effects on smokers. The only reason the agency was compiling EIS reports in the first place was because NORML, environmental groups, and other concerned Americans forced it to.

Indeed, the EIS requirement probably prevented a great deal of collateral damage, both to people and the environment, as it compelled the DEA to outline its plans for the safe application of herbicides. In the 1985 EIS, the agency produced illustrated diagrams that showed how and where the chemicals would be applied, indicating an effort to minimize drift, keep herbicides away from homes, use buffer zones to protect water supplies, and alert the public to sprayed areas.[97] But in its discussion of the various methods for applying these chemicals, the DEA admitted that spraying could contaminate legitimate crops, destroy surrounding vegetation, and kill wildlife, as well as pose a minimal health risk to "heavy smokers."[98] The DEA continued to spray cannabis growing on nonfederal lands, and as late as 1989 the administration found up to 10 percent of street samples from five California cities to be contaminated with paraquat and glyphosate.[99]

Indoor Indica

The Reagan administration and state governments across the country poured unprecedented resources into the drug war, and in the process it trampled on constitutional rights, destroyed hundreds of thousands of plants, sprayed toxic chemicals on public and private lands, and arrested thousands of people. Yet the all-out strategy failed to achieve its primary goal: reducing the growth, use, and traffic of cannabis within and outside the United States. For instance, the DEA estimated in 1985 that there were twenty million cannabis users in the country.[100] Another estimate in *Mother Jones* magazine from the same year put the number of pot smokers at thirty-five million.[101] Meanwhile, under increasing pressure from state and federal law enforcement, most cannabis growers fled to either the safety of the indoors or the vast, unenforceable stretches of US public land.

By 1985 NORML estimated that a quarter of all marijuana grown in the nation was produced indoors.[102] Two years later, a DEA survey cited by CAMP reported a 49 percent increase in indoor growing operations from 1986 to 1987.[103] The importance of this shift in cannabis growing cannot be overstated. Forcing growers indoors not only made it harder for federal and state authorities to enforce prohibition, but it also inspired the innovation necessary to turn American grass from Mexican and Afghani transplants to the polygenetic pride of the pot-puffing world. Unsurprisingly, one of the first reports of indoor cannabis growth comes from California, where in 1957 Marin College student Salvadore Sorra and his wife Maryle grew marijuana underneath a "sun lamp" on a small plot in his basement.[104] Sorra's method was certainly more secure than the most common strategy of his day—outdoor cultivation—but it was not until the 1980s that it became a necessity in the face of amped-up federal enforcement.

In the relative safety of their homes, Americans discovered that cannabis was a lot more adaptive than they thought. Not only could it grow in basements under artificial light, but it could take just about as much light, water, nutrients, and even CO_2 that growers wanted to give it. The right combinations yielded indoor-adapted varieties of cannabis with bigger flowers and more potent resin.[105] Breeders crossed tropical and temperate varieties of cannabis, and came up with new strains with new names, including Skunk #1, Northern Lights, Big Bud, Train Wreck, and OG Kush—the genetic bases of today's cannabis crops.[106] American growers traveled to Amsterdam, where cannabis laws were notoriously lax—although the substance is not technically legal—and networked with growers from around the world at events like the *High Times*–sponsored Cannabis Cup.[107] The first American cannabis breeders were those trying to come up with a strain that would tolerate the cold dampness of the Pacific Northwest, but as the drug war pushed growers indoors, anyone anywhere could experiment with cannabis breeding and cultivation. As Tom Alexander told *Mother Jones* in 1985, "you can grow $30,000 worth of top-grade sinsemilla in a space as small as your master bedroom."[108]

One such experiment was apparently underway sometime after 1982 in Fort Collins, Colorado. In 2006, Greg Smoak, history professor at Colorado State University, bought a home on the city's southwest side that was built in 1982. While searching for a bad cable splitter in Smoak's basement, a cable company tech made a startling discovery: there appeared to be a false wall in one of the closets. Smoak started pushing and pulling on the wall, which turned out to be a hidden door on hinges. It opened into a small room containing several electrical outlets and ceiling hooks, most likely for powering and hanging grow lights. Smoak noticed that "all the drywall seams were sealed on the inside with duct tape, probably to prevent odors from escaping." In the grow room, the cable techs found and replaced the bad splitter; Smoak used the space to store valuables while he was out of town until he sold the house in 2010.[109] As journalist Jim Rendon notes, secret grow rooms like the one in Smoak's basement were not just quaint sanctuaries of outlaw horticulture in the 1980s—they became the backbone of the illegal cannabis trade.[110]

Growing indoors removed two key obstacles to high-quality cannabis growth: the once-a-year harvest and the removal of male plants to produce the coveted sinsemilla. Indoors, growers fooled cannabis plants into flowering by turning off their "sun"—the high-powered lamps—for twelve hours per day, mimicking the natural change in daylight hours outside. Although outdoor growers produce sizeable yields, greater control over their plants' conditions allows indoor growers to harvest multiple crops year round. Outdoor-grown bud also often lacks the specifically tailored aesthetics that higher-end customers prefer, and which indoor growers can deliver— clean-looking, rounded flowers, for example.[111] As long as they don't have any male plants and don't shock the female plants into producing male parts, indoor growers also don't have to deal with random fertilization; outdoors, where pollen from male plants floats on the wind, this threat looms larger.[112] Indoors, breeders looking to create hybrid strains also had better control over the transfer of pollen from one plant to another.[113]

Indoor-grown cannabis, as it developed in the 1980s, may be the favorite of many customers, but it comes at a high cost to the environment. Large-scale indoor growing operations require enormous amounts of fossil fuel energy to power lighting and advanced climate control systems. Current estimates claim that as much as 3 percent of California's energy goes to indoor cultivation each year and the total cost to power indoor marijuana sits at $6 billion.[114] In 2015, the *Denver Post* reported that indoor marijuana cultivation was responsible for nearly half of the city's 1.2-percent increase in electrical use each year since 2012.[115] In the Pacific Northwest, the Northwest Power and Conservation Council noted in 2016 that, "as a result of the legalization of cannabis production in Washington and Oregon, indoor agriculture is anticipated to contribute to between 100 and 200 average megawatts of increased electricity demand over the next twenty years."[116]

The shift to energy-intensive indoor growing in the 1980s represented a period of coevolution of cannabis culture and the plant itself, a feat that was not without positive and negative consequences for both. Growers operating indoors, free from government persecution, endlessly hybridized different varieties and selected for certain traits, such as higher THC content or a particular smell, taste, or effect. The results of this are some two-thousand-and-counting different strains of marijuana today. This human-engineered biodiversity was not the product of mainstream agricultural science, which has recently been focused on creating genetically engineered, chemically dependent monocrops. Rather, modern marijuana sprang out of an amalgam of traditional knowledge and American innovation, as growers across the nation, led by those in the West, reacted to intense pressure from law enforcement.

Into the Forest

The crackdown of the Reagan administration, and the Bush administration after that, on foreign drug smuggling led to another shift in cannabis cultivation.[117] By the mid-1980s, some foreign-tied "drug trafficking organizations" (DTOs), as the Forest Service calls them, started growing high-quality weed on federal lands.[118] A far cry from the hippies of the 1970s, these growers were armed and dangerous, as the CAMP reports attested. Near the end of the 1980s, growers on federal lands in California protected their crops with "trip-wired explosives, spear-like stakes, and wired plants," and some even lined their plants with razor blades.[119] Meanwhile, in Huerfano County, Colorado, growers on public lands posted armed guards, kept pit bulls, and hung fishing line with "hooks at eye level" near their crops.[120]

Along with these deadly obstacles, rangers, DEA agents, and other law enforcement personnel had the impossible task of patrolling some 193 million acres of national forest land for pot crops.[121] In 1988, despite doubling its number of cannabis plants destroyed and upping drug-related arrests on its lands by 300 percent, the Forest Service noted its efforts had "not reduced cannabis cultivation on US public lands."[122] Federal eradication campaigns, as well-funded as they were under Reagan and Bush, simply could not keep up with illegal cultivation on public lands, which continues through the present.

Forest Service agent Daryl Rush, who handles all drug enforcement operations in California's national forests, noted that when he started in the mid-1990s, cannabis patches were "few and far between" and had no more than three hundred plants. Very few growers lived with their plants in the woods. But now, he said, the number of plants in one patch routinely reaches into the thousands, and more growers are setting up on-site camps. Rush said most of these current growers are involved in smaller drug-trafficking organizations, but the Forest Service has not been able to link very many of them to larger cartels.

Living in the woods allows growers to constantly watch over their crop, and Rush notes that they have become extremely adept at hiding themselves in the forests, picking out unnatural sounds like footsteps, and hanging fishing wire around grow sites as an informal alarm system—although most are not stringing up hooks on fishing wire or using other booby traps anymore. "Those people who grow, they know the woods better than we do," Rush said. His main concern with illegal grow sites is how they affect the local environment. Many careless growers leave behind plastic bottles and other trash, and runoff from the rodenticides that are commonly used to keep small mammals away can contaminate nearby water sources.[123] Researchers working with the Forest Service have found toxic pesticides from marijuana grows in the dead bodies of fishers, foxes, deer, and owls. Often, the plastic bottles found at grow sites contain remnants of hazardous pesticides, such as malathion, an insecticide closely related to the nerve gas sarin. And the chemicals don't just pose a threat to wildlife; law enforcement personnel have reported headaches and other mild symptoms of toxicity while removing pesticide-treated cannabis, and many agents undergo monthly blood tests for chemical exposure.[124]

The experiences of Rush and others dispatched to pull up cannabis on public lands show that, while they may no longer be rigged with booby traps, today's industrially minded, outlaw marijuana growers pose a significant threat not only to the environment and law enforcement, but also to anyone who stumbles across their toxic sites. Cannabis growth on public lands today appears to be even more problematic than it has been in the past, even as marijuana legalization unfolds across the country.[125] Despite the best efforts of Rush and others, illegal cannabis growth on public lands will likely continue in some form until it has no market to serve. Far from a justification of prohibition, the environmental destruction wreaked by outlaw growers strengthens the impetus for federal regulation. The question remains: Will the federal government consider this threat to America's public lands a worthy reason to revise its policy toward marijuana?

Drug-Policy Fatigue

Americans tend to sour on any war when it drags on too long. It happened with engagements in Vietnam, Iraq, and Afghanistan, and it also happened with the war on drugs. Although they weren't quite ready to legalize cannabis and call home the troops, by the late 1990s, Americans in the cannabis-growing hotbeds of Oregon, Washington, and especially in prohibition-hammered California would show that they were at least open to the idea of some kind of legitimate market for the plant.

In the meantime, the absolutist drug policy of the federal government was about to be shaken to its core by a group of people whom it never expected to mount such an effective challenge to its authority—a sickly population of gay San Franciscans.

CHAPTER 6

Legalizing It

Medical Cannabis and the Push for a Sustainable Future

Noah Hirsch is twenty-five going on thirty-five. With a warm, bearded smile and an intelligent, deliberate style of speaking, the UC–Santa Cruz graduate has the air of a college professor. And he is, of sorts. Hirsch is an instructor in cannabis horticulture at Oaksterdam University in Oakland, the nation's first educational institution devoted entirely to cannabis. After an experiment with closet growing when he was eighteen, Hirsch raised his first serious cannabis crop in college. He grew ninety-nine plants in the spare bedroom of his off-campus apartment.[1]

"I like to anecdotally say that I majored in anthropology but minored in cannabis horticulture," Hirsch said. His bedroom crop was legal; back then he had obtained a medical marijuana recommendation for insomnia, a condition he could not beat even with high doses of Lunesta and Ambien, two powerful prescription drugs. "I would smoke a little bit or eat a little bit right before bed and that's what did it for me," Hirsch said. "I didn't think it was any kind of ceremonial or amazing occurrence—it was kind of mundane and bland: I had some problems sleeping and weed helped."

As he pursued his degree in forensic anthropology, Hirsch continued researching and experimenting with his crop. Then, in his junior year, Hirsch's father was diagnosed with severe lung cancer. After undergoing several surgeries that removed half a lung and some lymphatic tissue, his dad had a hard time breathing and suffered chronic pain. "He was taking outrageously concentrated drugs—opiates—and still feeling awful because of the radiation from the chemo," said Hirsch, who during his senior year made weekly trips back to his parents' home in Antioch, California.

By that point, Hirsch had been cultivating for several years and felt comfortable enough to recommend medical cannabis to his dad. He even bought him a vaporizer—a noncombustion device that heats cannabis flowers or oil just enough to turn the resin into a vapor—and showed him how to use it. "It was something he started to pick up on, and it really helped as far as his pain management goes. He wasn't having to take the highest dose of opiates—of hydrocodone—he was taking at the time," Hirsch said.

Hirsch's father was able to attend his graduation from UC–Santa Cruz, but he passed away a year later. "I remember very vividly the night before he passed away—we vaped together one last time. It was at that point that I didn't really know what to do next. I felt very lost," Hirsch said. He had previously considered pursuing a doctorate in anthropology, but his heart was no longer in it. Then his mother recommended he start a career in cannabis. "She told me, 'You know, for all these years you've been growing pot in your spare bedroom and you never really thought you could do that as a real job. Why don't you think about this as a career?'"

So he did. Through his brother, Hirsch got in touch with a former grower in Oakland who wanted to give him a job but told him to take a few classes at Oaksterdam first. Hirsch took his first class at the institution in 2013, then began an internship there in January 2014. Within two weeks he was hired to fill in as the Horticulture Lab Technician, and later he was doing IT work for the school. Instead of going into the business, Hirsch decided to stay at Oaksterdam and teach. While he began his growing career indoors, Hirsch is now a strong proponent of greenhouse cultivation. He maintains that natural sunlight produces the highest-quality cannabis, and now teaches a course on greenhouse growing. "Even though for the most part I've been an indoor cultivator of cannabis, I find in general that that is a dying practice," Hirsch told a class in August 2015. "I would seriously think that in about ten to fifteen years, there will be no more indoor cannabis cultivators. It is not a sustainable practice."[2] As someone who has benefited from medical cannabis and is educating a new crop of growers on sustainable cultivation, Hirsch reflects the cannabis movement's medical legacy as well as the legal cannabis industry's recent lurch toward a more environmentally friendly business model.

Taking the Initiative

Since 1996, twenty-three states and the District of Columbia have legalized some form of medical cannabis, but the first great push began in the West. Seven of the first eight states to pass medical cannabis measures

Oaksterdam University in Oakland, California, was founded in 2007 by Bay Area medical marijuana user and activist Richard Lee. The nation's first educational institution exclusively dedicated to cannabis, Oaksterdam is open to anyone who pays enrollment fees and offers professionally taught courses on subjects ranging from cannabis horticulture to law and business. Recently, Oaksterdam's horticulture instructors have focused more on sustainable cannabis cultivation. Author photo.

between 1996 and 2000 were western states—California (1996), Arizona (1996), Alaska (1998), Oregon (1998), Nevada (1998), Washington (1998), and Colorado (2000). All but Arizona went on to legalize the adult use of cannabis in the 2010s. By and large, these campaigns were grassroots endeavors that focused on the ballot initiative process—so-called "direct democracy"—rather than winning support in state legislatures.[3]

The first medical measures varied greatly in consequence and staying power. California's medical program remains the most famous (or infamous) in the nation, while the Colorado, Washington, and Oregon programs all lasted until those states legalized adult cannabis use in 2012 and 2014. Arizona's, meanwhile, was overturned by the legislature the same year it was approved (pro-cannabis organizations in the Grand Canyon state took that lesson to heart and got another initiative passed in 1998 that blocked the legislature from overturning it).[4] Possession and use of medical cannabis was legal in Nevada for fifteen years before the legislature allowed dispensaries to open.[5] In fiercely libertarian Alaska, cannabis had basically been legal since 1975, when the State Supreme Court approved personal use and cultivation.

The West has since added Montana (2004) and New Mexico (2007) to its list of states that have relegalized medical cannabis.[6] Today, medical cannabis programs across the West, including Hawai'i, serve about one million patients.[7] Conditions that make one eligible for the programs vary from state to state, but some of the most common include glaucoma, AIDS/HIV, cancer, chronic pain, and nausea.[8] As Hirsch's story and many others attest, these medical programs have helped millions of people cope with such afflictions.

But like most significant events, the increasing popularity and acceptance of cannabis in the West after 1996 had a dark side. With prices kept high by federal prohibition, more and more people got into cannabis growing, not to produce for themselves or for patients, but for the hefty black-market profits. As with most other forms of unregulated capitalism, this proved environmentally and socially destructive. In northern California, southern Oregon, and many other places, growers clear-cut land and polluted rivers and forests with chemicals and trash; indoor growers burned coal, diesel, and other fossil fuels in their efforts to replicate the sun and the seasons. The underground cannabis market became flooded with dangerous pesticides and fungicides. Growers became suspicious and resentful of their neighbors, law enforcement, and each other. Law enforcement did not help by harassing citizens, arresting and imprisoning medical users, and targeting blacks, Latinos, and gays for cannabis crimes.

Nevertheless, thanks to the medical movement's legacy of strong, grassroots organizing, there appears be a brighter future for the American cannabis industry. By popular mandate of their constituents, governments in several states have legalized and regulated the industry. Although their new marijuana policies cannot be considered universally beneficial or environmentally responsible, these states have enjoyed benefits including tax windfalls, fewer incarcerated residents, and a huge, if temporary, boost in tourism.[9] By exposing some of the more troubling aspects of a once-underground industry, state-by-state legalization has also helped paved the way for a more responsible, sustainable model for cannabis farming, even though some problems from the black-market era, including the use of dangerous pesticides, persist. As more states consider entering the landscape of legal cannabis, many more Americans are bearing witness, yet again, to a transformation in the national perception of this peculiar plant.

Bay Area Blues

It is hard to argue that such a transformation did not begin in the Bay Area in the late seventies and early eighties. The cannabis and gay rights movements went hand-in-hand in San Francisco at that time, and would combine to turn cannabis from a political nonstarter to a rallying point for millions of Californians. The city by the bay had long been a hub for all things countercultural, a refuge for hippies, environmentalists, LGBT citizens, civil rights activists, and other progressive people who tended to be cast aside or maligned by mainstream culture.[10] Unsurprisingly, it was also one of the strongest pro-cannabis communities in the nation. One of the most influential activists for both gay rights and cannabis in the Bay Area was Dennis Peron, a gay Vietnam veteran who settled in San Francisco and opened a restaurant/informal psychedelic dispensary in the early 1970s. When the AIDS epidemic hit San Francisco's gay community in the early 1980s, Peron was perhaps the city's largest supplier of cannabis to AIDS patients.[11]

People with AIDS often suffer from a decreased appetite, which leads to extreme weight loss that can weaken their already compromised immune systems.[12] Cannabis helps AIDS patients because there is a high concentration of cannabinoid receptors in the hypothalamus, the part of the brain that regulates appetite—this is why weed induces the "munchies."[13] Many patients report a host of other positive effects from using the herb, such as relief of nausea and neuropathic pain as well as a reduction in the anxiety and depression that often accompanies the disease.[14] These therapeutic effects have been discovered and at least partially confirmed by modern studies largely because of the brave efforts of AIDS patients and others in the Bay Area during the 1980s, whom no number of police raids could silence. They were determined to tell the rest of the nation and world how cannabis made their lives better.

Anecdotal evidence for cannabis's therapeutic effects began getting more scientific support in the mid-1980s. When he couldn't get funding from the government to study the effects of cannabis on AIDS patients, Bay Area doctor Donald Abrams conducted his own studies, which verified that cannabis stimulated the appetite without weakening the immune system.

Abrams also found that it helped treat pain induced by peripheral neuropathy, a debilitating condition that affects not only AIDS patients but also cancer patients and diabetics.[15]

By 1990, other doctors and scientists had made many important breakthroughs regarding medical cannabis and how cannabinoids worked within the human body.[16] In 1973, while Peron was slinging weed in San Francisco, Dr. Tod Mikuriya, a physician who began studying drug cannabis abroad in the sixties, published *Marijuana: Medical Papers*, an anthology of medical reports that helped break the silence on the herb's medical potential.[17] Other studies began to document cannabis's effectiveness in treating nausea, cancer-related pain, and cancer itself.[18]

Then, in the late eighties and early nineties, scientists also began to better understand how drug cannabis works within the human brain. In 1988 professor Allyn Howlett of the St. Louis University School of Medicine discovered a receptor for THC in the brain and began mapping its concentrations in the brain's different regions. She found the receptors to be most plentiful in the areas of the brain responsible for processes that cannabis is known to affect: in the hippocampus, which controls memory; in the cerebral cortex, which is responsible for analytical and creative thinking; in the basal ganglia, which houses the mood-enhancing neurotransmitter dopamine, and in the amygdala, which is tied to emotional memories.[19] A lack of receptors in the brain stem, which is responsible for automated, essential functions like heartbeat and breathing, likely explains why cannabis itself has never induced a fatal overdose.[20]

Howlett's mapping of cannabinoid receptors was followed by another revolutionary discovery. Raphael Mechoulam, the Israeli scientist who first discovered THC in 1965, found the body's own endogenous cannabinoid, which he named anandamide.[21] Like THC in drug cannabis, anandamide interacts with the cannabinoid receptors discovered by Howlett. Scientists now had a more complete picture of a previously unknown system, which came to be called the endocannabinoid system. As it turns out, it's fairly important, as journalist Martin Lee relates:

> This molecular signaling system modulates how we experience pain, stress, hunger, sleep, our circadian rhythms, our blood pressure, body temperature, bone density, fertility, intestinal fortitude, mood, metabolism, memory retention, and more.[22]

It was the basis for all future attempts to understand the various ways, both positive and negative, that marijuana affects the human body.

By the time of Howlett's and Michoulam's discoveries, two other Americans began exploring cannabis's therapeutic potential for veterans. In the 1980s, Al Byrne, a retired naval officer who was exposed to Agent Orange in Vietnam, found as he counseled Vietnam veterans in Appalachia that cannabis helped them sleep, drink less, and in some cases quit harder drugs. Mary Mathre, Byrne's wife and an addiction specialist who was trained as a navy nurse during Vietnam, also counseled Vietnam veterans and advocated for their access to cannabis. A decade later, Mikuriya treated veterans of the Gulf War for PTSD and recommended that "Cannabis should be considered first in the treatment of post-traumatic stress disorder."[23]

All of these important medical discoveries and rediscoveries happened under the noses of tough-on-drugs presidents Ronald Reagan, George H. W. Bush, and Bill Clinton. Slowly but surely, the public was realizing that not only did cannabis not turn everyone into addicts or slackers, but it was actually helpful in many ways—those natural cannabinoid receptors in our brains, and the natural substance many used to activate them, were useful after all.

By the mid-1990s, national polls showed strong support for medical cannabis. But most state and federal lawmakers had not budged on anti-cannabis laws for two decades. California governor Pete Wilson vetoed a bill in 1994 that would have allowed physicians to prescribe cannabis.[24] Frustrated with intransigent lawmakers, the surging medical movement in California took advantage of the opportunity to turn public opinion into political gain. In 1995 the movement campaigned hard for Proposition 215, the initiative to re-legalize medical cannabis in the Golden State. On November 5, 1996, the measure passed with 56 percent of the vote, receiving support from liberals, conservatives, and independents.[25] A slew of western—and some non-western—states followed suit over the next four years.

Weed on the Western Ballot

What, besides scientific and anecdotal evidence, made medical cannabis politically viable in the late twentieth century? Certainly some of the support came from citizens, especially Californians, who had been besieged for over a decade by CAMP and other intense enforcement campaigns. Drug policy historian Kathleen Ferraiolo also has a good explanation:

In the 1990s, medical marijuana supporters successfully shifted the terms of debate from concerns about addiction, apathy, and listlessness to feelings of sympathy and compassion for normal Americans with chronic pain for whom the drug offered relief from suffering.[26]

Though accurate, this explanation only speaks to contemporary reasons for the movement's success. A more complete understanding of why the medical cannabis movement took hold in the American West requires delving deeper into the history of the region.

For centuries before 1853, when the United States laid claim to the last piece of land that makes up today's American West, the region had been shaped by the ideas and interactions of people from many cultures and backgrounds, from indigenous to Spanish, French, Mexican, and even Russian.[27] This cultural amalgam continued during the American period, as industrial and agricultural opportunities in the West drew thousands of newcomers during the nineteenth and twentieth centuries.[28] However else one wishes to define it, the West has always been a destination. Whether it was gold, glory, land, labor, health, climate, or even the current draw of legal grass, thousands of people have acted on the belief that something better waits in the West. As Western historian Donald Worster wrote, "no region settled in modern times has had so much optimism in its eyes."[29]

In the cultural hodgepodge of the West, many had one thing—and often only one thing—in common: a belief in the region's mythical promise of self-determination, the prospect of making (or remaking) something of oneself. Moreover, in the nineteenth century the federal government lacked the considerable power it would gain in the region during the twentieth. This real lack of order merged with the West's persistent promise of self-reinvention to produce a defiant political spirit that has repeatedly expressed itself in drives for self-determination. The region's nineteenth-century "frontier justice"—the lynchings and other forms of vigilante justice carried out across the West before the arrival of courts—was a particularly bloody expression. But in the early twentieth century, western states began adopting a more civilized expression of self-determination—the ballot initiative, a process whereby citizens can create and change laws by drafting, signing, and voting on individual measures.

South Dakota became the first state to add a ballot initiative process in 1898, but the first state to use it was Oregon in 1904.[30] In the decades that followed, western states were not the only ones to adopt the process, but they were among the first and most numerous. Along with Oregon, Utah and Montana were the only other states to approve the initiative process before 1907; Colorado, California, Arizona, Nevada, Idaho, and Washington adopted it by 1912.[31] While the type of initiative process varied from state to state, by 1915 citizens in most western states could now invent or change laws without the approval of the state legislature.

In many states, the approval of the ballot initiative was due in no small part to the Progressive Movement, a coalition of reformers fed up with the excesses of monopolistic banking, railroad, and energy industries and the corrupt politicians who supported them. Progressives both in and outside state governments worked to improve the lives of ordinary citizens by transferring power from industry-backed government into the hands of citizens and professionally trained experts.[32] This was the same Progressive impulse that drove the standardization and professionalization of disciplines such as agriculture and medicine, resulting in medical journals and USDA bulletins, like *Farmers' Bulletin* 663. Socially, Progressives advocated for better working conditions, voting rights for women, better education, and restrictions on the use of alcohol, among other things.

The first sets of ballot initiatives in the West reflected these Progressive goals. One of the first three initiatives approved by Oregon voters was a local option liquor law in 1904 that allowed municipalities to hold elections to determine the legality of booze. In 1906 Oregonians considered, but ultimately rejected, a ballot initiative to create an amendment to the state constitution that would grant women the vote.[33] Montanans said yes to a state bond issue for higher education in 1908 and approved the construction of a mental health facility in 1912.[34] In 1914 Washingtonians approved a ban on the production of liquor and on employment fees, but rejected measures to enact mandatory workers' compensation and an eight-hour workday.[35] The same year, Californians approved measures that abolished the poll tax, expanded the authority of railroad regulators, gave tax breaks to colleges, and authorized the legislature to establish a minimum wage for women and minors.[36]

The initiative wasn't always used to advance Progressive causes. Also among the approved California initiatives in 1914 were a *suspension* of the state's prohibition amendment and provisions that made it cheaper and easier for residents to buy and sell land.[37] Progressive or not, for better or worse, use of the initiative process spiked during the 1920s and 1930s, fell off during World War II, and returned to favor in the 1970s.

A variety of motivating factors compelled state governments in the West to allow the initiative process, but once established, the process fed into a regional tradition of self-determination.[38] This tradition was apparent in other events throughout the twentieth century, such as when western ranchers and sympathizers joined multiple "sagebrush rebellions"—rural, locally orchestrated uprisings against federal land management policies.[39] It is also evident in the back-to-the-land movement of the 1970s, when many northern Californians grew cannabis for their livelihoods in spite of state and federal law. Of course, continued and liberal use of the ballot initiative itself is an indicator of westerners' affection for direct democracy.[40] On strictly geographic terms, the area west of the eastern borders of Montana, Wyoming, Colorado, and New Mexico is the only region in the continental United States where every state allows for some kind of initiative.[41] In general, the adoption of ballot initiatives in the West allowed a population inclined toward self-determination to make end-runs around their elected officials on all kinds of popular issues, from guns to gay marriage to ganja.

Seen through the lens of history, it's clear that the compassion-centered rhetoric of the medical cannabis movement in the late twentieth-century West did not alone lead to the movement's success; rather, that message resonated because it summoned the power of the ballot initiative, which had long been used in service of the strong desire for self-determination in the West. The movement also harnessed another potent historical force: the skepticism and frustration toward federal drug policy that developed in the 1960s and 1970s.

Although polls showed poor support for recreational cannabis in California in 1996, the template for outright legalization had been set: use the initiative, year after year, to keep the conversation going, and reframe the argument.[42] Mason Tvert, director of communications for the Marijuana Policy Project in Denver, and those who worked with him to legalize recreational cannabis in Colorado did exactly that. They called their efforts the "Campaign to Regulate Marijuana Like Alcohol." On November 6, 2012, Colorado voters legalized the adult use of cannabis by approving a constitutional amendment; Washingtonians did the same via a ballot initiative.[43]

Oregon, Alaska, and Washington, DC, enacted similar voter-approved laws in November 2014, and California, Nevada, and Massachusetts followed suit two years later.[44]

State Cannabis Regulations: The Green, the Bad, and the Ugly

True to form, Anthony Silvaggio doesn't mince words when describing state regulators' approach to cannabis cultivation in Colorado and Washington. "The models that we see in Colorado and Washington state, with this push toward indoors, is an ecological nightmare," the sociologist says. "But the state wants indoor production. You can hide it—security—and you get three to four cycles a year, and you get revenue, revenue, revenue."[45]

That's not to say all states that legalized were blind to environmental issues. As it developed plans to implement Initiative 502, the Washington State Liquor Control Commission—the agency in charge of regulating cannabis—commissioned BOTEC analysis corporation to conduct an environmental impact study.

The report, compiled by public policy experts at the University of California, noted that "increased cannabis cultivation indoors will likely be a noticeable fraction (single-digit percentages) of the state's total electricity consumption." The authors also listed "other environmental effects of cannabis . . . including water use, fertilizer greenhouse-gas emissions, and chemical releases," though they noted that "environmental risks from cannabis production are nowhere near as salient as . . . the explosive and toxic hazards of methamphetamine, or the environmental costs of large-scale agriculture, mining, metallurgy, and other industries." Legal, regulated indoor cultivation, the study reported, is still preferable to illegal indoor cultivation, which "often entails off-grid diesel or gasoline fuel generators" that "are often 3–4 times greater than the relatively low-carbon electricity available in the Pacific Northwest or California."[46]

The report authors made a number of policy recommendations based on their research, including "adjusting the excise tax on indoor-cultivated marijuana to reflect about 9 [cents] per gram worth of global warming impact, labeling low GHG [greenhouse gas] marijuana as such, encouraging efficient LED lighting development and use, allowing outdoor cultivation," and "making energy-efficient production a condition of licensing."[47] The state responded by allowing outdoor production, both in greenhouses "with rigid walls, a roof, and doors" or expanses "of open or cleared ground fully enclosed by a physical barrier" at least eight feet high.[48] It capped the maximum area of any cannabis farm at two million square feet.[49]

Some proponents of sustainable cannabis farming in Washington also take issue with the fact that the state liquor control board is regulating the industry. David Rice, Washington grower and founder of the pro-outdoor Washington Sungrowers Industry Association (WSIA), says cannabis should be regulated by the department of agriculture. "On the state level we don't have cannabis recognized as an agricultural activity," Rice said.[50]

The state left it up to individual counties to decide how to zone cannabis operations, meaning that growers could be intentionally zoned out of agricultural areas. The best climate for producing cannabis outdoors in Washington, Rice says, is in the eastern part of the state, which is largely conservative and opposed the passage of I-502. The law therefore makes it easy for eastern counties to bar the outdoor production of cannabis in the state's most heavily agricultural areas, confining production to the western part of the state where unsustainable indoor production is more viable. "Seventy years of prohibition is a hard thing to wipe away," Rice said. "Particularly when you have phrases coming out of the judiciary for years that [say] we're 'manufacturing a controlled substance.' When you go to a county council member and start talking about how I want to go to your [agriculturally zoned] area and set up my pot farm, they're like 'no way, you're going to be manufacturing a controlled substance.'"[51] Outdoor growers in Washington face an uphill battle, but the third-party environmental review and the state's allowance of outdoor cultivation shows that Washington not only considered the environmental effects of commercial cannabis production but also sought to create public policy that mitigated those effects.

The same cannot be said about Colorado. On March 13, 2013, the state's Amendment 64 Implementation Task Force published its final, 166-page report. The report covers everything from regulatory framework to consumer safety to the monitoring of scientific literature on the health effects of cannabis use. But despite the fact that the report discusses the regulation of a plant, the word "water" is nowhere to be found. Nor did the task force outline any plans or call for the study of the industry's effect on energy consumption or carbon dioxide emissions.[52] The task force also failed to consult readily available studies, such as Evan Mills's 2011 report, that would have alerted them to the problematic effects of indoor cultivation.[53] The environmental oversight was curious in a state that, like many in the West, faces water-supply challenges and is already dealing with the effects of climate change.

Colorado's laws also encourage unsustainable cannabis growth on a personal and commercial level. While the state allows anyone over the age of twenty-one to grow up to six plants (three flowering), the state's website maintains that the "plants must be kept in an enclosed, locked area that can't be viewed openly. . . . whether indoors or outdoors."[54] While the law ostensibly permits growing in backyard greenhouses, many growers lack the space and/or the resources to obtain a permit for a greenhouse. Like Washington, Colorado leaves zoning up to the counties. But greenhouses require a huge initial investment from commercial growers, so the first wave of recreational growers snapped up Denver warehouse space like hotcakes; a recent report found that one in eleven industrial buildings in Denver contain cannabis farms.[55]

The effects of Colorado's inattention to the environmental costs of cannabis production began showing up in 2015, when Denver officials reported that the city's 354 grow operations used 86 million more kilowatts in 2013 than they used in 2012.[56] Statewide, more than twelve hundred growers reflected nearly half of new electricity demand between 2012 and 2014.[57] Noting that the majority of electricity powering commercial marijuana comes from coal plants, Boulder County officials estimated that a typical five-thousand-square-foot indoor grow sends "approximately 43,731 pounds of carbon dioxide" into the atmosphere. In response, county officials now require cannabis growers to "either offset their electricity use with renewable energy, or pay a 2.16 cent charge per Kwh [kilowatt hour]. The fee is put into the Boulder County Energy Impact Offset Fund," a fund explicitly created to lessen the environmental impact of the local cannabis industry.[58]

While Colorado and Washington struggle to define cannabis as an agricultural product and curb its unsustainable growth, Oregon is taking steps to ensure more environmentally sensitive regulation. For instance, unlike lawmakers in Olympia, who commissioned one third-party study, or in Denver, who ignored environmental issues completely, the state legislature in Salem created the Task Force on Cannabis Environmental Best Practices. Consisting of Oregon lawmakers, a consultant from the cannabis industry, and representatives of the state's departments of energy, water resources, agriculture, and public utility, the task force studied agricultural practices associated with marijuana production, including existing best practices from other states. In the final draft of its report, issued in August 2016, the task force recommended that Oregon lawmakers consider four major avenues "to encourage use of environmental best practices in cannabis production"—provide growers access to information on best practices; support third-party certification programs; encourage cannabis-related research, including on best cultivation practices; and reconsider existing regulations that currently make it difficult for small-scale marijuana producers to obtain a water right.[59] In addition, Oregon's law caps indoor production at ten thousand square feet and allows outdoor grows to cover up to forty thousand square feet, thus encouraging the largest growers to set up outdoor farms.[60]

Meanwhile, as this book is being published, lawmakers in California are under a January 2018 deadline to produce a regulatory framework for their own cannabis market, estimated to be worth some $7 billion—roughly four times the combined markets in Colorado and Washington.[61] In June 2017, the state legislature passed a set of regulations that require, among other things, that pot farmers "identify the source of water they use. And if the state Department of Food and Agriculture determines there to be adverse impacts related to cultivation, it would have the authority to limit the issuance of unique identifying tags, which are required for all legally grown plants." The bill, which as of this writing has gone to the governor's desk for signature, also sets organic standards for California growers and includes protocols to lab-test marijuana products for banned pesticides.[62]

As the four largest legal markets for drug cannabis in the United States, the successes and failures of California, Colorado, Oregon, and Washington will undoubtedly help guide the creation of regulatory frameworks in other states, especially in other parts of the arid West, where the effects of climate change are already being felt.[63] But while tackling the carbon footprint and water use of cannabis growth are major steps toward a more sustainable industry, there remain other important challenges. Among the most pressing is the need to rein in a massive underground market in chemical pesticides that have been dumped and sprayed on illegal cannabis plots for decades.

Probing for Pesticides

Paraquat, thankfully, is a problem of the past; the biggest chemical threat to marijuana smokers today comes not from government spraying programs but from the growers themselves. Again, just ask Silvaggio: "You go into the grow stores [in California] and you look around on the tables and on the shelves, and they're selling toxic shit for marijuana agriculture," he said. Around the time when indoor cannabis cultivation took off in the 1980s, garden supply shops, happy to have an entirely new customer base, began selling lights, equipment, fertilizers, and pesticides to growers.[64] The problem, Silvaggio says, is that many of the pesticides growers bought and continue to buy from these stores were meant for ornamental plants, like rose bushes. "Nothing's ever been tested for inhalation, for combustion," he said.[65]

Cannabis plants are prone to a variety of insect infestations, including spider mites, hemp russet mites, aphids, and fungus gnats, as well as diseases including gray mold, powdery mildew, leaf spot, and others.[66] Failure to recognize and eliminate these infestations can result in more than just crop loss—a 2011 study from the National Institute of Health described an association between two patients' medical marijuana use and subsequent development of chronic pulmonary aspergillosis, a debilitating and life-threatening lung disease that is caused by the fungus *Aspergillus*.[67] The UK-based Aspergillus & Aspergillosis website, a vetted online resource for doctors and patients, states that aspergillosis in cannabis users "is thought to be due to the direct inhalation of fungal spores that are present on the surface of the plant."[68]

Chemical pesticides and fungicides do keep these threats at bay, but because of federal prohibition, their impact on humans who smoke the affected pot has yet to be empirically studied.[69] According to a 2015 publication from the Colorado Department of Agriculture, although the Environmental Protection Agency (EPA) admits that "some pesticides may have broadly written label language that would allow use on marijuana," the plant's classification as a "controlled substance . . . currently makes it difficult to address the issue of considering it a crop."[70] Because the herb is not federally recognized as "an herb, a spice, or a vegetable"— categories the EPA uses to label pesticides—the agency is powerless to determine whether there are any safe or unsafe pesticides for pot.[71]

Many smokers aren't aware of the kinds of pesticides being sprayed on cannabis crops, Silvaggio says, and others simply care more about things like the levels of THC and other cannabinoids. "It's strange as a sociologist because back in the seventies and the early eighties with the threat of paraquat . . . you [had] pot activists having demonstrations," he said. "Now, there is none."[72]

Colorado began earnestly confronting the pesticide issue in March 2015, when crops from ten different Denver dispensaries were either destroyed or quarantined after an investigation by the Denver Department of Environmental Health. One dispensary had to quarantine sixty thousand plants.[73] The major chemical offender was Dow Chemical's Eagle 20EW, a popular fungicide among cannabis growers that the maker warns "may be fatal if swallowed and enters airways" and "is suspected of causing cancer."[74] The hazards that the chemical poses to pot smokers are not well known because—like paraquat in the 1970s and early 1980s—it hasn't been tested for combustion.[75] In response to the raids, Governor John Hickenlooper issued an executive order in November 2015 directing state agencies to address pesticide use on marijuana plants.[76] By the following March, the Colorado Department of Agriculture had adopted rules that only allow cannabis cultivators to use pesticides whose "product label expressly allows use on crops or plants intended for human consumption."[77] On its website, the state now provides growers with lists of approved and unapproved pesticides for cannabis.[78]

The pesticide problem is not limited to California or Colorado. In June 2015, a study published by the nonprofit Cannabis Safety Institute revealed that "pesticides can now be found on close to half of the cannabis sold in Oregon dispensaries." The study tested 389 samples of cannabis flowers and 154 samples of concentrates, such as hash oil used in vape pens, and found that 14 percent of flower and 46 percent of concentrates had levels of pesticides (or PBO, a chemical added to pesticides to boost their effectiveness) that would violate EPA rules. The study's authors considered this "strong evidence that the production of cannabis extracts leads to the concentration of pesticides in the final product."[79] Like Colorado, Oregon's Department of

Agriculture has since published a list of approved pesticides and conducts lab testing of cannabis products to ensure growers are using appropriate amounts of approved pesticides.[80] The state issued its first pesticide-related recall of marijuana products in March 2017, after a marijuana business west of Eugene reported a failed pesticide reading on Oregon's online cannabis tracking system. A state-certified lab found that samples of the company's bud contained higher-than-allowed levels of pyrethrin, a low-toxicity insecticide that can nonetheless cause irritation of the skin and respiratory passages, as well as tissue damage in the nasal and respiratory passages.[81] In Washington, the state department of agriculture provides similar lists of approved pesticides, and the department of health requires that "pesticide screening by a certified third-party lab approved by the Liquor and Cannabis Board must be completed at the time of harvest for all marijuana flowers, trim, leaves, or other plant matter."[82]

The response to the pesticide issue in Colorado, Oregon, Washington, and California suggests that while state regulators may not have initially considered marijuana an agricultural product, they are increasingly seeing and regulating it as such. But while it is good that states are regulating pesticide use, the question remains whether nonorganic pesticides should be used in marijuana cultivation at all. Historian Michelle Mart notes that most Americans have an ongoing love affair with chemical pesticides, despite decades of mounting evidence of their capacity for environmental and personal harm.[83] Like the mainstream farmers and gardeners Mart cites in her book, marijuana cultivators might also have an irrational affinity for synthetic pesticides (and fertilizers), as the chemicals aid them in their continual search for more efficient ways to produce bigger buds.

Another potential problem with state-regulated marijuana pesticides is that each state has to develop its own lists of approved and unapproved substances, as well as testing and enforcement procedures. This means that chemicals (or thresholds for chemicals) not allowed in some states might be approved in others, so marijuana consumers may be exposing themselves to chemicals in Colorado that they would not be in Oregon, or vice versa. And while many states try to align their pesticide standards for marijuana to those of mainstream agriculture, the lack of research on how chemical pesticides uniquely affect marijuana consumers reduces the factual basis of such alignment to guesswork (if it's fine to use on apples, why not weed?)[84]

Guidance and research from the EPA would go a long way toward clari-
fying which chemical pesticides at which levels are safe for marijuana consumers, but the federal government has proved unwilling to legalize and
regulate cannabis, rendering the EPA powerless to assist states attempting
to set up rules. States can do their best—and in many cases they are—but at
some point they will need the same uniform federal guidance that directs
pesticide application in legitimate agriculture. Meanwhile, one of the best
ways to keep plants pest-free is to make sure they are as healthy and stress-
free as possible, and many cannabis growers in the West are advocating for
more organic, sustainable methods that ensure exactly that.

"Greening Corporate Cannabis": The Industry's Push for Sustainability

The negative environmental effects of large-scale cannabis cultivation and
the threats posed by un- or underregulated chemical pesticides are certainly concerning, but current trends in the legitimate cannabis industry
indicate a shift toward a more organic, environmentally sustainable model.
While indoor growers have long argued that creating an enclosed, highly
controlled environment is the best way to produce high-quality cannabis,
advances in greenhouse technology and improved cultivation techniques
have wiped out that advantage. And by using natural sunlight, greenhouse growers can produce the same high-quality bud at a fraction of the
cost—and with virtually no carbon footprint. Basically, the huge warehouse
growers can make their money and burn their electricity now, but over the
next ten to fifteen years they will have to adjust to market realities or face
extinction.[85]

Of course, converting the largely indoor industry to greenhouses is
not as easy as it sounds. Federal prohibition, the reason growers moved
indoors to begin with, remains intact, which discourages outdoor cultivation in all states that have not legalized. The shadow of prohibition also
looms over states that have legalized, prompting them to regulate cannabis
growers as if they were producing weaponry instead of plants. In Colorado
and Washington, for example, growers must comply with a host of stringent security requirements as well as restrictive zoning laws that discourage greenhouse construction and confine growing facilities to warehouses
and other industrial buildings. Such regulations reflect the desire of cannabis-friendly states to walk a line between carrying out the will of their

constituents and showing the feds that they have the situation under control.

Nonetheless, legitimate growers facing such regulations are still incorporating more efficient techniques. Like Colorado, Nevada's laws keep most cannabis growers indoors (an exceptionally hot and dry climate makes outdoor cannabis cultivation nearly impossible, anyway). To help keep his electrical costs down—and by proxy reduce his business's carbon footprint—Aron Swan, operator of Silver State Relief, Nevada's first medical dispensary, said his growers use only LED lights, which are far more efficient than traditional High-Pressure Sodium (HPS) lights.[86] Although LEDs are more expensive, they make for smaller electric bills in the long run. Because they run cooler than HPS lights, LEDs have the added benefit of saving growers money on cooling systems, further reducing their carbon footprints. Swan's staff includes a plant physiologist who specializes in grapes, a close cousin of cannabis, as well as a salesperson with experience in (non-cannabis) herbal medicine. He also said Silver State Relief plans on hosting public classes on cannabis science, among other topics.

As it turns out, Swan is getting some good advice regarding sustainability. He partners with Denver Relief, a consulting agency for the industry and one of the longest-running cannabis companies in the Mile High City. Nick Hice, who oversaw Denver Relief's growing operation before the company sold its cultivation facility to a group led by Willie Nelson, is a major proponent of organic, sustainable cannabis agriculture.[87]

The cultivation center Hice used to manage is located in a warehouse in an industrial part of northeast Denver. During a tour of the facility in August 2015, Hice showed me grow rooms that still featured mostly HPS lights, but they were mixed with twenty thousand panels of LEDs, and in one room the company was testing newer, more efficient lights from BIOS lighting (on its website, BIOS claims that these new lights are 40 percent more efficient than standard HPS lights).[88] Hice even had a high-tech water recycling system installed so the grow facility had almost no waste water.

The facility had separate rooms for each stage of the plant's growth: cutting, vegetative, flowering, and final maturation. Like other indoor cannabis farms, Denver Relief's facility was humming with lights and fans, and the grow rooms are no place for the claustrophobic. The scenery is reminiscent of a factory—in the maturation room, where the plants spend their final weeks pushing as much resin onto their flowers as they can, silver ducts and black wires droop from the ceiling, spanning heavy-duty light fixtures. A suspended grid of thin, white-roped trellises keeps the plants erect under the weight of dense, heavy buds that appear in various shades of green or purple. Most are glistening with resin and covered in hundreds of red-orange or yellow hairs called pistils, which are part of the female plant's reproductive anatomy. One plant—a strain called "Gorilla Glue," apparently for its ability to fasten one's behind to the sofa—has slender green leaves, purple stems, and eye-catching, purplish-green flowers. Hice ticked off the names of some of the other strains that were just about ready to harvest. "The Girl Scout Cookie are completely dark purple, you can see the Gumbo over there has some good purple color . . . this is Glass Slipper, this big one, and this one under here is Golden Goat," he said, pointing to a cluster of brilliant green flowers sporting a thick mass of tiny yellow hairs.

Each plant sat in a permeable organic container filled with a natural soil mixture that included worm castings, cocoa fiber, and perlite, a glasslike lava rock that absorbs moisture and allows the plant to take in more water and nutrients. The containers were arranged in rows on grooved tables. Pipes delivered a water-nutrient solution into the grooves, which functioned like irrigation troughs. The tables also held monitoring equipment that kept tabs on how much water each plant used, helping Hice cut back on wastewater while maintaining the proper water and nutrient levels for each plant. For pest control, Hice used neem oil, which is pressed from the seeds of an evergreen tree and used as a popular organic treatment for cannabis that can effectively replace chemical pesticides, especially on healthy plants.[89] Like other cultivation facilities, each room in Denver Relief's facility had small trays of soapy water near the door; employees had to clean their shoes after leaving each room to avoid transferring any pests or mold spores to another room. In the curing room, hundreds of harvested marijuana branches hung upside down, and thousands of trimmed buds sat on stacked trays drying out. Once cured, the buds either went to a special "kitchen" to have their THC extracted for edibles and concentrates or were packaged and shipped to the dispensary.

At the time, Denver Relief had drawn up plans to add greenhouses to the property. Before it went full-time in the consulting business, Denver Relief only had one retail location for its marijuana—a small dispensary on

This photo shows the final maturation room at Denver Relief Cultivation Facility in August 2015, about a year before the company sold its cultivation facility to a cannabis firm led by Willie Nelson. Mature flower clusters poke above white-roped trellises that hold the plants upright. Above, High Pressure Sodium (HPS) lights are interspersed with smaller, more efficient LED lights, while wall-mounted fans keep the plants cool and grooved tables supply a water-nutrient mix to the roots. Author photo.

Broadway, just south of downtown. Hice and his partners, Ean Seeb and Kayvan Khalatbari, wanted it that way, as it allowed them to have more control over the company and cater more to a niche market for high-quality cannabis. "Much like the craft beer industry. You'll talk to a lot of people that say, well you have to scale up and grow, grow, grow or you're gonna die in this industry, because that's the way it's going. . . . We don't want to scale up that big," Hice said at the time.[90]

Having transformed their cultivation facility into one of Denver's most sustainable indoor marijuana farms, Hice and his partners set out to spread their sustainable model across the West. Swan was one of the group's first consulting clients; Denver Relief designed the layout for Silver State Relief's cultivation facility, which is capable of handling about two thousand plants and features smaller grow rooms to help contain any pest infestations. As they started traveling more, it became difficult for Denver Relief's founders to maintain their Denver operations. Hice and his partners always wanted the company to remain between the three of them, but keeping their small-scale operation competitive amidst Colorado's burgeoning weed industry became difficult. They began entertaining buyout offers. "We realized that if we didn't sell when we did sell, we would have to consider taking on outside investors to be able to continue to grow and be competitive in the state. There's so much merger and acquisition happening, and it's just harder to keep that market share."[91]

When I visited in 2015, Hice had a black filing cabinet in his office that held files for Denver Relief's consulting clients—there were just two drawers, one labeled "Nevada" and one "Illinois" (Illinois legalized medical marijuana in 2013). Today, Denver Relief's consulting portfolio includes some twenty-five cannabis businesses and counting, including operations in Washington, Oregon, Colorado, and Canada. Although the size of the average legal marijuana farm has increased greatly over the last several years (mirroring a similar trend in mainstream agriculture that began in the mid-twentieth century), Hice and his consulting team apply the same sustainable standards to every client. "[We're] trying to get zero waste water, trying to be more sustainable with our energy efficiency," he said. "With every buildout and every design and engineering process we are constantly improving." For instance, Hice said that greenhouse growers used to make up only 10 to 20 percent of the firm's client base, but "on any of the facilities that we build from here out, I would say 50 percent or more of those are going to be greenhouse production."[92]

Beyond consulting, Denver Relief is also working to make the marijuana industry more sustainable through its involvement in the Resource Innovation Institute (RII), which on its website states that its mission is "galvanizing leaders to make cannabis the most sustainable industry on the planet."[93] Hice is a member of RII's Technical Advisory Committee, while his partner Khalatbari is an RII board member. Denver Relief also remains a force for cannabis sustainability in the Colorado capital; in 2016 Khalatbari helped the city's Department of Environmental Health establish a Cannabis Sustainability Workgroup, which in mid-2017 was working to manualize best practices for the city's 160-plus cultivators.[94]

While Denver Relief works to establish best practices through its consulting network, other sustainable growers across the West are looking for ways to let consumers know their products are naturally and responsibly produced. Oregon has its own grower-led organization advocating for "sun-grown" cannabis, the Oregon Sungrown Growers' Guild.[95] In 2014, David Rice's Washington-based outdoor cannabis farm, San Juan Sun Grown, became the first organically certified farm in the state via Certified Kind, an Oregon-based group.[96] Rice himself also helped found an initiative called Greening Corporate Cannabis (GCC), which, like the RII, describes itself as "a coalition of like-minded individuals, consultants, businesses, and certifiers that are committed to reduced carbon footprint cannabis production."[97] GCC members include Scott Zeramby, coauthor of the 2011 cannabis-energy study "Up in Smoke," as well as representatives from greenhouse companies and growers from several states. During the 2015 convention of the National Cannabis Industry Association (NCIA) in Denver, members of GCC gave a well-attended, four-hour presentation on strategies to make the cannabis industry more environmentally sustainable. Presenters included Alex Cooley, a grower in Seattle who entered the industry as an indoors-only cultivator but has since added greenhouses and more efficient LED lighting as he tries to convert his whole company, Solstice Grown, to sustainable cannabis. "A warehouse facility, in my opinion, will not be viable in ten years at the longest. At the shortest it won't be viable in five years," Cooley told attendees.[98]

One of Colorado's most interesting proponents of organic cannabis has a far wider and more ambitious goal for the plant. John-Paul Maxfield, a ten-year veteran of organic farming, comes from a long line of farmers; his great-grandfather was one of the largest sheep ranchers in the country during the 1920s. A thoughtful speaker with a friendly grin and a deep knowledge of all things horticulture, the thirty-seven-year-old Denver native doesn't smoke marijuana, but he has nonetheless started an organic certification program—the Organic Cannabis Association (OCA)—for his home state's most lucrative cash crop.[99]

"[Cannabis] grows out here are the equivalent of feedlots," he said. "It was novel at first but now it's gluttonous." Believing that many Coloradans would appreciate knowing whether the cannabis they buy is truly organic, Maxfield set up a rigorous pesticide inspection program that certifies pesticide-free growers and informs customers what kinds of chemicals have been applied to the bud they're purchasing. By August 2016, Maxfield's certification program had more than a dozen growers in line for inspections and hundreds of inquiries.[100] But in June 2017 the OCA took the opportunity to expand its efforts by merging with another nonprofit, the Portland, Oregon–based Ethical Cannabis Alliance, to create the Cannabis Certification Council (CCC).[101] Representing a cooperative effort between organic weed enthusiasts in two of the cannabis industry's pioneer states, the CCC immediately began drafting a new set of standards and plans to start certifying organic cannabis products by late 2017.[102]

The challenge, Maxwell said, is that while the FDA has done an excellent job of getting people to trust the "organic" brand, the word is thrown around far too loosely in the cannabis community. For instance, one of the dispensaries that had its crop quarantined in 2015 for using the potentially hazardous Eagle 20 fungicide was named "Organic Greens."[103] Reviving a truly "organic" brand in the cannabis community will take more than just cooperative growers, Maxfield says. It will also take an educated customer base that cares about how its drug product is produced—much like the organic food market, which is incredibly popular all over Colorado and the West Coast.[104]

Unsurprisingly, Maxfield is a staunch opponent of mainstream, industrial agriculture and believes in the power of cannabis to help reconnect people with not only the land but also with sustainable food production. Agriculture is a biological process, Maxfield maintains, that Big Ag has attempted to strip down and make uniform with monoculture, genetically modified plants, and an assortment of synthetic chemicals. "Biological processes depend on diversity," he said. "And because of that it's awfully hard to industrialize [those processes] successfully" without fundamentally manipulating them through artificial means. "The answer to the food system," he said, echoing the homestead growers of the 1970s, "is getting back to the land and growing plants."

That belief explains Maxfield's passion for organic agriculture and his desire to help bring cannabis out from under the lights. "Marijuana is a complement to a diverse farm," Maxfield said. "I've said to farmers, 'You're letting drug dealers in the city grow something that you can grow; you can diversify your farm and make money.'" He acknowledged how enthusiastic and excited many cannabis farmers get when working with or talking about their plants, and he believes incorporating organic cannabis into the rest of organic agriculture can help everyone—farmers, pot growers, and consumers—reconnect with nature. "Agriculture has this power to raise consciousness," he said.

Although he lives nearly one thousand miles away, Oaksterdam instructor Noah Hirsch is exactly the type of farmer that Maxfield hopes to cultivate with the CCC. "I grow cannabis, but I also grow tomatoes, peppers, and other plants because it's really invigorated this love of horticulture that I can't express enough," Hirsch said. "There's absolutely this way of interacting with this crop that is so different from the norm. In a world where so many products are industrially manufactured, even the crops that you eat, [growing] something in your backyard or in your closet, in a secluded space just so you have access to it, puts you back in touch with that process of growing something from start to finish."[105]

Is It Too Late for the Eel?

The trends toward environmentally sustainable cannabis across the American West are encouraging, but are they enough to save the Eel River and its endangered coho salmon? Scott Greacen, executive director of the local environmental group Friends of the Eel, doesn't think so. But it's not legal cultivation in places like Colorado, or even California, that worries him. Rather, it is the inability of California to wrap its arms around an illegal, gray- and black-market cannabis industry that has been increasing in size every year since the 1990s. Without federal legalization, which would drive down the price and destroy the national black market, California authorities are simply powerless to contain the environmental damage from illegal pot farming, no matter how committed they might be.

"I think it's really important to make it clear that it's not the plant itself; it's the kind of development people are doing to grow it easily here," Greacen said. "It is still a green rush. [Growing] activity is still more this year than it was last year. And that's what we can't actually deal with; that's what we can't get our arms around; that's what we can't regulate. If the sheriff is gonna bust fifty or sixty operations this year and we've got probably two hundred to three hundred new ones being set up every year—or maybe a thousand—where is this going?"[106]

Greacen notes that even if there were tighter restrictions on growers, California's multilayered, complex web of water- and land-use laws makes it nearly impossible for state and county agencies to effectively coordinate on enforcement campaigns. And even if they could, those agencies do not have nearly enough staff to physically confront more than ten thousand

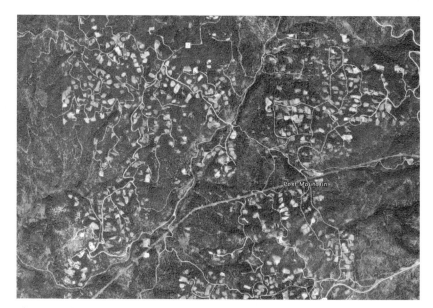

This screenshot of the Basin Gulch area in northern California shows one of the most intense concentrations of marijuana farms in the region. Over the last decade or so, hundreds of illegal marijuana farms have been clear-cut into the hillsides, contributing to environmental degradation. In addition to trash and chemical pollution, among the worst effects of high-density, unregulated marijuana growing is the sediment dislodged from clear-cutting and traffic on dirt roads. The dirt piles into nearby waterways and disrupts not only the local ecology but also downstream ecosystems. Source: Google Maps.

illegal growers in northern California, many of whom are well-armed and leery of anyone with a government uniform.

What the north coast salmon really need, Greacen says, is federal legalization. "[We need] a situation where weed is selling for $100-$500 per pound, and you can buy it legally anywhere in the country," he said. "You can't grow it profitably for $500 per pound in the hills here."[107]

Anthony Silvaggio agrees that federal prohibition lies at the heart of the problem. As an example, he cites the fate of Mendocino County's lauded zip-tie program, enacted in 2010. The county required growers to put a zip tie around every plant linked with a medical operation—up to ninety-nine, as stipulated by the Compassionate Use Act of 1996. The program's administrative costs were paid by a fifty-dollar-per-plant fee charged to growers. This allowed the sheriff's office to clearly determine whether a grower was complying with state regulations, including environmental regulations, and clamp down on noncompliant ones. County officials promised skeptical growers that their information wouldn't be released to the federal government.

But the feds wrecked it. In the summer of 2011, the DEA conducted a highly publicized raid on a compliant grower near Ukiah and later subpoenaed all of Mendocino County's information about growers in its zip-tie program. The county shut the program down and was forced to release growers' information to the DEA. Understandably, registered growers were outraged, and have since been even more reluctant to comply with any kind of local regulations.[108]

Silvaggio praises Friends of the Eel and other grassroots environmental organizations for taking on extractive industry in the region and publicizing cannabis-related environmental issues. "If it wasn't for them, these policymakers would have their heads up their asses even more," he said. But he admits that, like the fish they seek to defend, Greacen and other environmentalists are swimming against what seems like an insurmountable current. "We have a culture that has normalized environmental degradation," Silvaggio said. "It's normalized because we see it every day. You hear the logging trucks going down the road. We see industrial fishing here. So when growers come here they're like, 'My footprint is smaller than those big logging companies and those big industrial fishing fleets.' So they think they're doing okay, they're trying their best. But really they're sucking water, they're clear-cutting."[109]

Greacen, who like Silvaggio has lived in the Emerald Triangle since the 1990s, agrees that there is a cultural layer to the problem. "There's this core belief in a lot of folks, in southern Humboldt especially, people who have been there for decades . . . that they are good people, and because they are good people and they love the land, they can't do bad things," Greacen said. "And it reminds me of nothing so much as the loggers and the ranchers I've encountered in other phases of my environmental work, who genuinely love the places they work and aren't really willing to admit to people on the outside that some of the things they've done has actually hurt the land, even if they know it."[110]

Greacen admits that, despite the incredible number of obstacles in front of them, state and county officials must not wait for federal legalization before they act to contain the environmentally destructive practices associated with cannabis agriculture. But he remains doubtful that such efforts will be effective in the Emerald Triangle, with its overwhelming army of environmentally negligent growers. The salmon have caught a break with the recent cessation of the drought, but wanton bulldozing and other unplanned weed development over the previous four or five years meant that the rains of 2016 to 2017 only pushed all that loose sediment into the river systems, nullifying any habitat improvement from the increased rainfall.[111] "I think we're probably going to lose coho in the south fork Eel, just based on the biological realities we face," he said. "I think we are going to eventually end up with a more sustainable cannabis industry, but it might not be in Humboldt."[112]

Accounts from sustainable growers across the West suggest that Greacen is on to something. While people like Nick Hice, Jean-Paul Maxfield, and Noah Hirsch are "greening" the legal cannabis industry, all the good that may come from their efforts simply stops where the unregulated woods of northern California begin. Like the earlier fishing and logging industries, the booming cannabis industry in the Emerald Triangle will have come at a terrible environmental cost. If the Eel River's salmon are indeed doomed, perhaps their sacrifice will galvanize the region into thinking twice before allowing another extractive industry to take over its economy. However, as both Silvaggio and Greacen point out, Californians aren't too big on learning from their own environmental history. "We should learn from the history of the timber industry and everything else," Silvaggio said. "But politicians and capitalists have their own views on these things"—as do outlaw growers.

Our Best Root Forward

Weed and Wine in the Applegate

Silvaggio and the rest of the marijuana researchers at HSU are not the only academics with a front-row view of the environmental effects of illegal weed production. Chelsea Rose, an archaeologist at Southern Oregon University in Ashland, has lived among cannabis farmers in Oregon's Applegate Valley for more than a decade. In early August 2015, Rose gave me a tour of the Applegate, one of the lesser-known but significant weedscapes in the State of Jefferson.

I met the archaeologist on a flawless morning some fifteen miles west of Medford, down a gravel road that runs past a group of homesteads. She led me on foot to the base of a steep hill, and not too far up we came to the spot where Rose had found remnants of an illegal marijuana grow, likely dating to the early 1990s. Easily discernible beneath the dry, yellow grass were several circular depressions, each about five feet across with a deeper hole in the center. "The deeper holes are for the taproots," Rose explained. Each hole would accommodate a large, bushy cannabis plant typical of many outdoor grows.

We continued up the hillside, where an ample cover of poison oak made me regret wearing shorts and the tangled branches of low-growing madrone trees necessitated an uncomfortable stoop. There we came across more evidence of illicit farming—a couple of abandoned hoop houses with four black plastic tubes arched over black plastic planters, some embedded in the ground, others tipped over and half-buried. Each house held about a dozen containers, arranged in four rows of three and filled with dirt and weeds (the regular kind). The crude structures weren't more than four or five feet tall at the top of their arches—with the forest in full growth, the hoop houses would have been invisible from the air. Around the base of the arches, black and white plastic covers lay tattered and crumpled. I tried to imagine trudging up this steep hill with heavy bags of potting soil and other supplies, as the growers here probably did.

Tramping even farther up the hill, we discovered another hoop house that Rose had not been aware of. This one was a bit larger than the previous two, with six arched tubes covering about fifteen buried planters. After sharing a moment of subdued elation that only an archaeologist or cannabis historian would understand, we headed back downhill. A thick black hose, which allowed the grower to pump water up the hill from an adjacent homestead, ran underneath the leaf litter from the bottom of the hillside to the last of the hoop houses. The whole setup was quite innovative, but it was ugly. If I lived in the area—and my guide wasn't an archaeologist intent on keeping the sites exactly the way she found them—I might have come back with a few large trash cans and cleaned up the hillside. I wondered how many other sites like this were strewn about the valley and how many pounds of nondegradable plastic trash were left at each one.

Following a quick thorn and burr removal—and reassuring myself that I did not contract poison oak—I rode shotgun in Rose's car on a tour of the Applegate Valley. At the height of a scorching summer, the forests on the surrounding hills were clearly dry, but the valley was flushed green with agriculture. The warm, dry climate makes it a perfect area for wineries; grape vines don't even need to be cultivated to thrive there. We whisked past vineyards, organic nurseries, and sprawling ranches, with the gleaming ribbon of the Applegate River winding close to the road to greet us, then playfully swerving away. In the distance, the blue-green silhouettes of hills rolled underneath sparse, puffy clouds drifting through a stunningly blue sky. The drive alone, absent any related insight into the region's pot culture, made the entire visit worthwhile.

Still, I knew that hidden behind and in between this Edenic patchwork of vineyards and grassy meadows was a smattering of (mostly) illegal marijuana grows. Medical cannabis cultivation was legalized in Oregon in 1998, but as in California, it is loosely regulated. Plants are supposed to be grown only for patients with medical cannabis cards, but most agree that the large amounts of pot being grown is far too much to be strictly for patient consumption. Rose also said that she finds today's growers in the Applegate, like many in northern California, to be far more brazen and less neighborly than their predecessors who brought the crop to the valley in the 1970s. They attempt to do stupid things like plant fence posts in the middle of roads. One grower has an obnoxiously loud fan system; another has a

This abandoned hoop house was used by an outlaw marijuana farmer on a hillside in southern Oregon, likely in the 1990s. Note the sunken black planters and low-growing madrone trees, which kept the grow site hidden from above. A nearby hose ran up the hillside and was formerly connected to a pump on a nearby homestead. Author photo.

greenhouse full of obnoxiously bright lights, and almost all of them have aggressive guard dogs. Rose is appreciative of new local laws that limit fan and light operation between the hours of 7:00 a.m. and 7:00 p.m., but she said enforcement is lax and depends on neighbors filing complaints on each other—not exactly a recipe for a harmonious community.

As for the growers themselves, Rose said they come in about as many different varieties as the weed they produce, from the typical nice-guy neighbors to quirky, skittish types to the paranoid, armed, and downright dangerous. At one point, as we slowly rolled along a gravel road past the telltale high fences of a pot farm, I stuck my phone out the window to take a picture. "I wouldn't be too obvious about that," Rose cautioned, pointing to an eerie sign that read "Smile: You're on Camera." We passed another grow site, which Rose said is run by a kooky vet and some shady tweaker-types who have really made a mess of the property. I make out a US Marine Corps banner hanging from a decrepit trailer and see a horse grazing nonchalantly in the yard.

Like the growers mired in the CAMP conflict of northern California, some of the Applegate growers actively patrol their grow sites, screening every passing pedestrian or motorist. Rose said that archaeologists (and presumably other scientists who do field work in the area) are often surprised to stumble upon a grow site, and that can make for an uncomfortable situation. "The archaeologist in me thinks about these sites in the same vein as the isolated mountain stills during the Prohibition Era," she said. "But the citizen in me is annoyed that I have to worry about stumbling into a dangerous situation on public lands, or when driving or walking in a rural area."

After passing a couple more grow sites, rendered invisible by the dense forest, we headed out to the main road, Oregon Highway 238, that runs through the town of Applegate. We were going to the famous Applegate River Lodge, run by Joanna Davis, her ex-husband Richard, and their two sons, Dusty and Duke. Rose said Richard would be a good person to talk to about the valley's cannabis history, given the time he's spent there and his affinity for the herb. Richard, who hand built the lodge with his family some twenty-three years ago, grows and smokes cannabis; he was berated for it on a 2014 episode of celebrity chef Gordon Ramsey's show "Hotel Hell." The rustic, yet eccentric, lodge is a popular local music venue and has its own resident mascot—a bandana-sporting, cannabis-eating deer named Sugar Bob.

We wound our way to the lodge, flying past more vineyards, ramshackle homesteads, and orchards. We saw plenty more properties with tall fences and greenhouses. Rose had tried to contact some of the local growers to see if they'd let us talk with them but didn't have much luck. Despite legalization unfolding in Oregon, Applegate weed growers are still a cloistered bunch. It's not immediately clear why, because their activities underwrite the entire local economy. Growers and their labor forces, she said, have brought a much-needed influx of cash to the area, which has allowed for the establishment of new creative businesses and restaurants. And while illegal growers are often thought of or portrayed as villains—and some do act the part—many are simply poor, rural people who have grown weed illegally for decades to help support themselves and make some money on the side. "It's hard to make a living out here," Rose said. "Almost everybody has at least one plant out here, no matter what their background is." The situation is almost identical to northern California, just on a smaller scale: Illegal growers, whatever their attitude is toward the environment or their

Many outlaw growers in Oregon's Applegate Valley build fence extensions to conceal the canopy of their illicit crop. Parts of this grower's fence have fallen down, allowing a glimpse at white PVC trellises (center) built to hold up bud-laden marijuana plants. Author photo.

neighbors, simply aren't going to pay a licensing fee to grow marijuana; they aren't going to fill out a bunch of forms or let state bureaucrats inspect their properties. It goes against the grain of the culture of rural Oregon—and rural America more generally, in fact—to force these people to conform to state regulations. As Greacen and Silvaggio point out, the only thing black-market growers are going to respond to is price. And the only thing that can solve the price problem is federal legalization.

Richard wasn't there when we reached the lodge; Joanna was preparing to host a wedding and had sent him away. Determined to have a conversation about cannabis with someone in the valley, Rose drove me out farther into Applegate wine country. She arranged to meet with Greg Paneitz, owner of Wooldridge Creek Vineyard and Winery. Paneitz is among several area vintners who seek to bring the wine industry into dialogue with the newly legalized cannabis industry to ensure a mutually beneficial relationship. It makes sense—cannabis and grapes are both popular crops used to produce mind-altering substances; they are also biologically similar and share a niche in the Mediterranean climates of the West, where their popularity has run up against the region's limited water supply. For instance, as of January

2016, all water rights holders in California are required to submit annual reports on water diversions, a mandate that has many vineyards and wineries bristling at the steep costs of bringing their measurement and reporting systems up to the new standard.[1]

After rolling through Paneitz's sixty acres of vineyards, we found the owner enjoying his lunch in the open-air tasting section of the winery. A pleasant breeze under the shade of the winery roof broke the heat of the afternoon, while the stunning vistas of the Applegate stretched blissfully to the south under a cloudless sky. Michael Bublé crooned in the background.

Paneitz, who moonlights as a firefighter in the Applegate Valley, wants to bring the grape and cannabis industries into dialogue to discuss important agricultural issues such as water rights, spray drift, and land use, and to make sure that nobody's afraid of each other. "At the moment there's an awful lot of fear about what they do and why they do it, and a lot of misinformation," he said. His biggest fear is not an unhinged weed economy but rather developers moving into unused, unplanted land, looking to capitalize on the scenic beauty of the valley. "When you do something with the land that is profitable, you don't build condos on it," Paneitz said. "I'd like to see the Applegate known as a bastion of agriculture. This is a wonderful place to grow food and produce hedonistic products, like wine or sinsemilla." And lest one get the impression that those two crops are mutually exclusive, as of April 2017 at least two winemakers in southern Oregon have also begun legally planting marijuana.[2]

Several weeks before we met, Paneitz said he went to a meeting of the valley's vintners, where there was significant desire for interaction with the area's pot farmers. He said he's also spoken with the Oregon Sungrown Growers Association about cooperation between the industries. "Our hope is to facilitate a conversation," he said. "I'd love to see an agricultural coalition with sinsemilla, hemp, grape, cattle, and milk, to tell the world we're here and we're open for business. If there was a group that could lobby for everybody, that would be enormous."[3]

Paneitz's vision of marijuana farmers joining forces with ranchers and winemakers is admirable, if utopian. It relies on full cooperation from pot growers, a diverse group that includes legal as well as illegal producers, who are notoriously reclusive and uncooperative. Ultimately, the same reason that some enterprising grower decided to sully a beautiful Oregon hillside with black plastic trash is the same reason why California can't get its salmon-killing pot industry under control—federal prohibition.

Pot, Past and Present

If there's anything to be learned from visiting the weedscapes of California and Oregon and digging through the agricultural history of cannabis, it's that environmental degradation is an overlooked consequence of federal prohibition. Despite the fact that the plant has been grown in this part of the country for more than one hundred years, only since the ratcheting-up of the drug war in the 1980s has marijuana farming become a threat to the environment in the West. By doubling down on prohibition, a policy that has failed since 1937, the federal government created and maintains the enormous incentive for industrial outdoor cannabis farming, armed and paranoid growers, and the energy-sucking indoor industry. This has produced some strange situations within the federal bureaucracy itself. For instance, the US Department of Fish and Wildlife now has to deal with California fishers dying of anticoagulant poisoning, a mess that can be directly traced to the refusal of its parent institution to legalize and regulate cannabis production. Nationwide legalization would break up the concentrated agricultural footprint of today's outdoor marijuana crop and relieve pressure on sensitive ecosystems such as the Eel River.

Prohibition also stands in the way of badly needed research on both marijuana and the cannabis plant. Since the late nineteenth century, physicians, pharmacologists, botanists, government officials, and other scientists and professionals have attempted to unlock the mysteries of this cryptic plant, but more often than not their efforts produced more questions than answers. Of course, some of these questions have been settled, such as the difference between marijuana and hemp plants. But many others, such as "what constitutes a safe, medically effective dose of marijuana?" and "what exactly accounts for the different effects of marijuana obtained from different plants?" still perplex growers and researchers today. *Grass Roots* clearly demonstrates that millions have found the herb medically valuable, giving the argument for medical marijuana a historical weight that renders any contrary statement from lawmakers or the DEA irrelevant. The American scientific and medical community needs to get the green light on all facets of marijuana research—the limited and biased work of NIDA, which fundamentally ignores any potential benefits of marijuana, is not enough. Nearly 60 percent of Americans live in a state where cannabis products of some type are legal.[4] That means that, now more than ever, the federal government has a responsibility to base its marijuana policy on facts and truly objective analysis instead of its monolithic assumption that nothing good can ever come from this plant.

This is not to say that ending prohibition alone will effectively address the environmental problems associated with cannabis. The whole point of toppling prohibition is undermined when the detrimental practices it encouraged are allowed to go on after legalization. Now that we have empirical evidence of the huge carbon footprint of indoor cannabis production, there's simply no good reason for states that legalize marijuana to tolerate it. Moreover, strict and unthought-out packaging requirements for legal weed in places like Colorado have left the city of Denver littered with plastic cylinders. How does that differ from the thousands of pounds of black plastic left by hundreds of illegal grow sites in the hills of southern Oregon? (Ironically, hemp plastic may actually provide a solution to that problem.[5]) Put simply, the more aware we are of cannabis's agricultural history and environmental legacy, the more proactive we can be about its environmental impact in the present and future.

Such an awareness is most urgently needed in the West, where residents are bringing another water-intensive cash crop into the legal economy just as the region enters an age of unprecedented water crisis. Authors of initiatives to legalize marijuana and public officials in the West cannot afford to ignore the plant's history as a water-sucking beneficiary of the irrigation and massive reclamation projects that allowed agriculture and cities to expand in many parts of the region. If cannabis legalization is to occur side-by-side with increasing drought, western states must enforce best practices and limits on cultivation in order to keep both marijuana and industrial hemp from becoming the next big agricultural drain on the region's water supply. Agricultural coalitions, like the one Paneitz is advocating in the Applegate Valley, do seem like an excellent way to reduce weed growers' reflexive suspicion, promote harmony among pot growers and other farmers, and ensure that best practices in mainstream agriculture transfer over to the cannabis sector.

It's not uncommon to find plastic marijuana containers littering the streets of Denver. Coincidentally, this joint case was found at the corner of Evans Avenue and High Street. Author photo.

It's important to keep in mind that environmental ignorance is not the only ugly holdover from the days of blanket marijuana prohibition. Race played a major role in the establishment of prohibition, and it also determined who suffered most under the policy and who stands to benefit most from cannabis legalization. Remember that, despite the major role that black and brown Americans played in the dissemination of marijuana across the United States, it was not until a movement of mostly white, middle-class Americans began growing and smoking the herb in the 1960s that cannabis became anything more than a political nonstarter—the white body politic's tolerance of white people going to jail for nonviolent drug offenses was apparently far more limited than its tolerance of black and brown people going to jail for the same crimes. During the revamped war on drugs of the 1980s, white, middle-class growers in the suburbs certainly risked a lot by deciding to break the law, but they nonetheless reaped the benefits of high black-market marijuana prices without suffering the disproportionate, relentless, and brutal enforcement tactics reserved for black and brown neighborhoods in the inner cities. White Americans also disproportionately possessed the resources to conduct cannabis breeding experiments and build elaborate indoor grow operations, like the one Greg Smoak discovered in Fort Collins. Without the intense police scrutiny and harassment present in minority communities, white growers and breeders were able to accumulate the horticultural knowledge that would allow them to succeed in a legal market.

It should not be surprising, then, to discover that 84 percent of legal dispensary owners in Colorado are white, or that young blacks and Latinos in the state are still arrested for underage marijuana use and possession at far higher rates than young whites.[6] Of course, the major drop in adult marijuana arrests in Colorado—and other states that have legalized—is a benefit to communities and families of color. But it's not an even drop; while marijuana arrests among whites fell by 51 percent from 2012 to 2014, they fell by just 25 percent among blacks and 33 percent among Latinos.[7] Just like the worst effects of prohibition, the spoils of legalization are not equally distributed across the color line. And while there are certainly no easy fixes for such disparity, the data from Colorado should remind those who would legalize and regulate cannabis that unsustainable growing is not the only prohibition-era problem that has continued into the age of legalization.

From the clandestine crops of Mexican laborers to the seed scattering of Johnny Pot and the outdoor gardens of modern growers like Washington's David Rice, we know that sustainable, sun-grown marijuana is possible. And not only is it possible, but people like Noah Hirsch in California, Nick Hice and John-Paul Maxfield in Denver, and scholars and environmentalists in Humboldt County are working to make it happen. They have the support of institutions and organizations such as Oaksterdam University, the Oregon Sungrown Grower's Guild, Greening Corporate Cannabis, the Resource Innovation Institute, and the Cannabis Certification Council, but they also need the support of their state governments and local communities, especially citizens who smoke and grow legal marijuana. Obtaining political support may be easier than it sounds—politicians may be reluctant to strictly regulate mining, oil and gas development, and other environmentally destructive industries, but when it comes to marijuana, most politicians would favor strict regulation. It is not farfetched to imagine the "green" wing of the cannabis movement allying itself with those politicians to ensure that the legal cannabis industry is held to high standards of sustainability. Meanwhile, those who use marijuana, whether medically or recreationally, should ask more questions about the weed they buy at dispensaries and demand a more sustainably grown product, if not for the health of the environment then for their own sake.

The goal is to set a sustainable standard for the nationwide relegalization of cannabis, a possibility that becomes more likely with every state that sheds prohibition. If we, as Americans, can reexamine and reform the way we grow a crop as immensely popular and culturally significant as cannabis, then there's no reason we cannot reform the way we grow other, arguably more important crops. That would certainly be an uphill climb fraught with challenges from powerful corporate and political forces, but it is no stoner's pipe dream—greener cannabis farming could indeed be a gateway to greener American agriculture.

Notes

Preface

1 See, for example, Crissy Van Meter, "The 'M' Word: The History of 'Marijuana,' and Should You Stop Saying It?" *The Kind*, November 18, 2015, http://www.thekindland. com/the-m-word-the-history-of-marijuana-and-should-you-219; "The Racist 'M' Word: Marijuana," May 15, 2015, http://naturalrevolution.org/its-time-to-strike-the-racist-m-word-from-our-vocabulary/; Michael Roberts, "Is the Word 'Marijuana' Offensive?" *Westword*, December 1, 2015, http://www.westword.com/news/is-the-word-marijuana-offensive-7387171.

2 Chris Duvall, *Cannabis* (London: Reaktion Books, 2015), 14–15.

3 I am far from the only cannabis writer to have dealt with this problem; see Isaac Campos, *Home Grown: Marijuana and the Origins of Mexico's War on Drugs* (Chapel Hill: University of North Carolina Press, 2013).

Introduction

1 Dr. Anthony Silvaggio, Humboldt Institute for Interdisciplinary Marijuana Research, Humboldt State University, conversation with author, July 26, 2014.

2 Allan A. Schoenherr, *A Natural History of California* (Berkeley: University of California Press, 1992), 228, 236, 249–59, 261–312.

3 Frank DeCourten, *The Geology of Northern California*, Cengage Learning, Custom Enrichment Module, 2009, 37, http://www.cengage.com/custom/regional_geology.bak/data/DeCourten_0495763829_LowRes_New.pdf, (accessed September 14, 2016).

4 See Andrew Thompson, "When Growing Marijuana Isn't Green," *NBC News*, April 22, 2016, http://www.nbcnews.com/business/business-news/when-growing-marijuana-isn-t-green-n560391.

5 Ibid., 11.

6 Ibid.; Glenda Anderson, "Marijuana's thirst depleting North Coast watersheds," *Press Democrat* (San Francisco), April 12, 2014, http://www.pressdemocrat.com/csp/mediapool/sites/PressDemocrat/News/story.csp?cid=1860712&sid=555&fid=181#page&gallery=2318622&artslide=0.

7 California Fish and Wildlife, "Impacts of Surface Water Diversion," 13.

8 State of California, "California Drought," http://ca.gov/drought/.

9 Lee Romney, "Trying to cultivate respect for water regulations among pot growers," *Los Angeles Times*, June 13, 2015, http://www.latimes.com/local/la-me-marijuana-regs-20150613-story.html; Scott Greacen, Executive Director, Friends of the Eel River, conversation with author, June 9, 2015.

10 California Fish and Wildlife, "Impacts of Surface Water Diversion," 2.

11 See Mourad W. Gabriel, Leslie W. Woods, et al., "Anticoagulant Rodenticides on our Public and Community Lands: Spatial Distribution of Exposure and Poisoning of a Rare Forest Carnivore," *PLOS ONE*, July 13, 2012; Zoe Schlanger, "Marijuana

Farms Are Poisoning this Mink-like Animal with Rodenticide," *Newsweek*, October 7, 2014.

12 US Fish and Wildlife Service, "West Coast Population of Fisher Will not be Listed Under Endangered Species Act," press release, April 14, 2016.

13 California Fish and Wildlife Department, "Impacts of Surface Water Diversions for Marijuana Cultivation on Aquatic Habitat in Four Northwestern California Watersheds," *PLOS ONE*, March 18, 2015, 1, doi:10.1371/journal.pone.0120016.

14 "Federal Laws & Penalties," National Organization for the Reform of Marijuana Laws, 2015, http://norml.org/laws/item/federal-penalties-2.

15 Max Daly, "The Stoners' Paradise of Humboldt County Is Dreading Weed Legalization," *Vice*, February 25, 2014, http://www.vice.com/read/the-us-weed-growing-town-dreading-weed-legalisation.

16 Anderson, "Marijuana's thirst depleting North Coast watersheds . . . ." For other crop estimates see Christopher Ingraham, "The marijuana industry could be bigger than the NFL by 2020," *The Washington Post*, October 24, 2014, https://www.washingtonpost.com/news/wonk/wp/2014/10/24/the-marijuana-industry-could-be-bigger-than-the-nfl-by-2020/; Matt Ferner, "Legal Marijuana Is the Fastest-Growing Industry in the US: Report," *Huffington Post*, January 26, 2015, http://www.huffingtonpost.com/2015/01/26/marijuana-industry-fastest-growing_n_6540166.html.

17 Jim Rendon, *Super-Charged: How Outlaws, Hippies, and Scientists Reinvented Marijuana* (Portland: Timber Press, 2012), 80–91, 102–20.

18 Evan Mills, "Energy Up In Smoke: The Carbon Footprint of Indoor Cannabis Production," *Journal of Energy Policy* 46 (2012): 58–67, evanmills.lbl.gov/pubs/pdf/cannabis-carbon-footprint.pdf.

19 US Geological Survey, "California Drought," updated August 3, 2016, http://ca.water.usgs.gov/data/drought/ (accessed August 27, 2016); see also Frani Halperin, "Meet the NASA Scientist keeping an eye on California's drought," *H2o Radio*, web exclusive, *High Country News*, August 26, 2016, https://www.hcn.org/articles/technology-groundwater-california-drought-water-h2oradio.

20 California Department of Water Resources, "Governor's Drought Declaration," updated June 17, 2016, http://www.water.ca.gov/waterconditions/declaration.cfm (accessed August 27, 2017).

21 Gregory P. Asner, Philip G. Brodrick, Christopher B. Anderson, Nicholas Vaughn, David E. Knapp, and Roberta E. Martin, "Progressive forest canopy water loss during 2012–2015 California drought," *Proceedings of the National Academy of Sciences*, December 28, 2015, E252; State of California, "California Drought," 2015, http://ca.gov/drought/ (accessed December 28, 2015); Ryan Sabalow, Dale Kasler, and Phillip Reese, "Feds: Winter salmon run nearly extinguished in California drought," *The Sacramento Bee*, October 28, 2015, http://www.sacbee.com/news/state/california/water-and-drought/article41684160.html.

22 Greacen, conversation with author, June 9, 2015; Silvaggio, conversation with author, July 26, 2014.

23 Humboldt County, Ordinance No. 2523, October 28, 2014.

24 Anthony Silvaggio, conversation with author, August 31, 2016.

25 National Organization for the Reform of Marijuana Laws, "State Info," http://norml. org/states (accessed September 3, 2016).

26 For discussion of the role of aridity in the history of American West, see Donald Worster, "The American West in the Age of Vulnerability," *Western Historical Quarterly* 45 (Spring 2014): 5–16; William deBuys, *A Great Aridness: Climate Change and the Future of the American Southwest* (New York: Oxford University Press, 2011); and Marc Reisner, *Cadillac Desert: The American West and its Disappearing Water*, rev. ed. (New York: Penguin Books, 1993).

For discussion of the West's unique cosmopolitanism, see Elliott West, "Reconstructing Race," in The Essential West: Collected Essays (Norman: University of Oklahoma Press, 2012), 100–126; Earl Pomeroy, The American Far West in the 20th Century, ed. Richard W. Etulain (New Haven: Yale University Press, 2008), 233–263; and Donald Worster, "Beyond the Agrarian Myth," in Trails: Toward a New Western History, eds. Patricia Nelson Limerick, Clyde A. Milner II, and Charles E. Rankin (Lawrence: University Press of Kansas, 1991), 16–18.

For discussion of the West as borderlands, see Anne F. Hyde, *Empires, Nations, and Families: A New History of the North American West, 1800–1860* (Lincoln: University of Nebraska Press, 2011), 5–15; Katherine Benton-Cohen, *Borderline Americans: Racial Division and Labor War in the Arizona Borderlands* (Cambridge, MA: Harvard University Press, 2009); Samuel Truett, *Fugitive Landscapes: The Forgotten History of the U.S.-Mexico Borderlands* (New Haven: Yale University Press, 2008); and Pekka Hämäläinen, *The Comanche Empire* (New Haven: Yale University Press, 2008).

For discussion of the West's boom-and-bust cycles and tourism economies, see Leah S. Glaser, "Beyond the Boom/Bust Cycle: Locating Enduring Stories in the Cultural Resources of the West," *Western Historical Quarterly* 41 (Summer 2010): 218–226; William Philpott, *Vacationland: Tourism and Environment in the Colorado High Country* (Seattle: University of Washington Press, 2013); and Hal K. Rothman, "Stumbling toward the Millennium: Tourism, the Postindustrial World, and the Transformation of the American West," *California History* 77, no. 3 (Fall 1998): 140–155.

For discussion of individualism/libertarianism and disdain for federal power in the West, see Marshall Swearingen, ed., *Sagebrush Rebellion: Evolution of a Movement* (Paonia, CO: High Country News, 2016); Jeffrey Lockwood, "Why the West Needs Mythic Cowboys," *High Country News*, June 9, 2008; Richard White, "The Current Weirdness in the West," *Western Historical Quarterly* 28, no. 1 (Spring 1997): 4–16.

27 For cannabis histories written by journalists, see Martin A. Lee, *Smoke Signals: A Social History of Marijuana: Medical, Recreational, Scientific* (New York: Scribner, 2012); Martin Booth, *Cannabis: A History* (New York: Picador, 2003); Rendon, *Super Charged*; Michael Pollan, *The Botany of Desire: A Plant's-Eye View of the World* (New York: Random House, 2001); Emily Brady, *Humboldt: Life on America's Marijuana Frontier* (Melbourne, AU: Scribe, 2013); Peter Hecht, *Weed Land: Inside America's Marijuana Epicenter and How Pot Went Legit* (Berkeley: University of California Press, 2014). For cannabis histories written by historians and other academics, see

Ray Raphael, *Cash Crop: An American Dream* (Mendocino, CA: Ridge Times Press, 1985); Richard J. Bonnie and Charles H. Whitebread, *The Marijuana Conviction: A History of Marijuana Prohibition in the United States* (New York: The Lindesmith Center, 1999. Reprint: Charlottesville: University of Press of Virginia, 1974); James Mills, *Cannabis Britannica: Empire, Trade, and Prohibition* (Oxford, UK: Oxford University Press, 2003); Isaac Campos, *Home Grown: Marijuana and the Origins of Mexico's War on Drugs* (Chapel Hill: University of North Carolina Press, 2012); Robert C. Clarke and Mark Merlin, *Cannabis: Evolution and Ethnobotany* (Berkeley: University of California Press, 2013); Duvall, *Cannabis*.

28   This book draws from and builds on important frameworks and concepts advanced by other historians. Foremost among them are William Cronon's "paths out of town" analysis and John B. Jackson's "vernacular landscape," as well as discussions of hybrid landscapes, urban ecology, and the roles of race and class in agricultural development, labor, and ideas about nature. See William Cronon, "Kennecott Journey: The Paths out of Town," in *Under an Open Sky: Rethinking America's Western Past*, eds. William Cronon, George Miles, and Jay Gitlin (New York: W.W. Norton & Co., 1992), 28–51, and John Brinckerhoff Jackson, *Discovering the Vernacular Landscape* (New Haven: Yale University Press, 1984).

For discussions of hybrid landscapes, see Richard White, "From Wilderness to Hybrid Landscapes: The Cultural Turn in Environmental History," *The Historian* 66, no. 3 (Fall 2004): 557–564, and Mark Fiege, *Irrigated Eden: The Making of an Agricultural Landscape in the American West* (Seattle: University of Washington Press, 1999).

For discussion of urban ecology and its role in the history of the American West, see Matthew Morse Booker, *Down By the Bay: San Francisco's History Between the Tides* (Berkeley: University of California Press, 2013); Zachary S. Falck, *Weeds: An Environmental History of Metropolitan America* (Pittsburgh, PA: University of Pittsburgh Press, 2010); Matthew Klingle, *Emerald City: An Environmental History of Seattle* (New Haven: Yale University Press, 2007); and Jared Orsi, *Hazardous Metropolis: Flooding and Urban Ecology in Los Angeles* (Berkeley: University of California Press, 2004).

For discussions of the roles of race and class in agricultural development, labor, and ideas about nature, see Mark Fiege, "King Cotton: The Cotton Plant and Southern Slavery," in *Republic of Nature: An Environmental History of the United States* (Seattle: University of Washington Press, 2012); Thomas Andrews, *Killing for Coal: America's Deadliest Labor War* (Cambridge, MA: Harvard University Press, 2008); Linda Nash, *Inescapable Ecologies: A History of Environment, Disease, and Knowledge* (Berkeley: University of California Press, 2006); Jake Kosek, *Understories: The Political Life of Forests in Northern New Mexico* (Durham, NC: Duke University Press, 2006); Douglas Sackman, *Orange Empire: California and the Fruits of Eden* (Berkeley: University of California Press, 2005).

29   For discussions on regionalism and the West, see Mark Fiege, "The Nature of the West and the World," and Robert D. Johnston, "There's No 'There' There:

Reflections on Western Political Historiography," *Western Historical Quarterly* 42, no. 3 (Autumn 2011): 305–312, 331–337.

30   See W. W. Stockberger, "Commercial Drug Growing in the United States in 1918," *Journal of American Pharmaceutical Association* 8, no. 1 (January 1919): 809.

31   Cynthia Almaguer, Christina Schönberger, Martina Gastl, Elke K. Arendt, and Thomas Becker, "Humulus lupulus—a story that begs to be told," *Journal of the Institute of Brewing* 120 (2014): 289–314; See also Duvall, *Cannabis*, 10–12.

32   For scholarly perspectives on Cannabis taxonomy, see Jason Sawler, Jake M. Stout, Kyle M. Gardner, Darryl Hudson, John Vidmar, Laura Butler, Jonathan E. Page, and Sean Myles, "The Genetic Structure of Marijuana and Hemp," *PLOS ONE* 10, no. 8, February 20, 2015, doi:10,1371/journal.pone.0133292; Karl W. Hillig, "Genetic evidence for speciation in Cannabis (Cannabaceae)," *Genetic Resources and Crop Evolution* 52 (2005): 161–180; John McPartland, "Corrected vernacular nomenclature: indica, afghanica, sativa," *O'Shaughnessy's* (Journal of the California Cannabis Research Medical Group) Autumn 2014: 1, http://www.os-extra.cannabisclinicians. org/wp-content/uploads/2015/12/Corrected-Vernacular.png; Clarke and Merlin, *Evolution and Ethnobotany*, 311–323. For a more accessible discussion, see Phillip Smith, "Is marijuana a single species?: While you're searching for the perfect high, scientists go deeper," *Salon*, September 28, 2015, http://www.salon.com/2015/09/28/ is_marijuana_a_single_species_while_youre_searching_for_the_perfect_high_ scientists_go_deeper_partner/; Mitchell Colbert, "Indica, Sativa, Ruderalis—Did We Get It All Wrong?" *The Leaf Online*, January 26, 2015, http://theleafonline. com/c/science/2015/01/indica-sativa-ruderalis-get-wrong/.

33   John M. McPartland, correspondence with author, August 22, 2016; see also John M. McPartland and GW Guy, "A question of rank: using DNA barcodes to classify Cannabis sativa and Cannabis indica," *Proceedings of the 24th Annual Symposium on the Cannabinoids* (Research Triangle Park, NC: International Cannabinoid Research Society, 2014), 54.

34   Ibid.; McPartland, "Corrected vernacular nomenclature"; the term *Cannabis sativa* was originally coined by the Swedish botanist Carl Linnaeus in the eighteenth century; see Carl Linnaeus, *Species plantarum*, vol. 2 (1753): 1027.

35   Hillig, "Genetic evidence for speciation"; Clarke and Merlin, *Evolution and Ethnobotany*, 312; Hillig's taxonomy is also adopted by cannabis historian Chris Duvall; see Duvall, *Cannabis*, 20–21.

36   The hemp industry in the United States peaked in the mid-nineteenth century; see Duvall, *Cannabis*, 81. Today, hemp covers just 6,900 acres nationwide; see Kristen Wyatt, "3 Years into nation's hemp experiment, crop's future is hazy," Associated Press, August 12, 2016. For historical and current discussions of hemp in the United States, see James F. Hopkins, *A History of the Hemp Industry in Kentucky* (Lexington: University Press of Kentucky, 1951); Ernest L. Abel, "'That Valuable Article:' Hemp," *American History Illustrated* 11, no. 3 (1976): 27–33; Sterling Evans, *Bound in Twine: The History and Ecology of the Henequen-Wheat Complex for Mexico and the American and Canadian Plains, 1880–1950* (College Station: Texas A&M University

Press, 2007), 27–30; Doug Fine, *Hemp Bound: Dispatches from the Front Lines of the Next Agricultural Revolution* (White River Junction, VT: Chelsea Green Publishing, 2014); Duvall, *Cannabis*, 80–87; Clarke and Merlin, *Evolution and Ethnobotany*, 182–84.

37 Clarke and Merlin, *Evolution and Ethnobotany*, 24–25.

38 Ibid., 31.

39 Ibid.

40 Bruce D. Smith, *The Emergence of Agriculture* (New York: Scientific American Library, 1995), 20–21; for a detailed discussion of crop domestication, see Jared Diamond, *Guns, Germs, & Steel: The Fates of Human Societies* (New York: W. W. Norton, 1999), 114–130.

41 Clarke and Merlin, *Evolution and Ethnobotany*, 33.

42 Duvall, *Cannabis*, 7.

43 Clarke and Merlin, *Evolution and Ethnobotany*, 21–22, 50–51; in McPartland's taxonomy, these are *Cannabis sativa ssp. indica* (tropical-Mediterranean) and *Cannabis indica ssp. afghanica* (temperate-mountain); in the taxonomy adopted by Hillig, Clarke, and Merlin, these are simply different varieties of *Cannabis indica*.

44 Duvall, *Cannabis*, 23–25.

45 Mel Frank, *Marijuana Grower's Insider's Guide* (Los Angeles: Red Eye Press, 1988), 124–27, 132.

46 Clarke and Merlin, *Evolution and Ethnobotany*, 16.

47 Frank, *Insider's Guide*, 74–83.

48 Robert C. Clarke, *Marijuana Botany* (Oakland, CA: Ronin, 1981), 4–8; Clarke and Merlin, *Evolution and Ethnobotany*, 16–17.

49 Clarke and Merlin, *Evolution and Ethnobotany*, 16; David W. Pate, "Chemical ecology of Cannabis," *Journal of the International Hemp Association* 2, no. 29 (1994): 32–37; Pollan, *Botany of Desire*, 156.

50 Clarke, *Marijuana Botany*, 16; Pollan, *Botany of Desire*, 134–35.

51 Ibid., 83; Ed Rosenthal, *Marijuana Pest and Disease Control* (San Francisco: Quick American Archives, 2012).

52 Clarke and Merlin, *Evolution and Ethnobotany*, 51.

53 Kate McLean, "Pot and Pesticides: A Bustling Illegal Trade," *The Bay Citizen* (San Francisco), May 26, 2010; Colorado Green Lab, "Eagle 20 and Myclobutanil in the Context of Cannabis Cultivation and Consumption," May 14, 2015, http://www.coloradogreenlab.com/blog/eagle-20-and-myclobutanil-in-the-context-of-cannabis-cultivation-and-consumption.

54 Oregon Department of Agriculture, "Guidelist for Pesticides and Cannabis," updated Aug. 10, 2016, https://www.oregon.gov/ODA/shared/Documents Publications/PesticidesPARC/GuidelistPesticideCannabis.pdf; Washington State Department of Agriculture, "Section 3 Federally Registered Pesticides," updated June 29, 2016, http://agr.wa.gov/pestfert/pesticides/docs/PesticidesallowedforuseonmarijuanainWashington20160629.pdf; Colorado Department of Agriculture, "Pesticides allowed for use in Cannabis production

in accordance with the PAA rule," updated August 4, 2016: https://www.colorado.gov/pacific/sites/default/files/atoms/files/Pesticides%20allowed%20for%20use%20in%20cannabis%20production%208-4-16.pdf.

55 See Paige Raibmon, "Picking, Posing, and Performing: Puget Sound Hop Fields and Income for Aboriginal Workers," in Raibmon, *Authentic Indians: Episodes of Encounter from the Late Nineteenth-Century West Coast* (Durham, NC: Duke University Press, 2005), 79–97; Artemis Oscar, "What It's Like to Be a Professional Marijuana Trimmer," *ALternet*, via *O'Shaugnessy's*, October 26, 2012, http://www.alternet.org/drugs/what-its-be-professional-marijuana-trimmer.

56 See George T. Griffing, "Endocannabinoids: Endocannabinoid System Roles," *Medscape*, updated February 5, 2015, http://emedicine.medscape.com/article/1361971-overview#a4 (accessed August 27, 2016).

57 For discussion of "set" and "setting" as it relates to cannabis and other drugs, see Campos, *Home Grown*, 23–26.

58 Pollan, *Botany of Desire*, 139–42.

59 The lungs have long been one area of concern, but recent studies have not found any link between cannabis exposure and cancer or other severe pulmonary impairment. See, for instance, the following report, which concludes, "habitual use of marijuana alone does not appear to lead to significant abnormalities in lung function": Donald P. Tashkin, "Effects of Marijuana Smoking on the Lung," *Annals of the American Thoracic Society* 10, no. 3 (2013): 239–47 (Special Article), http://www.atsjournals.org/doi/pdf/10.1513/AnnalsATS.201212-127FR;

60 Robert McCoppin, "Could medical marijuana users become addicted to pot?" *Chicago Tribune*, October 19, 2015, http://www.chicagotribune.com/lifestyles/health/ct-illinois-medical-marijuana-addiction-met-20151018-story.html.

61 Nora D. Volkow, Ruben D. Baler, Wilson M. Compton, and Susan R. B. Weiss, "Adverse Health Effects of Marijuana Use," T*he New England Version of Medicine* 37 (2014), 2219–27; Eva Hoch, Udo Bonnet, Rainer Thomasius, Florian Ganzer, Ursula Havemann-Reinecke, Ulrich W. Preuss, "Risks Associated With the Non-Medicinal Use of Cannabis," *Deutsches Arzteblatt International* 112 (2015), 271–78.

62 Hoch et al., "Risks Associated With the Non-Medicinal Use of Cannabis," 271.

63 See Stephen P. H. Alexander, "Review: Therapeutic potential of cannabis-related drugs," *Progress in Neuro-Psychopharmacology & Biological Psychiatry* 64 (2016): 157–66; Laura M. Borgelt, Kari L. Franson, Abraham M. Nussbaum, and George S. Wang, "The Pharmacologic and Clinical Effects of Medical Cannabis," *Pharmacotherapy* 33, no. 2 (2013): 195–209; Julie Holland, ed., *The Pot Book: A Complete Guide to Cannabis* (Rochester, VT: Park Street Press, 2010), 287–90; Marcel O. Bonn-Miller, Kimberly A. Babson, Ryan Vandrey, "Using cannabis to help you sleep: Heightened frequency of medical cannabis use among those with PTSD," *Drug and Alcohol Dependence* 136 (2014): 162–65.

64 Christopher Ingraham, "The government is stifling medical marijuana research, major think tank declares," *Washington Post*, October 20, 2015: https://www.washingtonpost.com/news/wonk/wp/2015/10/20/the-federal-government-is-stifling-medical-research-major-think-tank-declares/.

Chapter 1

1   "Stronger than Opium: Attempt to Smuggle 'Mariguana' Into Yuma Prison," *Tombstone Prospector* (Tombstone, AZ), September 15, 1897.

2   Ibid.

3   Isaac Campos, *Home Grown: Marijuana and the Origins of Mexico's War on Drugs* (Chapel Hill: University of North Carolina Press, 2012), 90, 98–9; "4th Quarterly Reports of the Asst. Superintendent and Physician of the Territorial Prison," *Arizona Sentinel* (Yuma, AZ), January 12, 1895; see also "Had the Way Paved For Descent to Freedom: Discovery of Attempt to Break Jail," *Arizona Republican*, June 17, 1909, in which the paper reported that "the search was undertaken" at the county jail "for the purpose of ascertaining if any drugs had been smuggled into jail, more especially Indian hemp of cannabis indica which is in much favor with Mexican prisoners who call it 'miriwana.'"

4   "Stronger than Opium . . ."

5   "The Medicine Closet," *The Argus* (Holbrook, AZ), November 18, 1899.

6   "Stronger than Opium . . . "

7   For discussion of Cannabis's sinister reputation in Mexico, see Campos, *Home Grown*, 81–102. For discussion of European stereotypes about tropical cannabis, see Chris Duvall, *Cannabis* (London: Reaktion Books, 2014), 148–149. For general discussion of European stereotypes about tropical environments, see Nancy Leys Stepan, *Picturing Tropical Nature* (London: Reaktion Books, 2006).

8   For discussion of growing disdain for Mexicans in the Southwest at the turn of the century, see Katherine Benton-Cohen, *Borderline Americans: Racial Division and Labor War in the Arizona Borderlands* (Cambridge, MA: Harvard University Press, 2009), 85–90.

9   Martin A. Lee, *Smoke Signals: A Social History of Marijuana—Medical, Recreational, Scientific* (New York: Scribner, 2012), 7.

10   Legal historians Richard Bonnie and Charles Whitebread coined the term "marihuana menace" to describe the general idea that drug cannabis led users to madness and violence; see Richard J. Bonnie and Charles H. Whitebread II, *The Marijuana Conviction: A History of Marijuana Prohibition in the United States* (Charlottesville: University Press of Virgina, 1974. Reprint, New York: The Lindesmith Center, 1999).

11   See Duvall, *Cannabis*, 108–109; Bonnie and Whitebread, *Marijuana Conviction*, 32–38, 42–47.

12   Pure Food and Drug Act, 770.

13   Bonnie and Whitebread, *Marijuana Conviction*, 48.

14   Dale H. Gieringer, "The Origins of Cannabis Prohibition in California," *Contemporary Drug Problems* 26, no. 2 (Summer 1999): 33; Bonnie and Whitebread, *Marijuana Conviction*, 48–49.

15   "Marihuana is Cause of Half of Crimes Here, Says Officer," *Arizona Republican*, March 31, 1920, 8.

16   Bonnie and Whitebread, *Marijuana Conviction*, 48–49.

17   Ibid., 52.

18 "Military Police Start War Against Marihuana Users," *The Evening Herald* (Albuquerque, NM), September 6, 1917, 3; "Marihuana Is Cause of Half of Crimes Here, Says Officer," *Arizona Republican*, March 31, 1920, 8; "Menace as Great as Opium Looms on Mex. Border," *Daily Journal* (Telluride, CO), August 16, 1921; "Narcotic Weed Believed Cause of Fatal Shooting," *Denver Post*, November 28, 1921, 8; "Marijuana Confiscated By County Sheriff," *Corona Courier* (Corona, CA), August 26, 1921, 1; "Mexican Confesses Growing Marijuana," *Helena Independent* (Helena, MT), November 20, 1928.

19 Duvall, "Race, class, and post-Columbian Cannabis diffusion," 1.

20 Ibid., 32; "Results from the 2013 National Survey on Drug Use and Health: Summary of National Findings," Center for Behavioral Health Statistics and Quality, US Department of Health and Human Services (September 2014), 27.

21 *The Pharmacopoeia of the United States* (Philadelphia: Lippincott, Grambo & Co., 1851), 50.

22 Martin A. Lee, *Smoke Signals: A Social History of Marijuana—Medical, Recreational, Scientific* (New York: Scribner, 2012), 31.

23 Fitz Hugh Ludlow, *The Hasheesh Eater: Being Passages from the Life of a Pythagorean* (New York: Harper & Brothers, 1857) 51, 67.

24 Ibid., 85.

25 Ibid., 91.

26 Alicia Puglionesi, "Proving It: The American Provers' Union documents certain ill effects," *The Public Domain Review*, September 4, 2013, http://publicdomainreview. org/2013/09/04/proving-it-the-american-provers-union-documents-certain-ill-effects/.

27 The American Provers' Union, *Provings of Cannabis Indica* (Philadelphia: King & Baird Printers, 1859), 5–6.

28 Ibid., 8, 16–17.

29 Ibid., 15–19; Laura M. Borgelt, Kari L. Franson, Abraham M. Nussbaum, and George S. Wang, "The Pharmacologic and Clinical Effects of Medical Cannabis," *Pharmacotherapy* 33, no. 2 (2013): 199–202; see Mark S. Wallace and Ben Platt, "Pain Management," in *The Pot Book: A Complete Guide to Cannabis*, ed. Julie Holland, MD (Rochester, VT: Park Street Press, 2010), 328-35.

30 H. H. Kane, *Drugs That Enslave: The Opium, Morphine, Chloral, and Hashisch Habits* (Philadelphia: Presley Blakiston, 1881), 208–210.

31 Ibid., 212–217.

32 Ibid., 210–211; Horatio C. Wood, "On The Medical Activity of the Hemp Plant," *Proceedings of the American Philosophical Society*, Vol. 11, No. 81 (January 1869): 226–232.

33 E. W. Scripture, "Consciousness Under the Influence of Cannabis Indica," *Science*, Vol. 22, No. 560 (October 27, 1893): 233–234.

34 "Alcohol Must Go! Drugs That are Being Used as Stimulants. New York Druggists on the Subject—Habitual Users Grow Secretive as Regards Their Vice," *Sausalito (CA) News*, December 5, 1890.

35 A.A. Stevens, A.M., M.D., *Modern Materia Medica and Therapeutics* 5th ed. (Philadelphia: W.B. Saunders, 1909), 101.

36 "Safety with edibles," Colorado.gov, 2015: https://www.colorado.gov/pacific/marijuana/safety-edibles (accessed October 21, 2015).

37 "Indigestion Acute or Gastric Tympanitis (Address by Dr. F.H. Cassells at the recent meeting of the Washington Medical Veterinary Association)," Ranch and Range (North Yakima, Washington), July 30, 1898, 6–7.

38 "If You Cannot Sleep at Night Read This," *San Francisco Call*, January 16, 1898, 18.

39 Helen Watts McVey, "The Home Department: Good Things to Know," *The Commoner* (Lincoln, NE), vol. 11, no. 48 (1901), 8.

40 "Pages from Harriet Hubbard Ayer's Book Health and Beauty," *The San Francisco Call*, February 17, 19.01; "Little Cures for Our Aches and Pains," *The Morning Oregonian*, March 24, 1907; Mme. Lina Cavalieri, "My Secrets of Beauty—Care of the Feet," *The Spokane Press*, January 9, 1910.

41 "Scientific Notes," *Pacific Pharmacist* 3 (1909–1910), 232.

42 Borgelt et al., "The Pharmacologic and Clinical Effects," 202–203; Amanda Reiman, "Cannabis as a substitute for alcohol and other drugs," *Harm Reduction Journal* 6, no. 35 (2009).

43 Daniel Freeman, Graham Dunn, Robin M. Murray, Nicole Evans, Rachel Lister, et al., "How Cannabis Causes Paranoia: Using the Intravenous Administration of Delta-9 Tetrahydrocannabinol (THC) to Identify Key Cognitive Mechanisms Leading to Paranoia," *Schizophrenia Bulletin* 41, no. 2 (2015), 391–399.

44 Stephen Wishnia, "Smoke vs. Snack: Why Edible Marijuana Is Stronger Than Smoking," *The Daily Beast*, June 13, 2014, http://www.thedailybeast.com/articles/2014/06/13/smoke-vs-snack-why-edible-marijuana-is-stronger-than-smoking.html.

45 Gieringer, "Origins of Cannabis Prohibition in California," 3–4.

46 Clarke and Merlin, *Evolution and Ethnobotany*, 36, 46, 298.

47 Wood apparently used an extract from male plants to create his ingestible tincture; see Wood, "The Medicinal Effects of the Hemp Plant," 226; see also R. P. Walton, "Description of the Hashish Experience," in *Marihuana: America's New Drug Problem* (Philadelphia: J.E Lippincott, 1938), 83–113.

48 Gieringer, "The Origins of Cannabis Prohibition in California," 7–8; see *The San Francisco Call*, June 24, 1895.

49 W. W. Stockberger, "Drug Plants Under Cultivation," *Farmers' Bulletin* No. 663, US Department of Agriculture, June 5, 1915, 19.

50 Ibid., 3.

51 See Linda Nash, *Inescapable Ecologies: A History of Environment, Disease, and Knowledge* (Berkeley: University of California Press, 2006), 94, 96–97; Jared Orsi, *Hazardous Metropolis: Flooding and Urban Ecology in Los Angeles* (Berkeley: University of California Press, 2004), 38–43.

52 "Cultivating Drugs: New Government Experiment in This State," *The Watchman and Southron* (Sumter, SC), April 13, 1904, 1.

53 Ibid.

54 Stockberger, "Drug Plants Under Cultivation," 1915, 3.

55 W. W. Stockberger, "Commercial Drug Growing in the United States in 1918," *Journal of American Pharmaceutical Association* 8, no. 1 (January 1919): 809.

56 Ibid.

57 George P. Koch, "The Cultivation of Medicinal Plants," *Journal of American Pharmaceutical Association* 8, no. 1 (January 1919): 280.

58 Stockberger, "Commercial Drug Growing," 811.

59 W. W. Stockberger, "Drug Plants Under Cultivation," *Farmers' Bulletin* No. 663, US Department of Agriculture, Revised August 1920, 25.

60 See Emily Brady, *Humboldt: Life on America's Marijuana Frontier* (Melbourne, Australia: Scribe, 2013), 69–70; Martin A. Lee, *Smoke Signals: A Social History of Marijuana—Medical, Recreational, Scientific* (New York: Scribner, 2012), 176; Jim Rendon, *Super Charged—How Outlaws, Hippies, and Scientists Reinvented Marijuana* (Portland: Timber Press, 2012), 56.

61 "Fighting Weed Vendor Gets Stiff Jolt," *Weekly Journal-Miner* (Prescott, AZ), April 16, 1919, 2.

62 "Marihuana Crop Nipped," *Bisbee Daily Review*, June 29, 1919, 4.

63 "Make Marihuana Raid," *Arizona Republican*, June 6, 1920, 14.

64 Stockberger, "Drug Plants," 1920, p. 25; W. W. Stockberger, "Drug Plants Under Cultivation," *Farmers' Bulletin* No. 663, US Department of Agriculture, Revised August 1927, 17.

65 Average price calculated from Stockberger, "Drug Plants," 1927.

66 For discussion on the role of Mexican marijuana folklore in US prohibition, see "Postscript: Mexican Ideas Move North," in Campos, *Home Grown,* 203–223.

67 As late as 1914 members of the American Pharmaceutical Association opined that "probably not one laymen in five thousand every [sic] heard of cannabis indica, and it is doubtful if the Hashish habit will ever be in vogue in this country"; see H.C. Fuller, "Conservation in Relation to Pharmaceutical Chemistry," *The Journal of the American Pharmaceutical Association* 3 (January-December, 1914): 134; Gieringer, "The Origins of Cannabis Prohibition in California," 14.

68 Advertisements for T. Puente & Son in *La Revista de Taos*, November 22, 1912, February 14, 1913, and December 10, 1915.

69 "Poisonous Weeds of Mexico Cause Death," *El Paso Herald*, May 9, 1914, 8-D.

70 "Use for Deadly Weed: Mexican Marihuana Plant to Be Grown in Texas for Drug Purposes," *Florida Star* (Titusville, FL), October 16, 1908, 3. See also "Marihuana to be Grown in Texas," *Pacific Drug Review* 21, no. 5 (May 1909): 68.

71 Ibid.

72 "Grand Jury Recommends That Steps Be Taken To Stop Sale of Marihuana," *El Paso Herald*, October 4, 1913; see "Hop and Dope Fiends Fast Being Recruited From Better Families: Juarez Has a Hellhole of Temptation, *El Paso Herald*, June 15, 1912; "Crazed By Weed, Man Murders," *El Paso Herald*, January 2, 1913, 1.

73 "Marihuana Sale Now Prohibited: Council Passes Emergency Ordinance to Stop Sale of Mexican Drug," *El Paso Herald*, June 3, 1915.

74   "Declares American Diplomacy Is Laughing Stock Of The World; Commends *El Paso Herald*'s Stand,*" El Paso Herald*, May 14, 1915.

75   "Little Interviews," *El Paso Herald*, June 4, 1915.

76   "New Anti-Marihuaua [sic] Ordinance Very Stringent," *El Paso Herald*, June 7, 1915.

77   Doctor in Detroit Wants to Know About Marihuana," *El Paso Herald*, December 18, 1916.

78   "Little Interviews," *El Paso Herald*, December 10, 1917, 6.

79   Ibid.

80   "Legislature to Halt, March 18," *El Paso Herald*, March 10, 1919.

81   "Military Police Start War Against Mariahuana [sic] Users," *The Evening Herald* (Albuquerque, NM), September 6, 1917. For discussion of the 1917 liquor ban in New Mexico see Jason Silvernman, *Untold New Mexico: Stories from a Hidden Past* (Santa Fe, NM: Sunstone Press, 2006), 35.

82   "Marihuana Smokers Shut Off From Their 'Makins,'" *El Paso Herald*, September 13, 1917; "New Mexico State News," *Clovis (NM) News*, September 27, 1917.

83   "Drug Bill is Vetoed in Arizona," *Casper Daily Tribune* (WY), February 16, 1921, 12.

84   Ibid.

85   Campos, *Home Grown*, 207–215.

86   See Duvall, "Race, class, and post-Columbian Cannabis diffusion," 4.

87   Bonnie and Whitebread, *Marijuana Conviction*, 8–9, 14.

88   Ibid., 14–15.

89   Kane, *Drugs that Enslave.*

90   "Greek Hashish Drug; Culture and Exportation of This Strong Narcotic Plant Growth," *Daily East Oregonian* (Pendleton, OR), January 31, 1908, 5.

91   "Narcotics Sold To Boys; Juvenile Court With Decoys Gets Evidence," *Morning Oregonian*, March 13, 1915, 9; "Drug Sale Questioned; Clerk Held to Grand Jury For Letting Boy Have Hashish," *Morning Oregonian*, March 31, 1915, 9; "Law would block hashish sale," *Morning Oregonian*, May 22, 1915, 7; "Hashish Sale Prohibited; Council Unanimous in Vote to Put Opiate Under Ban," *Morning Oregonian*, May 27, 1915, 1.

92   "Fear that Marijuana Will Start Another Dope Craze in U.S.," *Bakersfield Californian*, November 3, 1925.

93   Winifred Black, "Marijuana, 'Flivver' of Drug Family, Described by Miss Black: Humble Texas Weed Drives Men to Slay," *San Antonio Light*, February 25, 1928.

94   Ibid., 207–208; Luigi Stella, Maria Redenta Vitelli, Enza Palazzo, Patrizia Oliva, Vito De Novellis, Annalisa Capuano, Maria Antoinetta Scafuro, Liberato Berrino, Francesco Rossi, and Sabatino Maione, "Datura Stramonium Intake: A Report on Three Cases," *Journal of Psychoactive Drugs* 42, no. 4 (December 2010): 510–511; Marcello Pennacchio, Lara Jefferson, Kayri Havens, *Uses & Abuses of Plant-Derived Smoke* (New York: Oxford University Press, 2010), 7; Amy M. Arnett, "Jimson Weed (Datura stramonium) Poisoning," *Clinical Toxicology Review* 18, no. 3 (December 1995).

95   Enno Freye, "Toxicity of Datura Stramonium," in Enno Freye and Joseph V. Levy, *Pharmacology and Abuse of Cocaine, Amphetamines, Ecstasy and Related Designer Drugs* (Netherlands: Springer, 2009), 217–218.

96   Juitao Wang, Lingzhen Song, Qui Zhang, Wei Zhang, Lei An, Yamei Zhang, Dewen Tong, Baoyu Zhao, Shulin Chen, Shanting Zhao, "Exposure to swainsonine impairs adult neurogenesis and spatial learning and memory," *Toxicology Letters* 232 (2015): 263–270.

97   "Stronger than Opium . . ."

98   "Locooed," *The Weekly Herald* (Amarillo, Texas), November 28, 1907, 2.

99   "The Deadly Loco Weed," *Socorro Chieftain*, August 31, 1907.

100 "Poisonous Weeds of Mexico Cause Death," *El Paso Herald*, May 9–10, 1914, 8-D.

101 Stockberger, "Drug Plants Under Cultivation," 35.

102 See "To Farm Insanity Plant," Yampa Leader (Routt County, CO), March 5, 1909; "Madness in Plants," *Bandon (OR) Recorder*, May 25, 1905; "Talavatchi," (Toloache) in *The New Standard Encyclopedia*, eds. William A. Colledge, Nathan Haskell Dole, and George J. Hagar (New York: The University Society, 1907), 224.

103 "To Farm Insanity Plant," Yampa Leader, 1909; "Madness in Plants," *Bandon Recorder*, 1905.

104 "Old Fable Revived: No Truth in the Poisoning of the Empress Carlota," *Brownsville (TX) Daily Herald* via *The Mexican Herald*, April 10, 1901, 1.

105 "Is The Mexican Nation 'Locoed' By A Peculiar Weed?" *The Ogden (UT) Standard*, September 25, 1915.

106 Don M. Coerver, "Plan of San Diego," *Handbook of Texas Online* (Texas State Historical Association: June 15, 2010, http://www.tshaonline.org/handbook/online/articles/ngp04).

107 "Is The Mexican Nation 'Locoed'. . ."

108 Ibid.

109 Campos, *Home Grown*, 208.

110 Coerver, "Plan of San Diego."

111 Ibid.

112 Andrew J. Peters, "T.D. 35719: Drugs," US Treasury Department, September 25, 1915; see Bonnie and Whitebread, *The Marijuana Conviction*, 53–54.

113 "Marihuana Evil is Growing In Colorado Says George Collins," *Denver Post*, February 21, 1927, 14.

114 "Smuggling of Mexican Drug into Pueblo Schools Charged," *Denver Post*, February 18, 1927.

115 "Whisky, Arms Taken in Raid," *Salt Lake Tribune*, March 13, 1928.

116 Bruce Grant, "A Home-Grown New Drug That Drives Its Victims Mad," *Denver Post*, December 30, 1928, 6.

117 Ibid. On the photocopy of the newspaper I obtained, it is impossible to tell whether the plants described as "marijuana" are indeed cannabis; nevertheless, a photograph that visually declared a deadly drug to be lurking on one's city block undoubtedly had a powerful effect on American readers.

118 Ibid.

119 For American attitudes toward Mexican laborers, see David G. Gutiérrez, *Walls and Mirrors: Mexican Americans, Mexican Immigrants, and the Politics of Ethnicity* (Berkeley: University of California Press, 1995), 46–47.

120 Gérard Niveau and Cécile Dang, "Cannabis and Violent Crime," *Medicine, Society, and the Law* 43, no. 2 (April 2003); Mikkel Arendt, Raben Rosenberg, Lone Fjordback, Jack Brandholdt, Leslie Foldager, Leo Sher, Povl Munk-Jorgensen, "Testing the self-medication hypothesis of depression and aggression in cannabis-dependent subjects," *Psychological Medicine* 37, no. 7 (July 2007); Philip H. Smith, Gregory G. Homish, Kenneth E. Leonard, R. Lorraine Collins, "Marijuana withdrawal and aggression among a representative sample of U.S. marijuana users," *Drug and Alcohol Dependence* 132 (2013): 63–68.

121 Michael K. Ostrowsky, "Does Marijuana Use Lead to Aggression and Violent Behavior?" *Journal of Drug Education* 41, no. 4 (December 2011): 369–389.

122 Eliana Dockterman, "Marijuana Now the Most Popular Drug in the World," *Time*, June 29, 2012, http://newsfeed.time.com/2012/06/29/marijuana-now-the-most-popular-drug-in-the-world/.

123 Patrick Frye, "Marijuana Crime Statistics in Colorado Drop, Denver Police Claim Tactics Change is Responsible, Not Legal Pot," *The Inquistr*, July 6, 2014, http://www.inquisitr.com/1338610/marijuana-crime-statistics-in-colorado-drop-denver-police-claim-change-in-tactics-is-responsible-not-legal-pot/; "Marijuana Legalization in Washington State: One-Year Status Report," *The Drug Policy Alliance*, July 6, 2015, http://newsfeed.time.com/2012/06/29/marijuana-now-the-most-popular-drug-in-the-world/.

124 S. Macdonald, P. Erickson, S. Wells, A. Hathaway, B. Pakula, "Predicting violence among cocaine, cannabis, and alcohol treatment clients," *Addictive Behaviors* 33 (2008): 201–205.

125 Adam R. Winstock, "The Global Drug Survey 2014 Findings," *Global Drug Survey*, 2014, http://www.globaldrugsurvey.com/facts-figures/the-global-drug-survey-/2014-findings/.

126 Campos, *Home Grown*, 179–180.

127 Search of available newspapers from Arizona, New Mexico, and Texas, in Chronicling America, the Library of Congress's collection of digitized newspapers, http://chroniclingamerica.loc.gov/search/pages/results/?state=Arizona&state=New+-Mexico&state=Texas&dateFilterType=yearRange&date1=1900&date2=1919&language=&ortext=marihuana&andtext=&phrasetext=&proxtext=&proxdistance=5&rows=20&searchType=advanced. The search returned 185 mentions; twenty were subtracted as duplicates.

128 W. A. Evans, "Hashish as Public Menace," in "How to Keep Well," *Salt Lake Tribune*, November 3, 1926, 6.

129 Ibid.; Wood, "On The Medical Activity of the Hemp Plant."

130 Willa Gibbs, "Ruth Judd, Dillinger Described by Visitor," *The Bakersfield Californian*, September 20, 1935, 1, 4.

131 Ibid., 4.

Chapter 2

1   "$4,000 Trees Weren't Weeping Willows," *Long Beach Press Telegram* (CA), July 19, 1956.

2   Ibid.

3   "14-Foot Shade Bush Actually Marijuana," *Long Beach Press Telegram*, August 13, 1954, B-8.

4   "This One Five Feet Tall: Another Woman Finds Overgrown Marijuana," *Long Beach Press Telegram*, September 27, 1956.

5   "The Newsreel," *Redlands Daily Facts*, May 2, 1959, p. 8.

6   Frank and Bill Moore, "With a Grain of Salt," *Redlands Daily Facts*, May 14, 1959, 12.

7   Sampling of articles obtained by author from Newspaperarchive.com; see Nick Johnson, "Mapping Cannabis Cultivation in California, 1900–60," *Hempirical Evidence* (blog), June 12, 2015: http://hempiricalevidence.blogspot.com/2015/06/mapping-cannabis-cultivation-in.html.

8   See Zachary S. Falck, *Weeds: An Environmental History of Metropolitan America* (Pittsburgh, PA: University of Pittsburgh Press, 2010), 76–89.

9   "The Light and Heavy Sides of News Today," *Corona Independent* (CA), August 9, 1956, 1; "Jury Frees Woman in Dope Possession Case," *Bakersfield Californian*, October 22, 1958.

10   For discussion of hemp used as birdseed, see Chris Duvall, *Cannabis* (London: Reaktion Books, 2015), 74; J.C. Callaway, "Hempseed as a nutritional resource: An overview," *Euphytica* 140 (2004): 65–6.

11   Marihuana Tax Act; Alaine Lowell, "Hemp: The miracle plant that can save the planet," *Pasadena Weekly*, October 22, 2010.

12   In 1938, for example, officers in Red Lodge, Montana burned some 32,000 plants of a fiber company's experimental hemp crop; the town's mayor denounced the burnings as "a big mistake." See "Marijuana Crop Mowed, Burned," *Oakland Tribune*, October 6, 1938, 10-D and "'Marihuana' Burning Denounced; Plant Was Fibre Company's Hemp," *Montana Standard*, October 14, 1938, 3. Authorities continued to conflate hemp and marijuana into the 1950s; see "Marijuana Blamed on Faulty Bird seed," *Long Beach Press Telegram*, April 8, 1950.

13   See Richard J. Bonnie and Charles H. Whitebread II, *The Marijuana Conviction: A History of Marijuana Prohibition in the United States* (Charlottesville: University Press of Virgina, 1974. Reprint, New York: The Lindesmith Center, 1999), 28–31.

14   For discussion of authorities targeting transient and minority populations under anti-cannabis laws, see Falck, *Weeds*, 79–80.

15   Bonnie and Whitebread, *Marijuana Conviction*, 42–43, 70–78; Martin A. Lee, *Smoke Signals: A Social History of Marijuana—Medical, Recreational, Scientific* (New York: Scribner, 2012), 42, 50–52; Jim Rendon, *Super Charged: How Outlaws, Hippies, and Scientists Reinvented Marijuana* (Portland: Timber Press, 2012), 122; Larry Sloman, *Reefer Madness: A History of Marijuana* (New York: St. Martin's Griffin, 1979), 30–31; Martin Booth, *Cannabis: A History* (New York: Picador, 2003), 177–184.

16   "The War on Marijuana in Black and White," American Civil Liberties Union, June 2013: https://www.aclu.org/files/assets/aclu-thewaronmarijuana-rel2.pdf

17   Ibid., 32; "Results from the 2013 National Survey on Drug Use and Health: Summary of National Findings," Center for Behavioral Health Statistics and Quality, US Department of Health and Human Services (September 2014), 27.

18   Orsi, *Hazardous Metropolis*, 77–79; Donald Worster, *Dust Bowl: The Southern Plains in the 1930s* (New York: Oxford University Press, 1982); Nash, *Inescapable Ecologies*, 88–91; Ted Steinberg, *Down to Earth: Nature's Role in American History* 2nd ed. (New York: Oxford University Press, 2009), 247–251.

19   Sloman, *Reefer Madness*, 29–32.

20   Lee, *Smoke Signals*, 48.

21   Sloman, *Reefer Madness*, 46.

22   Ibid., 35; "State Laws Urged to Cut Growing Use of Hashish," *Helena Independent*, October 4, 1931. Between 1931 and 1936, Anslinger and the FBN pushed for cannabis to be included in Uniform State Laws (identical laws passed individually by the states); see Sloman, *Reefer Madness*, 47.

23   Lee, *Smoke Signals*, 49.

24   Sloman, *Reefer Madness*, 48–51.

25   Ibid., 38–39, 45.

26   Ibid., 5.

27   Lee, *Smoke Signals*, 45, 47; Falck, *Weeds*, 79.

28   Sloman, *Reefer Madness*, 63–64.

29   See Isaac Campos, *Home Grown: Marijuana and the Origins of Mexico's War on Drugs* (Chapel Hill: University of North Carolina Press, 2012), 179–180; Adam R. Winstock, "The Global Drug Survey 2014 Findings," *Global Drug Survey*, 2014; Mikkel Arendt, Raben Rosenburg, Lone Fjordback, Jack Brandholdt, Leslie Foldager, Leo Sher, and Povl Munk-Jorgensen, "Testing the self-medication hypothesis of depression and aggression in cannabis-dependent subjects," *Psychological Medicine* 37 (January 2007): 935–945.

30   "Drive is on to Stamp out Marihuana Weed, Grown as Narcotic," *Denver Post*, August 15, 1934, 11.

31   Lee, *Smoke Sigals*, 51–52; Sloman, *Reefer Madness*, 58–60.

32   David G. Gutiérrez, *Walls and Mirrors: Mexican Americans, Mexican Immigrants, and the Politics of Ethnicity* (Berkeley: University Press of California, 1994), 72.

33   Historians Brian Gratton and Emily Merchant estimate that between 1930 and 1933 the Hoover administration deported about 9,768 more Mexicans per year than were deported during the period of 1925–1929; see Gratton and Merchant, "Immigration, Repatriation, and Deportation: The Mexican-Origin Population in the United States, 1920–1950," *International Migration Review* 47, no. 4 (Winter 2013): 955.

34   Marihuana Tax Act of 1937, Pub. L 238 (1937).

35   Bonnie and Whitebread, *Marijuana Conviction*, 173–174; Lee, *Smoke Signals*, 54.

36   Bonnie and Whitebread, *Marijuana Conviction*, 174.

37   Eugene Stanley, "Marihuana as a Developer of Criminals," Additional Statement of H.J. Anslinger, Commissioner of Narcotics, Department of the Treasury, Hearings on H.R. 6385 before the Committee on Ways and Means, Seventy-Fifth Congress, April 27, 1937.

38   Statement of H.J. Anslinger, Commissioner of Narcotics, Bureau of Narcotics, Department of the Treasury, Hearings on H.R. 6385 before the Committee on Ways and Means, Seventy-Fifth Congress, April 27, 1937.

39   Letter from Floyd K. Baskette to United States Treasury Department Bureau of Narcotics, September 4, 1936.

40   Statement of H.J. Anslinger, April 27, 1937.

41   Brian A. Catlos, *Infidel Kings and Unholy Warriors: Faith, Power, and Violence in the Age of Crusade and Jihad* (New York: Farrar, Straus and Giroux, 2014), 267.

42   Statement of H.J. Anslinger, April 27, 1937.

43   Statements of Clinton M. Hester, Assistant General Counsel for the Department of the Treasury, and Dr. James C. Munch, Pharmacologist, Temple University, Hearings on H.R. 6385 before the Committee on Ways and Means, Seventy-Fifth Congress, April 27, 1937.

44   Statement of James C. Munch, April 27, 1937.

45   Barbara J. Weiland, Rachel E. Thayer, Brendan E.Depue, Amithrupa Sabbineni, Angela D. Bryan, and Kent E. Hutchison, "Daily Marijuana Use Is Not Associated with Brain Morphometric Measures in Adolescents or Adults," *The Journal of Neuroscience* 35, no. 4 (January 2015): 1505–1512; "violent irritability" or aggression is not a commonly observed side effect of cannabis use, though it has been occasionally observed in users with a long history of depression. See Mikkel Arendt, Raben Rosenburg, Lone Fjordback, Jack Brandholdt, Leslie Foldager, Leo Sher, and Povl Munk Jorgensen, "Testing the self-medication hypothesis of depression and aggression in cannabis-dependent subjects," *Psychological Medicine* 37 (January 2007): 935–945; see also Eva Hoch, Udo Bonnet, Rainer Thomasius, Florian Ganzer, Ursula Havemann-Reinecke, Ulrich W. Preuss, "Risks Associated With the Non-Medicinal Use of Cannabis," *Deutsches Arzteblatt International* 112 (2015): 271–278.

46   W.L. Treadway, "Answers to Marijuana Questionnaire," Hearings on H.R. 6385 before the Committee on Ways and Means, Seventy-Fifth Congress, April 27, 1937.

47   Statement of Herbert J. Wollner, Consulting Chemist, Office of the Secretary of the Treasury, Hearings on H.R. 6385 before the Committee on Ways and Means, Seventy-Fifth Congress, April 27, 1937.

48   Statement of Dr. William C. Woodward, Hearings on H.R. 6385 before the Committee on Ways and Means, Seventy-Fifth Congress, May 4, 1937.

49   Ibid.

50   Ibid.

51   Ibid.

52   Ibid.

53   Ibid.

54   Ibid.

55   Statement of H.J. Anslinger, Hearings on H.R. 6385 before the Committee on Ways and Means, Seventy-Fifth Congress, April 27, 1937.

56   Robert C. Clarke and Mark Merlin, *Cannabis: Evolution and Ethnobotany* (Berkeley: University of California Press, 2013), 49, 52.

57   "Bird Seed Field Found To Be Dope Producer," *Woodland Daily Democrat*, August 12, 1933, 1.

58   See Associated Press, "Deer stomp down barbed wire to eat hemp in southern Oregon," *Oregonian*, September 7, 2015, http://www.oregonlive.com/pacific-north-west-news/index.ssf/2015/09/deer_devour_hemp_crop_in_south.html;   Ricardo Baca, "This video of a marijuana-munching deer needs to be seen to be believed," *The Cannabist* in *Denver Post*, December 11, 2014, http://www.thecannabist.co/2014/12/11/video-marijuana-deer-oregon/25116/; Robert Bergman, "Will Deer Eat My Outdoor Marijuana Plants?" *The Weed Blog* (blog post), May 13, 2014, http://www.theweedblog.com/will-deer-eat-my-outdoor-marijuana-plants/. The online forums for *Cannabis Culture* magazine include a discussion amongst growers on how to deal with Cannabis-eating deer; see http://forums.cannabisculture.com/forums/index.php?/topic/167525-do-deer-eat-cannabis/.

59   Marihuana Tax Act of 1937, Pub. L 238 (1937).

60   Statement of Joseph B. Hertzfield, Manager, Feed Department, The Philadelphia Seed Co., Hearings on H.R. 6385 before the Committee on Ways and Means, Seventy-Fifth Congress, April 30, 1937.

61   Ibid.

62   "Marijuana Blamed on Faulty Birdseed," *Long Beach Press Telegram*, April 8, 1950, A-3.

63   MJ Tax Act.

64   "Marijuana Crop Mowed, Burned," *Oakland Tribune*, October 6, 1938, 10-D; "'Marihuana' Burning Denounced; Plant was Fibre Company's Hemp," *Montana Standard* (Butte, MT), October 14, 1938, 3.

65   Rod Sterling, "Flamethrowers Fail to Destroy Lush Stand of Marijuana Found Here," *Denver Post*, August 21, 1951, 3.

66   "Huge Marijuana Field Burnt Up," *Hayward (CA) Daily Review*, August 8, 1957, 1.

67   Survey of news reports conducted by author; see Nick Johnson, "Instances of Cannabis Growth in the American West," custom Google map, 2015: https://www.google.com/maps/d/edit?mid=zIQvIFHnGktM.k4Gecc3Cfa6k&usp=sharing

68   A comprehensive survey of news reports on a wider scale was beyond the scope and budget of this book.

69   "Hemp for Victory," YouTube video, 14:11, from US Department of Agriculture Office of Public Affairs, 1942, posted by "Nuclear Vault," July 26, 2015: https://www.youtube.com/watch?v=d3rolyiTPro

70   Ibid.

71   "Statement of Dr. B. B. Robinson, Bureau of Plant Industry, Department of Agriculture," Marihuana Conference, December 5, 1938, Washington, DC: http://www.druglibrary.org/schaffer/hemp/taxact/mhc4.htm

72   Geoff Watts, "Cannabis confusions," *British Medical Journal* 332, no. 7534 (January 21, 2006): 175-76.

73   Alden P. Armagnac, "Can We Have Rope Without Dope? Plant Wizards Fight Wartime Drug Peril," *Popular Science*, September 1943: 62-3.

74 Brittain B. Robinson, "Marihuana investigations. IV. A study of marihuana tox-icity on goldfish applied to hemp breeding," *Journal of American Pharmaceutical Association* 30, no. 12 (December 1941): 616–19; H. E. Warmke, "Use of the Killfish, Fundulus heteroclitus, in the Assay of Marihuana," *Journal of the American Pharmaceutical Association* 33, no. 4 (April 1944): 122–25.

75 Armagnac, "Rope Without Dope?"

76 David P. West, "Hemp Under Attack," in *Fiber Wars: The Extinction of Kentucky Hemp* (unpublished manuscript: David P. West, 1995): http://www.newheadnews.com/hemp/fiberwars/chp8fr.html (last updated November 11, 2005).

77 US District Court, 10thcir., 1938–1952, case no.'s 8730–9151.

78 "New Charge Faced by Modesto Worker," *Bakersfield Californian*, August 31, 1937, 4.

79 "U.S. to Aid Rocky Mountain States Fight Marijuana," *Denver Post*, September 10, 1937.

80 "Denver Court Imposes First U.S. Marijuana Law Penalties," *Denver Post*, October 8, 1937.

81 United States v. Leo Acosta, F. (10th Cir. 1948); Pasquale Marranzino, "Marijuana Raid Shatters Haven of Drug Addicts," *Rocky Mountain News*, April 10, 1948.

82 United States v. Leo Acosta, F. (10th Cir. 1948): Defendant's Statement to Probation Officer.

83 United States v. Leo Acosta, F. (10th Cir. 1948): Judgment and Commitment.

84 "Marijuana Raid Jails Six Suspects," *Oakland Tribune*, October 26, 1940; "U.S. Agents Bought Dope to Trap Ring," *Denver Post*, August 30, 1948.

85 Bonnie and Whitebread, *Marijuana Conviction*, 210–212.

86 Ibid., 204, 214.

87 "Woman Held for Growing Marijuana," *Pasadena Independent*, November 11, 1957, 6; "Flower Pots Send Woman, 27, to Penitentiary," *Pasadena Star News*, December 19, 1957, 1.

88 "No Organized Crime in State, Says Brown," *Oakland Tribune*, December 8, 1952, 9.

89 Al Nakkula, "Illicit Marijuana Crops," *Rocky Mountain News* (Denver), June 1, 1951.

90 "Clothespin Gets Addict Extra Marijuana Puff," *Denver Post*, July 28, 1951, 2.

91 Lee, *Smoke Signals*, 73.

92 Ibid., 74; Michael Pollan, *The Botany of Desire: A Plant's-Eye View of the World* (New York: Random House, 2001), 152.

93 Lizbeth Cohen, *A Consumers' Republic: The Politics of Mass Consumption in Postwar America* (New York: Vintage Books, 2003), 126–127.

94 Ibid., 146–148, 153, 166–173.

95 Paul Goodman, *Growing Up Absurd* (New York: Vintage Books, 1956), 241.

96 Ibid., 170.

97 Ibid., 187.

98 Pollan, *Botany of Desire*, 149.

99 "Officer Winner Over Marijuana," *Billings Gazette*, February 19, 1958.

Chapter 3

1   "$60,000 Marijuana Confiscated And Alleged Wholesaler Arrested," *Rocky Mountain News*, June 13, 1946.

2   Ibid.

3   Ibid.

4   In 1946, sugar beet growers could expect to earn an average of $13.50 per ton of their crop, while moments before he was arrested, Hernandez sold a pound of marijuana to a customer for $100. See "Sugar Beet Growers May Be Guaranteed $14.50 Ton in 1947," *Farmers Weekly Review*, November 11, 1946, 3; "$60,000 Marijuana Confiscated . . . ," *Rocky Mountain News*, June 13, 1946.

5   "$60,000 Marijuana Confiscated . . . ," *Rocky Mountain News*, June 13, 1946.

6   The *Rocky Mountain News* reported $60,000; *Denver Post* reported $40,000.

7   *United States v. Manuel Hernandez* (F., 10th Cir. August 13, 1946)

8   See William Cronon, *Nature's Metropolis: Chicago and the Great West* (New York: W.W. Norton, 1991), 97–98.

9   See Jim Rendon, *Super Charged: How Outlaws, Hippies, and Scientists Reinvented Marijuana* (Portland: Timber Press, 2012); Martin A. Lee, *Smoke Signals: A Social History of Marijuana—Medical, Recreational, Scientific* (New York: Scribner, 2012), 174–180.

10   David T. Courtwright, *Forces of Habit: Drugs and the Making of the Modern World* (Cambridge, MA: Harvard University Press); See Chris Duvall, *Cannabis* (London: Reaktion Books, 2015), 91–92, 162–164; Mart Stewart, "Rice, Water, and Power: Landscapes of Domination and Resistance in the Lowcountry, 1790–1880," *Environmental History Review* 15 (Autumn 1991); Michael V. Angrosino, "Rum and Ganja: Indenture, Drug Foods, Labor Motivation, and the Evolution of the Modern Sugar Industry in Trinidad," in William Jankowiak and Daniel Bradburd, *Drugs, Labor, and Colonial Expansion* (Tucson: University of Arizona Press, 2003), 105; see also individual essays on coca, cannabis, and khat by Stephen Hugh-Jones, James H. Mills, and Axel Klein and Susan Beckerleg, in Jordan Goodman, Paul E. Lovejoy, and Andrew Sherrat, eds., *Consuming Habits: Global and Historical Perspectives on How Cultures Define Drugs*, 2nd ed. (London: Routledge, 2007), pp. 46–64, 178–193, 238–254.

11   For discussion of how boom periods took shape in the American West, see Kent Curtis, "Producing a Gold Rush: National Ambitions and the Northern Rocky Mountains, 1853–1863," *Western Historical Quarterly* 40, no. 3 (Autumn 2009): 275–297.

12   Taylor notes that "Between 1891 and 1907 'white laborers' were employed in a number of California beet-growing districts but 'they never formed a large part of the force in any district' . . . The immigration Commission attributed their disappearance to the 'disagreeable' nature of the work." See Taylor, "Hand Laborers," 22; A member of the California Agricultural Legislative Committee argued in 1930 that "'American whites have been educated away from hard, physical labor, particularly common labor'"; See David G. Gutiérrez, *Walls and Mirrors: Mexican Americans,*

Mexican Immigrants, and the Politics of Ethnicity (Berkeley: University of California Press, 1995), 48.

13   For a discussion of the various immigrant groups who worked beet fields in California, Colorado, and other states throughout the West, see Taylor, "Hand Laborers," 21–22, and Sierra Standish, "Beet Borderland: Hispanic Workers, the Sugar Beet, and the Making of a Northern Colorado Landscape," (master's thesis, CSU), 36. For discussion of upward social mobility of German-Russian and Japanese beet laborers, see Taylor, "Hand Laborers," 23–24, and Standish, "Beet Borderland," 36– 37. For discussion of the Immigration Acts of 1917 and 1924 that restricted European and Japanese immigration, see Michael E. Parrish, *Anxious Decades: America in Prosperity and Depression, 1920-1941* (New York: W.W. Norton & Co., 1992), 110–111.

14   For discussion of upward social mobility of German-Russian and Japanese beet laborers, see Taylor, "Hand Laborers," 23–24, and Standish, "Beet Borderland," 36– 37. For discussion of the Immigration Acts of 1917 and 1924 that restricted European and Japanese immigration, see Michael E. Parrish, *Anxious Decades: America in Prosperity and Depression, 1920-1941* (New York: W.W. Norton & Co., 1992), 110–111.

15   For discussion of the transition to farming from cattle ranching in South Texas and its effects on Mexican Americans, see Jim Norris, *North for the Harvest: Mexican Workers, Growers, and the Sugar Beet Industry* (St. Paul, MN: Minnesota Historical Society), 28–29. For discussion of the conditions of the Mexican working class before and after the revolution, see Gutiérrez, *Walls and Mirrors*, 44 and Norris, *North for the Harvest*, 27–28. For discussion of the Immigration Act of 1924, see Parrish, *Anxious Decades*, 112–13. For discussion of the sugar industry's role in the debate surrounding the Immigration Act of 1924, see Norris, *North for the Harvest*, 26–27, and Kathleen Mapes, *Sweet Tyranny: Migrant Labor, Industrial Agriculture, and Imperial Politics* (University of Illinois Press, 2009), 143–45. For statistics on the Mexican-born population's involvement in the sugar beet and other industries of the Southwest, see Gutiérrez, *Walls and Mirrors*, 45; In Colorado's South Platte River Valley, for instance, the number of betabeleros increased from 1,000 in 1909 to 14,300, or more than 59 percent of the workforce, in 1927; see Taylor, "Hand Laborers," 22–23.

16   Norris, *North for the Harvest*, 34; Johnston, "Wages, Employment Conditions," 325– 328; Standish, "Beet Borderland," 26.

17   Arthur Sherman, "Marijuana," Letter to the Editor, *Oakland Tribune*, August 17, 1938.

18   "Have 'New Booze,'" *Billings Gazette*, October 7, 1926; "Jags at Sidney Laid on Weeds," *Billings Gazette*, September 25, 1926.

19   "Rosebud Authorities Discover Marijuana," *Billings Gazette*, September 25, 1931, 6.

20   Ibid.

21   "Wyoming Officers Root Up Marijuana," *Billings Gazette*, August 8, 1935, 7.

22   "Blanket Order In Drug Battle," *Albuquerque Journal*, August 8, 1925, 1; "Marijuana Grove Seized at Wasco," *Bakersfield Californian*, November 8, 1923, 9; "Yolo Marijuana Field Raided," *Woodland Daily Democrat*, September 7, 1934, 1; "Officers Raid Two Marijuana Farms, Man Held," *Woodland Daily Democrat*, July 19, 1933;

"Officers on Guard Against Smuggling Of Drug in Valley," *Alamosa Daily Courier*, September 4, 1936; "Marijuana Maker Is Sent To State Asylum After Wild Outbreak," *Denver Post*, August 14, 1937, 8.

23 Sherman, "Marijuana."

24 Lisa Knopp, *What the River Carries: Encounters with the Mississippi, Missouri, and Platte* (Columbia: University of Missouri Press, 2012), 203–204.

25 United States Department of Labor, Children's Bureau. Child Labor and the Work of Mothers in the Beet Fields of Colorado and Michigan Bureau Publication no. 115. Washington, DC: Government Printing Office, 1923; Sierra Standish cited this report as part of a section on child labor in "Beet Borderland"; see Standish, "Beet Borderland," 50.

26 Standish, "Beet Borderland," 50.

27 Erik B. Oleson, Joseph F. Cheer, "A Brain on Cannabinoids: The Role of Dopamine Release in Reward Seeking," *Cold Spring Harbor Perspectives in Medicine* 2, no. 8 (August 2012).

28 Earlywine, *Understanding Marijuana*, 192.

29 "Marijuana is Found on Mexican Worker," *Las Animas Leader*, October 13, 1937.

30 "Marijuana Good For Rheumatism, He Says But Police Doubtful," *Yuma Morning Sun*, August 1, 1925.

31 Duvall, *Cannabis*, 91–92.

32 By "drink" he is referring to a tea-like preparation of Cannabis; see "Mexican Confesses Growing Marijuana," *Helena Independent*, November 20, 1928, and Duvall, *Cannabis*, 41–43.

33 See Angelo A. Izzo and Keith A. Sharkey, "Cannabinoids and the gut: New developments and emerging concepts," *Pharmacology & Therapeutics* 126 (2010): 29; Daniele De Filippis, Giuseppe Esposito, Carla Cirillo, Mariateresa Cipriano, Benedicte Y. De Winter, Caterina Scuderi, Giovanni Sarnelli, Rosario Cuomo, Luca Steardo, Joris G. De Man, and Teresa Iuvone, "Cannabidiol Reduces Intestinal Inflammation through the Control of Neuroimmune Axis," *PLOS One* 6, no. 12 (December 2011): http://www.ncbi.nlm.nih.gov/pmc/articles/PMC3232190/.

34 "Jury Frees Mexican in Marijuana Case," *Greeley Tribune*, February 19, 1958, 2.

35 Ibid.

36 Mapes, *Sweet Tyranny*, 145, 143–150; Gutiérrez, *Walls and Mirrors*, 46, 47–51; see also Standish, "Beet Borderland," 70–75.

37 ". . . Mexican workers would have no agricultural ladder," Mapes, *Sweet Tyranny*, 150.

38 Norris, *North for the Harvest*, 34; Michael M. Smith, "Beyond the Borderlands: Mexican Labor in the Central Plains, 1900–1930," *Great Plains Quarterly* 1, no. 4 (Fall 1981): 245.

39 See US Department of Labor, Bureau of Labor Statistics Bulletin 604, "History of Wages in the United States from Colonial Times to 1928" (Washington: US Government Printing Office, 1934. Reprint, Detroit: Gale Research Company, 1966).

40 The average net income reported by Americans in 1920 was $3,269.40; in 1925 it was $5,249.16: See US Department of Treasury, Statistics of Income from Returns of Net

Income for 1920, Internal Revenue Service, 1922, 2; US Department of Treasury, Statistics of Income from Returns of Net Income for 1925, Internal Revenue Service, 1927, 2.

41 Norris notes that "migrant housing was typically abysmal in the 1920s (and beyond)" (Norris, *North for the Harvest*, 34), while Standish describes the housing of beet workers in Fort Collins, Colorado as "temporary shacks," (Standish, "Beet Borderland," 65).

42 "Marijuana Ring Is Broken By Arrest of Five At Longmont," *Denver Post*, November 24, 1933, 28.

43 "Marijuana Grove Seized at Wasco," *Bakersfield Californian*, November 8, 1923.

44 "Whisky, Arms Taken in Raid," *Salt Lake Tribune*, March 13, 1928.

45 "Mexican Confesses Growing Marijuana," *Helena Independent*, November 20, 1928.

46 Associated Press, "Use of Loco Weed Growing Popular," *Kalispell Daily Interlake*, April 2, 1924.

47 "Have 'New Booze,'" *Billings Gazette*, October 7, 1926.

48 Survey of newspaper reports conducted by author; for discussion of methodology see Nick Johnson, "Mapping Cannabis Cultivation Across the American West, c. 1895–1950," *Hempirical Evidence* (blog), March 8, 2015, http://hempiricalevidence. blogspot.com/2015/03/mapping-cannabis-cultivation-across.html.

49 Officers Raid Two Marijuana Farms, Man Held," *Woodland Daily Democrat*, July 19, 1933.

50 "Mexicans Ordered From U.S. – Brothers Escape Prison By Agreement," *Woodland Daily Democrat*, October 23, 1933, 1.

51 "Marihuana Grower's Bond Fixed at $2,000 By Justice A. Ford," *Davis County Clipper* (UT), June 18, 1937; "Marihuana Burned By County Sheriff," *Davis County Clipper* (UT), March 10, 1939; "Mountain Hunt Fails for Hidden Mystery Field of Marijuana; Tomas Refuses To Aid Search," *San Mateo Times*, September 20, 1939, 11.

52 "Dope Raiders Jail 15 Colorado Suspects," *Denver Post*, January 12, 1941.

Chapter 4

1 "Johnny Pot Sows Marijuana," *Eureka Times Standard*, October 21, 1968.

2 Ibid.

3 Ray Raphael, "Green Gold and the American Way," in *West of Eden: Communes and Utopia in Northern California* eds. Iain Boal, Janferie Stone, Michaell Watts, Cal Winslow (Oakland, CA: PM Press, 2012), 188; Ray Raphael, *Cash Crop: An American Dream* (Mendocino, CA: Ridge Times Press, 1985), 35–36; Martin A. Lee, *Smoke Signals: A Social History of Marijuana—Medical, Recreational, Scientific* (New York: Scribner, 2012), 94–97.

4 Kathleen Ferraiolo, "From Killer Weed to Popular Medicine: The Evolution of American Drug Control Policy, 1937–2000," *Journal of Policy History* 19, no. 2 (2007): 157–158.

5 Matthew D. Lassiter, "Impossible Criminals: The Suburban Imperatives of America's War on Drugs," *Journal of American History* 102, no. 1 (June 2015): 126–140.

6   "Marijuana Law Reform Timeline," National Organization for the Reform of Marijuana Laws, 2015, http://norml.org/shop/item/marijuana-law-reform-timeline.

7   National Commission on Marijuana and Drug Abuse, *Marihuana: A Signal of Misunderstanding* (Washington, DC: US Government Printing Office, 1972).

8   deleted.

9   Raphael, "Green Gold," 188.

10 Paul F. Conkin, *A Revolution Down on the Farm: The Transformation of American Agriculture Since 1927* (Lexington: University Press of Kentucky, 2008), 112, 120–121.

11 See Lizabeth Cohen, *A Consumers' Republic: The Politics of Mass Consumption in Postwar America* (New York: Vintage Books, 2003), 112–165.

12 For discussion of postwar inequality, see Cohen, "Residence: Inequality in Mass Suburbia," in *Consumers' Republic*, 194–256.

13 See Cohen, *Consumers' Republic*, 121–123.

14 For discussion of Americans' deliberate manipulation of nature to produce "wilderness" and recreational hot spots, see William Cronon, "The Trouble with Wilderness; or, Getting Back to the Wrong Nature," in *Uncommon Ground: Rethinking the Human Place in Nature*, ed. William Cronon (New York: W.W. Norton & Company, 1996), 70–90; see also William Philpott, *Vacationland: Tourism and Environment in the Colorado High Country* (Seattle: University of Washington Press, 2013).

15 Cohen, *Consumers' Republic*, 124–127.

16 Andrew G. Kirk, *Counterculture Green: The Whole Earth Catalog and American Environmentalism* (Lawrence: University Press of Kansas, 2007), 13.

17 Kirk, *Counterculture Green*, 21-22; see also Mark Harvey, "Echo Park Dam Controversy," *Colorado Encyclopedia*, last modified September 9, 2016 (accessed June 14, 2017): https://coloradoencyclopedia.org/article/echo-park-dam-controversy.

18 Rachel Carson, *Silent Spring* (Cambridge, MA: Riverside Press, 1962); for discussion of suburban development, see Kirk, *Counterculture Green*, 23.

19 Jeff Lustig, "The Counterculture as Commons: the Ecology of Community in the Bay Area," in *West of Eden* eds. Boal et al., 31.

20 See Sherry L. Smith, *Hippies, Indians, and the Fight for Red Power* (New York: Oxford University Press, 2012) and John McMillian, *Smoking Typewriters: The Sixties Underground Press and the Rise of Alternative Media in America* (New York: Oxford University Press, 2011), 5.

21 McMillian, *Smoking Typewriters*, 6.

22 Felicity D. Scott, "Bulldozers in Utopia: Open Land, Outlaw Territory, and the Code Wars," in *West of Eden* eds. Boal et al., 58; for discussion of utopian thought in America, see James J. Kopp, "The American Utopian Tradition," in *Eden Within Eden: Oregon's Utopian Heritage* (Corvallis: Oregon State University Press, 2009), 22–38.

23 Miller, *The 60s Communes*, 206; Bernard Gavzer, "'Grass Grows on Many College Campuses," *Billings Gazette*, June 6, 1966, 7.

24 Richard J. Bonnie and Charles H. Whitebread II, *The Marijuana Conviction: A History of Marijuana Prohibition in the United States* (Charlottesville: University Press of Virginia, 1974. Reprint, New York: The Lindesmith Center, 1999), 237–238.

25 One estimate claims that in 1937 there were 50,000 users; see Lee, *Smoke Signals*, 55.

26 Edward M. Brecher and Editors of Consumer Reports Magazine, *Licit and Illicit Drugs: The Consumers Union Report on Narcotics, Stimulants, Depressants, Inhalants, Hallucinogens, and Marijuana—including Caffeine, Nicotine, and Alcohol* (Boston: Little Brown and Co., 1972), Part VIII, Chapter 57.

27 "Survey at CC Polls Dope Views," *Denver Post*, April 28, 1968.

28 "Students Using Marijuana, UM Paper Reports," *Helena Independent*, October 20, 1966.

29 Ibid.

30 Brecher et al., *Licit and Illicit Drugs*, Part VIII, Chapter 57.

31 "Panties and Other Unmentionables," *Helena Independent*, November 17, 1967, 4.

32 "A 'Popular' War," *Helena Independent*, December 7, 1962.

33 Patricia O'Connell, "Bozeman Wouldn't Want It," letter to the editor, *Billings Gazette*, November 22, 1967.

34 "Teacher Among Those Charged in 'Pot' Case," *Billings Gazette*, July 24, 1967.

35 Dick Gilluly, "MSU Professor Denies Drugs Found in Home," *Billings Gazette*, August 2, 1967.

36 Ibid.

37 Ibid.

38 Ibid.

39 Russell Baker, "Beatniks, Marijuana Dissenters Abound, But—Smog Can't Find Champion," *Independent* (Pasadena), February 9, 1967.

40 "Probation Officer Warns Area Parents," *Port Angeles Evening News*, May 8, 1968.

41 Jeff Lustig, "The Counterculture as Commons: The Ecology of Community in the Bay Area," in *West of Eden*, eds. Boal et al., 38.

42 Ibid., 29.

43 See Mark Matthews, *Droppers: America's First Hippie Commune* (Norman: University of Oklahoma Press, 2010); Timothy Miller, *The 60s Communes: Hippies and Beyond* (Syracuse, NY: Syracuse University Press, 1999); Miller, "California Communes," 8–9; see also Arthur Kopecky, *New Buffalo: Journals from a Taos Commune* (Albuquerque: University of New Mexico Press, 2004).

44 See Arthur Kopecky, *Leaving New Buffalo* (Albuquerque: University of New Mexico Press, 2006).

45 Raymond Mungo, "Living on the Earth," *New York Times* book review, March 21, 1971.

46 "Introduction."

47 Ibid., 134, 137.

48 Roberta Price, *Huerfano: A memoir of life in the counterculture* (Amherst: University of Massachusetts Press, 2004), 40.

49 Ibid., 306.

50 Smith, *Hippies, Indians, and the Fight for Red Power*, 127.

51 Ibid., 6–7, 119–122.

52 "Missing Girl Found in Hippie Colony," *Long Beach Press Telegram*, December 1, 1967.

53 Miller, *The 60s Communes*, 23–24.

54 Lee, *Smoke Signals*, 117, 174; Jim Rendon, *Super Charged: How Outlaws, Hippies, and Scientists Reinvented Marijuana* (Portland: Timber Press, 2012), 45.

55 John Brinckerhoff Jackson, *Discovering the Vernacular Landscape* (New Haven: Yale University Press, 1984), 149–150.

56 Ibid., 32.

57 Ibid., 39–40.

58 National Commission on Marijuana and Drug Abuse, "I. Control of Marihuana, Alcohol and Tobacco—History of Marihuana Legislation," in *Marihuana: A Signal of Misunderstanding* (Washington, DC: US Government Printing Office, 1972), http://www.druglibrary.org/schaffer/library/studies/nc/nc2_7.htm.

59 Lassiter, "Impossible Criminals," 132–133.

60 Bonnie and Whitebread, *Marijuana Conviction*, 239.

61 "Judge moved for statements on marijuana," *Redlands Daily Facts*, October 5, 1967.

62 Michael R. Aldrich, Tod H. Mikuriya, and Gordon S. Brownell, "Reasons for Escalating Enforcement Costs: California Drug and Marijuana Arrests, 1960–67," in *Preliminary Report: Fiscal Costs of California Marijuana Law Enforcement, 1960–1984*, by Michael R. Aldrich, Tod H. Mikuriya, and Gordon S. Brownell (Berkeley, 1986), Schaffer Library of Drug Policy, http://druglibrary.org/schaffer/ hemp/moscone/chap1.htm; see also Lassiter, "Impossible Criminals," 132.

63 *Leary v. United States*, 395 US 6 (1969).

64 "Legalize marijuana group established," *Corona Daily Independent*, October 11, 1967.

65 "ACLU plans to challenge marijuana law," *Port Angeles Evening News*, February 16, 1968; "State Supreme Court Rules on Marijuana," *Centralia Daily Chronicle*, May 15, 1970.

66 Lee, *Smoke Signals*, 118, 128.

67 Lee, *Smoke Signals*, 128–129.

68 "ABA favors removing pot penalties," *Eureka Times Standard*, August 10, 1973.

69 Richard Schneider, "Strang introduces legal marijuana bill," *Rocky Mountain News*, April 4, 1973; "Bill easing marijuana penalties sent to Lamm," *Rocky Mountain News*, June 20, 1975.

70 "Marijuana measure signed by Brown," *Eureka Times Standard*, July 10, 1975.

71 G.G. LaBelle, "Laws on marijuana are easing," *Billings Gazette*, July 17, 1975.

72 "Marijuana Law Reform Timeline," National Organization for the Reform of Marijuana Laws, 2015, http://norml.org/shop/item/marijuana-law-reform-timeline.

73 Ferraiolo, "From Killer Weed to Popular Medicine," 158.

74 National Commission on Marijuana and Drug Abuse, *Marihuana: A Signal of Misunderstanding* (Washington, DC: US Government Printing Office, 1972).

75 Ibid., Ch. II, "Marihuana Use and Its Effects," Summary.

76 Ibid., Ch. V, "Marihuana and Social Policy—A Final Comment."

77 Ibid., addendum IV.

78 "Richard Nixon War On Drugs 1972," YouTube video, 0:44, from a press conference, 1972, posted by Hunterhttpthompson, May 20, 2010, https://www.

youtube.com/watch?v=bsrxpVUKUK0; Lee, *Smoke Signals*, 121; see also Kevin Zeese, "Once-Secret 'Nixon Tapes' Show Why the U.S. Outlawed Pot," Alternet, March 20, 2002, http://www.alternet.org/story/12666/once-secret_%22nixon_tapes%22_show_why_the_u.s._outlawed_pot.

79   Lee, *Smoke Signals*, 134, 137–139; Carl Hart, "Why research is biased against pot to focus on its harm and not its benefits," *Dallas Morning News*, September 12, 2014, http://www.dallasnews.com/opinion/sunday-commentary/20140911-why-research-is-biased-against-pot-and-other-recreational-drugs.ece; Rob Hotakainen, "Feds accused of steering funding to anti-pot researchers," McClatchy DC, March 19, 2014, http://www.mcclatchydc.com/news/nation-world/national/economy/article24765427.html; Lee Fang, "Leading Anti-Marijuana Academics Are Paid By Painkiller Drug Companies," *Vice*, September 7, 2014: https://news.vice.com/article/leading-anti-marijuana-academics-are-paid-by-painkiller-drug-companies.

80   Lee, *Smoke Signals*, 140–141; Robert C. Randall, "Glaucoma: A Patient's View," in Mary Lynn Mathre, Ed., *Cannabis in Medical Practice: A Legal, Historical, and Pharmacological Overview of the Therapeutic Use of Marijuana* (Jefferson, NC: McFarland & Co., 1997), 94–102.

81   Randall, "Glaucoma," 99.

82   Ethan Russo, Mary Lynn Mathre, Al Byrne, Robert Velin, Paul J. back, Juan Sanchez-Ramos, and Kristin A. Kirlin, "Chronic Cannabis Use in the Compassionate Investigational New Drug Program: An Examination of Benefits and Adverse Effects of Legal Clinical Cannabis," *The Journal of Cannabis Therapeutics* 2, no. 1 (2002), 7.

83   Ibid.

84   Henry Jampel, "Position Statement on Marijuana and the Treatment of Glaucoma," American Glaucoma Society, August 10, 2009, http://www.americanglaucomasociety.net/patients/position_statements/marijuana_glaucoma.

85   See David Turbert, "Does Marijuana Help Treat Glaucoma?" Geteyesmart.org, last updated June 27, 2014, http://www.geteyesmart.org/eyesmart/living/medical-marijuana-glaucoma-treament.cfm; Stephen P.H. Alexander, "Therapeutic potential of cannabis-related drugs," *Progress in Neuro-Psychopharmacology & Biological Psychiatry* 64 (2016), 162; "Treating Glaucoma," The Glaucoma Foundation, https://www.glaucomafoundation.org/treating_glaucoma.htm (accessed December 20, 2015).

86   "The Dangers and Consequences of Marijuana Abuse," US Justice Department, Drug Enforcement Administration Demand Reduction Section (May 2014), 3–4, http://www.dea.gov/docs/dangers-consequences-marijuana-abuse.pdf.

87   Arthur J. Lingle, "Tucson becoming nation's marijuana smuggling capital," *Eureka (CA) Times Standard*, May 11, 1975.

88   Patrick Anderson, *High in America: The True Story Behind NORML and the Politics of Marijuana* (New York: Viking Press, 1981), Chapter 11; Rendon, *Super Charged*, 66–67.

89   See Eleanor Agnew, *Back from the Land: How Young Americans Went to Nature in the 1970s, and Why They Came Back* (Chicago: Ivan R. Dee, 2004); Miller, *The 60s*

Communes, 67–68; Rendon, *Super Charged*, 50–52; "Organized Crime Sets Sights on Haight-Ashbury," *Press-Courier* (Oxnard, CA) August 9, 1967.

90 "Organized Crime . . ."

91 Miller, *The 60s Communes*, 67–69.

92 Agnew, *Back from the Land*, 6.

93 Kirk, *Counterculture Green*.

94 Emily Brady, *Humboldt: Life on America's Marijuana Frontier* (New York: Grand Central Publishing, 2013) 65–66.

95 See W. Scott Prudham, *Knock on Wood: Nature as Commodity in Douglas Fir Country* (New York: Routledge, 2005), 223.

96 Brady, *Humboldt*, 65; Mandalit Del Barco, "Marijuana sales boost Northern California County," *NPR*, November 30, 2009.

97 Rendon, *Super Charged*, 44–45.

98 "Pot growers complain about deputies' raid," and David Anderson, "Cox denies any 'hippie harassment,'" *Eureka Times Standard*, August 28, 1973.

99 "Pot growers complain . . ."

100 "Pot growers complain . . ."

101 "Rotary Speaker," photo caption, *Ukiah Daily Journal*, July 26, 1967, 1.

102 Bill Drake, "About," *Panacea Chronicles* (blog), n.d. (accessed June 14, 2017): https://panaceachronicles.com/about/; Bill Drake, "The Cultivators Handbook of Marijuana—The Back Story," *Panacea Chronicles* (blog), July 4, 2015: https://panaceachronicles.com/2015/07/04/the-cultivators-handbook-of-marijuana-the-back-story/.

103 Bill Drake, *The Cultivator's Handbook of Marijuana* (Berkeley, CA: Bill Drake c/o Book People, 1970), 22-27, 38, 42-43, 59.

104 Ibid., 3, 7, 42-45, 59.

105 Bill Drake, "The Cultivators Handbook of Marijuana—The Back Story."

106 Ibid.

107 Ibid.

108 Ibid.

109 Lee, *Smoke Signals*, 150–151.

110 Rendon, *Super Charged*, 71–73; Mel Frank and Ed Rosenthal, *The Marijuana Grower's Guide* (Berkeley, CA: And/Or Press, 1978).

111 Ibid., 107–109; Jorge Cervantes, *Indoor Marijuana Horticulture* (Sacramento, CA: Van Patten Publishers, 1983).

112 For example, see The Macedonia Kid, "Who Put the 'High' in Ohio?" *High Times*, May 1981.

113 Rendon, *Super Charged*, 53, 64, 67; for an example of a Vietnam veteran returning with cannabis seeds, see Andrew Genzoli, "Ferndale Confession! Resident Says He Grew Marijuana, DA Knew It," *Eureka Times Standard*, December 2, 1970, 1–2.

114 "Pot growers complain . . ."

115 Ibid. Like other medicinal plants, cannabis produces more of its medicinal compounds when it is stressed by conditions such as heat, drought, or cold. See Dan Sullivan, "Global warming and the 'Green Rush,'" *Daily*

Climate,   May   13,   2015,   http://www.dailyclimate.org/tdc-newsroom/2015/05/
climate-change-marijuana-pot-global-warming-potent.

116 Brady, *Humboldt*, 107.

117 "Deputies' massive marijuana raid . . ."

118 "Couple Held for Growing Marijuana," *Eureka Times Standard*, April 23, 1968, 1.

119 For examples of sub-100 plant grows, see "3 Escapers Nabbed With Bonus Catch,"
     Eureka Times Standard, July 28, 1971, 1; "'Pot' Growth Jails Twosome," *Eureka Times
     Standard*, June 20, 1972, 12.; "Marijuana plants confiscated," *Eureka Times Standard*,
     March 21, 1974, 7.

120 "$50,000 'Pot' Raid in Eureka!" *Times Standard* (Eureka, CA), October 27, 1970, 1.

121 "Pot fields destroyed," *Times Standard* (Eureka, CA), August 2, 1973, 19.

122 "Deputies' massive marijuana raid confiscates plants; five arrested," *Times Standard*
     (Eureka, CA), September 30, 1976, 1.

123 "3,000 marijuana plants confiscated, nine arrested in raid by deputies," *Times
     Standard* (Eureka, CA), August 22, 1973.

124 "Property owners seeking information on marijuana raids," *Times Standard* (Eureka,
     CA), August 25, 1973, 1–2.

125 "3,000 marijuana plants confiscated . . ."

126 "For a high time, try burning green pot," *Eureka Times Standard*, August 24, 1973, 2.

127 "Property owners seeking information . . ."

128 "Allegations against sheriff's deputies brought up in county budget meeting," *Eureka
     Times Standard*, August 29, 1973; "Nine arraigned for pot," *Eureka Times Standard*,
     August 23, 1973.

129 Harold Kitching, "For a high time, try burning green pot," *Eureka Times Standard*,
     August 8, 1973, 1–2.

130 "Cox denies any 'hippie harassment . . ."

131 Ibid.

132 Allegations against sheriff's department brought up . . ."

133 "Marijuana trial faced," *Eureka Times Standard*, October 27, 1973; "Six have felony
     charges dropped from '73 pot raid," *Eureka Times Standard*, September 3, 1975.

134 See Raphael, *Cash Crop*, 159–160.

Chapter 5

1 Harry Harris, "Man arrested after cops find bumper crop of pot," *Oakland Tribune*,
   January 8, 1991.

2 Ibid.

3 See, for example, John Soluri, *Banana Cultures: Agriculture, Consumption, &
   Environmental Change in Honduras & the United States* (Austin: University of Texas
   Press, 2005), and Douglas Sackman, *Orange Empire: California and the Fruits of
   Eden* (Berkeley: University of California Press, 2007).

4 Michael Pollan, *The Botany of Desire: A Plant's-Eye View of the World* (New York:
   Random House, 2001), 131–132; Jim Rendon, *Super Charged: How Outlaws, Hippies,
   and Scientists Reinvented Marijuana* (Portland: Timber Press, 2012), 80–101; Robert

C. Clarke and Mark Merlin, *Cannabis: Evolution and Ethnobotany* (Berkeley: University of California Press, 2013), 130.

5   Jeremy Kuzmarov, *The Myth of the Addicted Army: Vietnam and the Modern War on Drugs* (Amherst: University of Massachusetts Press, 2009), 127.

6   Philip J. Landrigan, Kenneth E. Powell, Levy M. James, and Philip R. Taylor, "Paraquat and Marijuana: Epidemiologic Risk Assessment," *American Journal of Public Health* 73, no. 7 (July 1983): 784–788; Michael Isikoff, "DEA Finds Herbicides in Marijuana Samples," *Washington Post*, July 26, 1989, https://www.washington-post.com/archive/politics/1989/07/26/dea-finds-herbicides-in-marijuana-samples/1103a92e-31a5-42c0-9a92-19b3be05450e/.

7   Landrigan et al., "Paraquat and Marijuana," 784.

8   "Nation: Panic Over Paraquat," *Time* 111, no. 18 (May 1, 1978), 24; *High Times* no. 37 (September 1978).

9   Robert Levering, "The story behind the paraquat scare," *The Straight Creek Journal*, May 4, 1978.

10 Patrick Anderson, *High in America: The True Story Behind NORML and the Politics of Marijuana* (New York: Viking Press, 1981; eBook: Garrett County Press, 2015), 179, 218, 241–247.

11 Levering, "The story behind the paraquat scare . . ."

12 Ibid.

13 Ibid.

14 Alan Riding, "Mexico Says Marijuana Poison Scare Is Propaganda," *New York Times*, May 22, 1978.

15 Ibid.; Landrigan et al., "Paraquat and Marijuana," 786.

16 J. Routt Reigart and James R. Roberts, eds., *Recognition and Management of Pesticide Poisonings* 6th ed. (Washington, DC: US Environmental Protection Agency, 2013), 111, http://npic.orst.edu/RMPP/rmpp_ch12.pdf; Landrigan et al., "Paraquat and Marijuana," 786.

17 Michael Isikoff, "DEA Finds Herbicides . . ."

18 Rendon, *Super Charged*, 65–66.

19 "State of Jefferson," *Oregon Experience*, Oregon Public Broadcasting, aired November 17, 2014, http://www.opb.org/television/programs/oregonexperience/segment/state-of-jefferson/.

20 Jeff LaLande, "State of Jefferson," *Oregon Encyclopedia*, http://oregonencyclope-dia.org/articles/state_of_jefferson/#.VoQEz1nz7gk (accessed December 30, 2015); Kami Horton, "State of Jefferson," Oregon Public Broadcasting: *Oregon Experience*, September 29, 2014, http://www.opb.org/television/programs/oregonexperience/segment/state-of-jefferson/ (accessed December 30, 2015).

21 "State of Jefferson," Oregon Public Broadcasting.

22 "Where the Grass is Greener," *Time* 111, no. 24 (June 12, 1978): 22.

23 Ibid.; see also David Hooper, "Secret Harvest," *Pacific Northwest* (July-August 1983): 47–50.

24 Allen Hallmark, "Hot spot for Pot? Just how much of the potent weed is grown here?" *Mail Tribune* (Medford, OR), July 30, 1978, section C.

25 Mark Howard, "Marijuana may be big county business," *Mail Tribune* (Medford, OR), June 18, 1981, A-3.

26 Richard Reames, Oregon Sungrown Growers' Guild, conversation with author, June 5, 2015.

27 "Where the Grass is Greener"; Tom Towslee, "Marijuana found bearing 'Grown in Oregon' labels," *Mail Tribune* (Medford, OR), June 24, 1984, A-13.

28 Hooper, "Secret Harvest," 50.

29 Ibid.

30 "Where the Grass is Greener"

31 Campaign Against Marijuana Planting Final Reports, 1984–87, available at http://library.humboldt.edu/humco/holdings/CAMP.htm.

32 Elizabeth Watson, Humboldt Institute for Interdisciplinary Marijuana Research, conversation with author, July 26, 2014.

33 Ray Raphael, *Cash Crop: An American Dream* (Mendocino, CA: Ridge Times Press, 1985), 146; Peter Hecht, *Weed Land: Inside America's Marijuana Epicenter and How Pot Went Legit* (Berkeley: University of California Press, 2014), 36; Watson, conversation with author, July 26, 2014.

34 CAMP Final Report 1983 (Sacramento, CA: CAMP Headquarters, 1983), 22–23.

35 See CAMP Final Reports, 1983–89 (Sacramento, CA: CAMP Headquarters), available at http://library.humboldt.edu/humco/holdings/CAMP.htm.

36 For discussion of pesticide development and adoption by consumers in post-World War II America, see Michelle Mart, *Pesticides, A Love Story: America's Enduring Embrace of Dangerous Chemicals* (Lawrence: University Press of Kansas, 2015), 3, 21–25.

37 Clarke and Merlin, *Cannabis*, 227, 300.

38 Rendon, *Super Charged*, 56–57.

39 See James Mills, *Cannabis Britannica: Empire, Trade, and Prohibition 1800–1928* (New York: Oxford University Press, 2003), 51–55.

40 Martin Cizmar, "The Rise and Fall of *Sinsemilla Tips*, Corvallis' Legendary Marijuana Magazine," *The Potlander*, April 11, 2017.

41 Ibid.; Bob Labrasca and Dean Latimer, "Interview: Tom Alexander," *High Times*, December 1983, 35–37.

42 Cizmar, "Rise and Fall of *Sinsemilla Tips*"; "Magazine for Ambitious Marijuana Growers," Associated Press (via the *New York Times*), December 26, 1985.

43 Portland NORML, "Portland NORML notes," in "Excerpts from 'Interview: Tom Alexander,'" Marijuanalibrary.org (accessed June 15, 2017): www.marijuanalibrary.org/talexan_ht_1283.html; Cizmar, "Rise and Fall of *Sinsemilla Tips*."

44 Portland NORML, "Portland NORML notes."

45 Cizmar, "Rise and Fall of *Sinsemilla Tips*."

46 Van der Veer, "U-2 planes spy marijuana . . ."

47 Howard, "Marijuana may be big county business . . ."

48 See Joseph A. McCartin, *Collision Course: Ronald Reagan, the Air Traffic Controllers, and the Strike that Changed America* (New York: Oxford University Press, 2013); David Corn, "How I Got That Story," The Nation (April 6, 2015): 64–66.

49   "Ronald Reagan: 'Marijuana . . . is probably the most dangerous drug,'" Youtube video, 0:35, uploaded by akchuk on September 4, 2014, https://www.youtube.com/watch?v=VxHBx6H-xF0 (accessed December 29, 2015).

50   Martin A. Lee, *Smoke Signals: A Social History of Marijuana—Medical, Recreational, Scientific* (New York: Scribner, 2012), 137–138.

51   *An Analysis of Marijuana Policy* (Washington, DC: National Academy Press, 1982), 29–30, http://www.nap.edu/read/662/chapter/1.

52   Ronald Reagan, Radio Address to the Nation on Federal Drug Policy, October 2, 1982, http://www.presidency.ucsb.edu/ws/?pid=43085.

53   Bruce Barcott, *Weed the People: The Future of Legal Marijuana in America* (New York: Time Books, 2015), 53.

54   "Reagan Aide: Pot Can Make You Gay," *Newsweek*, October 27, 1986; see also Barcott, *Weed the People*, 53–54.

55   Comprehensive Crime Control Act of 1984, S.1762.

56   Ibid., 160.

57   *Illinois v. Gates* 462, US 213 (1983).

58   *United States v. 89 Firearms*, 465 US 354 (1984).

59   Lee, *Smoke Signals*, 191.

60   Ruud Van der Veer, "U-2 planes spy marijuana plots, say 2 experts," *Oakland Tribune*, July 13, 1980, A-1.

61   Ibid.

62   Carole Rafferty, "Marijuana Raids Angering Retirees," *New York Times*, June 10, 1984, http://www.nytimes.com/1984/06/10/us/marijuana-raids-angering-retirees.html.

63   Van der Veer, "U-2 planes spy marijuana . . ."

64   Rendon, *Super Charged*, 75; See also Paul Grabowicz, "Marijuana growers are under attack," *Oakland Tribune*, October 19, 1980, and George Estrada, "Fear and loathing in Mendocino," *Oakland Tribune*, October 19, 1980.

65   Lee, *Smoke Signals*, 178–179; "Kern County man pleads guilty to marijuana grow in Sequoia Forest," Porterville Recorder (CA), June 13, 2017.

66   CAMP Final Report 1983, 2–3.

67   Analysis of CAMP Final Reports, 1983–89.

68   CAMP Final Report 1985.

69   CAMP Final Report 1985, 25.

70   CAMP Final Report 1984, 17; CAMP Final Report 1985, 27

71   CAMP Final Report 1985, 26.

72   CAMP Final Report 1985 16; CAMP Final Report 1986 (Sacramento, CA: CAMP Headquarters, 1986), 14.

73   CAMP Final Report 1991 (Sacramento, CA: CAMP Headquarters, 1991), 10.

74   Analysis of CAMP Final Reports, 1983–91.

75   Tom Towslee, "Marijuana found bearing 'Grown in Oregon' labels, *Mail Tribune* (Medford, OR), June 24, 1984, 1–13.

76   Carole Rafferty, "Marijuana Raids Angering Retirees," *New York Times*, June 10, 1984.

77   See Dan Baum, *Smoke and Mirrors: The War on Drugs and the Politics of Failure* (Back Bay Books, 1997); for brief quotations on CAMP raids, see Radley Balko, "Raid(s) Of The Day: The CAMP Raids," *The Agitator* (Huffington Post blog), April 26, 2013, http://www.huffingtonpost.com/2013/04/26/raids-of-the-day-the-camp_n_3163932.html; see also Radley Balko, *Rise of the Warrior Cop: The Militarization of America's Police Forces* (New York: PublicAffairs, 2013), 147–152.

78   Deborah Frazier, "Pulling up pot plants pushes up price," *Rocky Mountain News*, October 6, 1986.

79   Ibid.; Pollan, *Botany of Desire*, 133.

80   Frazier, "Pulling up pot plants," *Rocky Mountain News*, October 6, 1986.

81   Jackson, *Discovering the Vernacular Landscape*, 39–40.

82   John Denver and Mike Taylor, "Rocky Mountain High," *Rocky Mountain High*, 1972.

83   Lee, *Smoke Signals*, 179, 189.

84   Ibid., 180; see also Ralph A. Weisheit, *Domestic Marijuana: A Neglected Industry* (New York: Greenwood Press, 1992).

85   Deborah Frazier, "Marijuana Colorado's No. 2 cash crop, group says," *Rocky Mountain News*, October 6, 1986.

86   Karen Merrill, "Cops, courts, and growers all weigh pot's profits and losses," *Mail Tribune*, July 24. 1983, C-1.

87   "Pot spraying effort is criminal," Editorial, *Mail Tribune* (Medford, OR), August 17, 1983, 4.

88   Kathy Smith Boe, "Paraquat Eradication: Legal Means for a Prudent Policy?" *Boston College Environmental Affairs Law Review* 12, no. 3 (May 1985): 492. "Marijuana Spraying Opposed," *New York Times*, September 2, 1983, http://www.nytimes.com/1983/09/02/us/marijuana-spraying-opposed.html.

89   "Paraquat Spraying Is Blocked," *New York Times*, September 14, 1983; "U.S. to Resume Using Paraquat on Marijuana," *New York Times* (Associated Press), July 14, 1988, http://www.nytimes.com/1988/07/14/us/us-to-resume-using-paraquat-on-marijuana.html.

90   Robert A. Jones, "US Revives Plan to Kill Marijuana With Paraquat," *LA Times*, July 28, 1985, http://articles.latimes.com/1985-07-28/news/mn-5386_1_marijuana-eradication; US Department of Justice, Drug Enforcement Administration, "Draft Environmental Impact Statement: Cannabis Eradication on Non-Federal and Indian Lands in the Contiguous United States and Hawaii" (Washington, DC: US Government Printing Office, May 1985), 1.

91   Drug Enforcement Administration, "Draft Environmental Impact Statement," 1, 12–13.

92   Ibid.

93   Ibid., 3.

94   Ibid., 5.

95   Ibid., 4–6.

96   Ibid., 6–7.

97   Ibid., 10.

98   Ibid., 15–21.

99 "US To Resume Using Paraquat on Marijuana,"; "The Nation," *LA Times*, July 26, 1989, http://articles.latimes.com/1989-07-26/news/mn-80_1_drug-enforcement-administration.

100 Drug Enforcement Administration, "Draft Environmental Impact Statement," 22.

101 Steve Chapple, "The Indoor Scoop on Pot," Mother Jones, November–December 1985, 11.

102 Ibid.

103 CAMP Final Report 1987 (Sacramento, CA: CAMP Headquarters, 1987), 2.

104 "Couple Raised Own Marijuana," *Bakersfield Californian*, January 3, 1957.

105 Pollan, *Botany of Desire*, 133–134; Rendon, *Super Charged*, 80–81.

106 Pollan, *Botany of Desire*, 132.

107 Rendon, *Super Charged*, 91–92.

108 Chapple, "The Indoor Scoop on Pot."

109 Gregory E. Smoak, communication with author, April 30, 2014. Smoak is now on the faculty at the University of Utah.

110 Rendon, *Super Charged*, 102–120.

111 Ibid., 15.

112 Pollan, *Botany of Desire*, 134–135.

113 Rendon, *Super Charged*, 86.

114 Ibid., 117–119.

115 Bruce Finley, "Marijuana growing spikes Denver electricity demand," *Denver Post*, July 22, 2015.

116 Northwest Power and Conservation Council, Seventh Northwest Conservation and Electric Power Plan (February 25, 2016), ch. 2, p. 6.

117 The Reagan administration, for instance, tripled the amount of money spent on preventing illegal drugs from entering the United States; see Lee, *Smoke Signals*, 159.

118 David L. Ferrell, "The Illegal Occupation of America's National Forests By Drug Trafficking Organizations (DTOs)," Powerpoint presentation, US Forest Service, 2012.

119 Peter G. Chronis, "Pot farmers getting more violent," *Denver Post*, August 22, 1988.

120 Ibid.

121 Ferrell, "The Illegal Occupation," US Forest Service, 2012.

122 Douglas Jehl, "Forest Service, Marijuana Growers Battle to Standoff," *LA Times*, October 14, 1989.

123 Daryl Rush, communication with author, November 27, 2013.

124 Julian Smith, "Illegal Pot Farms Are Poisoning California's Forests," *The Atlantic*, March 31, 2017.

125 "Total Plant Counts on NFS Lands," data table provided to author, US Forest Service, 2012.

Chapter 6

1   Noah Hirsch, Oaksterdam University, conversation with author, August 6, 2015.

2   Noah Hirsch, classroom lecture, Oaksterdam University, August 6, 2015.

3   Kathleen Ferraiolo, "From Killer Weed to Popular Medicine," *Journal of Policy History* 19, no. 2 (2007): 148.

4   Joanna Dodder Nellans, "Medical marijuana has long Arizona history," *Daily Courier* (Prescott, AZ), October 9, 2010, http://dcourier.com/main. asp?SectionID=1&SubSectionID=1&ArticleID=86114.

5   Chanelle Bessette, "Nevada's first medical pot dispensary now open in Sparks," *Reno Gazette Journal*, July 29, 2015, http://www.rgj.com/story/news/2015/07/29/ states-first-medical-marijuana-dispensary-open-friday/30863209/.

6   Ferraiolo, "From Killer Weed to Popular Medicine," 147; "New Mexico Medical Marijuana Law," NORML, http://norml.org/legal/item/new-mexico-medical-marijuana.

7   Analysis of NORML data on medical cannabis programs, compiled by author, August 21, 2015.

8   Ibid.

9   Matt Ferner, "Pioneer Pot States Have Collected More Than $200 Million in Marijuana Taxes," *Huffington Post*, August 26, 2015, http://www.huffingtonpost.com/entry/ washington-colorado-marijuana-taxes_55d6133be4b07addcb45e65d; Christopher Ingraham, "After legalization, Colorado pot arrests plunge," *Washington Post*, March 26, 2015; Washington State Office of Financial Management, Forecasting and Research Division, "Monitoring Impacts of Recreational Marijuana Legalization," February 2015, 19, http://www.ofm.wa.gov/reports/marijuana_impacts_2015.pdf; Julie Weed, "Book Your 'Bud and Breakfast,' Marijuana Tourism Is Growing In Colorado And Washington," *Forbes*, March 17, 2015, http://www.forbes.com/sites/ julieweed/2015/03/17/book-your-bud-and-breakfast-marijuana-tourism-is-grow-ing-in-colorado-and-washington/.

10 Martin A. Lee, *Smoke Signals: A Social History of Marijuana—Medical, Recreational, Scientific* (New York: Scribner, 2012), 223.

11 Ibid., 223–124.

12 "Loss of appetite," aidsmap.com, http://www.aidsmap.com/Loss-of-appetite/ page/1730430/ (accessed December 30, 2015).

13 Laura M. Borgelt, Kari L. Franson, Abraham M. Nussbaum, and George S. Wang, "The Pharmacologic and Clinical Effects of Medical Cannabis," *Pharmacotherapy* 33, no. 2 (2013), 196.

14 Diane Prentiss, Rachel Power, Gladys Balmas, Gloria Tzuang, and Dennis M. Isriaelsk, "Patterns of Marijuana Use Among Patients With HIV/AIDS Followed in a Public Health Care Setting," *Journal of Acquired Immune Deficiency Syndrome* 35, no. 1 (January 2004); Ronald J. Ellis, Will Toperoff, Florin Vaida, Geoffrey van den Brande, James Gonzales, Ben Gouaux, Heather Bentley, and J Hampton Atkinson, "Smoked Medicinal Cannabis for Neuropathic Pain in HIV: A Randomized, Crossover Clinical Trial,"*Neuropsychopharmacology* 34 (2009): 672–680.

15 Lee, *Smoke Signals*, 229–231; see also Julie Holland, ed., *The Pot Book: A Complete Guide to Cannabis* (Rochester, VT: Park Street Press, 2010), 252–260; Peter Hecht, *Weed Land: Inside America's Marijuana Epicenter and How Pot Went Legit* (Berkeley: University of California Press, 2014), 45–55.

16   Ibid., 214.

17   Lee, *Smoke Signals*, 123–130.

18   Mitch Earleywine, *Understanding Marijuana: A New Look at the Scientific Evidence* (New York: Oxford University Press, 2002), 176, 179–180, 192

19   Michael Pollan, *The Botany of Desire: A Plant's-Eye View of the World* (New York: Random House, 2001), 153; Earleywine, *Understanding Marijuana*, 136–141.

20   Ibid; Lee, *Smoke Signals*, 209–210.

21   Lee, *Smoke Signals*, 209–210.

22   Ibid., 211.

23   Ferraiolo, "From Killer Weed to Popular Medicine," 162; Lee, *Smoke Signals*, 121–124, 140–141; Holland, *The Pot Book*, 227–230, 287–290.

24   Ibid., 162–164.

25   Lee, *Smoke Signals*, 246–247.

26   Ferraiolo, "From Killer Weed To Popular Medicine," 167.

27   See Elliott West, "Reconstructing Race" and "The West Before Lewis and Clark: Three Lives," in Elliott West, *The Essential West: Collected Essays* (Norman: University of Oklahoma Press, 2012), 100–126, 129–153; Anne F. Hyde, *Empires, Nations, and Families: A New History of the North American West, 1800–1860* (Lincoln: University of Nebraska Press, 2011), 11–18; Donald Worster, "Beyond the Agrarian Myth," in *Trails: Toward a New Western History*, eds. Patricia Nelson Limerick, Clyde A. Milner, and Charles E. Rankin (Lawrence: University Press of Kansas, 1991), 18.

28   Major gold rushes, for example, drew thousands to California in 1848–1849, Colorado in 1858–1849, and Seattle (the Klondike Rush) in 1897–1898. Land rushes accompanied the gold rushes, facilitated by Indian removal, the Homestead Act of 1862, and the laying of railroad tracks across the region; see Elliott West, *Contested Plains: Indians, Goldseekers, and the Rush to Colorado* (Lawrence: University Press of Kansas, 1998); Klingle, *Emerald City*, 66–67, 95–97; Ted Steinburg, *Down to Earth: Nature's Role in American History* 2nd ed. (New York Oxford University Press, 2009), 117–123.

29   Worster, "Beyond the Agrarian Myth," 8.

30   Cody Hoesly, "Reforming Direct Democracy: Lessons from Oregon," *California Law Review* 1191 (July 2005): 1193.

31   Daniel A. Smith and Dustin Fridkin, "Delegating Direct Democracy: Interparty Legislative Competition and the Adoption of the Initiative in American States," *The American Political Science Review* 102, no. 3 (August 2008): 335.

32   For a detailed history of the ballot initiative, see Thomas Goebel, *A Government By the People: Direct Democracy in America, 1890–1940* (Chapel Hill: University of North Carolina Press, 2002); Hoesly, "Reforming Direct Democracy," 1192.

33   Oregon Secretary of State, "Initiative, Referendum and Recall: 1902–1906," *Oregon Blue Book*, updated 2016, http://bluebook.state.or.us/state/elections/elections10. htm.

34   Montana Secretary of State, "1906-Current Historical Ballot Initiatives and Referenda," updated 2016, http://sos.mt.gov/elections/ballot_issues/documents/

Statutory-Ballot-Issues-1906-Current.pdf; "Montana 1912 ballot measures," Ballotpedia, https://ballotpedia.org/Montana_1912_ballot_measures (accessed July 29, 2016).

35 "Washington 1914 ballot measures," Ballotpedia, https://ballotpedia.org/ Washington_1914_ballot_measures (accessed July 29, 2016).

36 "California 1914 ballot propositions," Ballotpedia, https://ballotpedia.org/ California_1914_ballot_propositions (accessed July 29, 2016).

37 California Secretary of State, "Initiatives Voted into Law," updated 2016, http:// elections.cdn.sos.ca.gov/ballot-measures/pdf/approval-percentages-initiatives. pdf; "Land Title Law," *Lompoc (CA) Journal*, October 17, 1914, http://cdnc.ucr.edu/ cgi-bin/cdnc?a=d&d=LJ19141017.2.10.

38 Ibid., 339–342. Smith and Fridkin note that interparty conflict, union and other Progressive influences, and racial makeup of a state's constituency all contributed to state legislatures' decisions whether or not to allow a vote on whether to adopt an initiative process.

39 See R. McGreggor Cawley, Federal Land, *Western Anger: The Sagebrush Rebellion and Environmental Politics* (Lawrence: University Press of Kansas, 1993); Paul Larmer, "Modern sagebrush rebels recycle old Western fanta-sies," *High Country News*, January 25, 2016, http://www.hcn.org/issues/48.1/ modern-sagebrush-rebels-recycle-old-western-fantasies.

40 Citizens of Arizona, California, Colorado, Oregon, and Washington were among the heaviest users of the ballot initiative between 1904 and 1996; see Hoesly, "Reforming Direct Democracy," 1195.

41 "States with initiative or referendum," Ballotpedia, https://ballotpedia.org/States_ with_initiative_or_referendum (accessed July 29, 2016).

42 Lee, *Smoke Signals*, 243.

43 Sadie Gurman, "Coloradans say yes to recreational marijuana," *Denver Post*, November 7, 2012.

44 Kory Grow, "D.C., Oregon, Alaska Vote to Legalize Marijuana as Florida Abstains," *Rolling Stone*, November 5, 2014.

45 Anthony Silvaggio, Humboldt Institute for Interdisciplinary Marijuana Research, conversation with author, July 26, 2014.

46 Michael O'Hare, Peter Alstone, and Daniel L. Sanchez, "Environmental Risks and Opportunities in Cannabis Cultivation," *Back of the Envelope Calculations*, September 7, 2013, 3–4, 7: http://lcb.wa.gov/marijuana/botec_reports.

47 Ibid., 3.

48 "FAQs on Rules," Washington State Liquor Advisory Board, http://liq.wa.gov/ mj2015/faqs-rules#growing (accessed December 31, 2015).

49 Chapter 314-55 WAC (2013), 11, http://www.liq.wa.gov/publications/rules/2013%20 Proposed%20Rules/OTS-5501-3Final.pdf.

50 David Rice, Washington Sungrown Industry Association, conversation with author, June 9, 2015.

51 Ibid.

52   State of Colorado, "Task Force Report on the Implementation of Amendment 64," March 13, 2013.

53   Evan Mills, "Energy Up In Smoke: The Carbon Footprint of Indoor Cannabis Production," *Journal of Energy Policy* 46 (2012): evanmills.lbl.gov/pubs/pdf/cannabis-carbon-footprint.pdf.

54   State of Colorado, "Home grow laws:" www.colorado.gov/pacific/marijuanainfodenver/marijuana-retailers-home-growers (accessed December 31, 2015).

55   Emilie Rusch, "One in 11 industrial buildings in central Denver now houses marijuana cultivation, CBRE report says," *Denver Post*, October 20, 2015.

56   Bruce Finley, "Marijuana growing spikes Denver electricity demand," *Denver Post*, July 1, 2015, http://www.thecannabist.co/2015/07/01/marijuana-electricity-demand-denver-led-lights-clean-power-plan/37304/.

57   Jennifer Oldham, "Energy-sapping marijuana cultivation a growing worry," *Bloomberg News*, December 21, 2015, http://www.thecannabist.co/2015/12/21/growing-marijuana-indoors-energy-use/45448/.

58   Boulder County, "Energy Impact Offset Fund," last modified 2017: bouldercounty.org/environment/sustainability/marijuana-offset-fund (accessed June 19, 2017).

59   Cannabis Environmental Best Practices Task Force, "08-16-2016: Working Document," August 16, 2016: Oregon.gov/olcc/marijuana/Documents/CEBP/workingdocument_CEBP_08162016.pdf (accessed June 19, 2017).

60   General Requirements Applicable to All Marijuana Licensees, Oregon Liquor Control Commission, http://www.oregon.gov/olcc/marijuana/Documents/TemporaryMarijuanaRules_adopted_122115.pdf.

61   See "California's new pot economy valued at $7 billion," Associated Press via the Los Angeles Times, January 29, 2017; Tom Huddleston, "Colorado Topped $1 Billion in Legal Marijuana Sales in 2016," *Fortune*, December 13, 2016; Washington reported $696 million in legal marijuana sales in 2016; see 502data.com (accessed June 19, 2017): $7 billion/$1.69 billion = 4.1.

62   Ben Adlin, "California Lawmakers Pass Changes to Cannabis Rules," Leafly.com, June 13, 2017, last modified June 15, 2017: leafly.com/news/politics/California-lawmakers-rush-put-cannabis-regulations-place (accessed June 19, 2017).

63   For data on how climate change is affecting the arid West, see DeBuys, *A Great Aridness*; Jonathan Waterman, *Running Dry: A Journey From Source to Sea Down the Colorado River* (Washington, DC: National Geographic Society, 2010); Maya L. Kapoor, "Climate change is unraveling natural cycles in the West," *High Country News*, May 11, 2017.

64   See Kate McLean, "Pot and Pesticides: A Bustling Illegal Trade," *The Bay Citizen* (San Francisco), May 26, 2010.

65   Anthony Silvaggio, conversation with author, July 26, 2014; McLean, "Pot and Pesticides . . ."

66   Nick Hice, Denver Relief, conversation with author, August 19, 2015; see Ed Rosenthal, *Marijuana Pest and Disease Control: How to protect your plants and win back your garden* (Quick American, 2012).

67 Yousef Gargani, Paul Bishop, and David W. Denning, "Too Many Mouldy Joints—Marijuana and Chronic Pulmonary Aspergillosis," *Mediterranean Journal of Hematology and Infectious Diseases* 3, no. 1 (January 14, 2011): https://www.ncbi.nlm.nih.gov/pmc/articles/PMC3103256/ (accessed June 22, 2017).

68 "Marijuana use and aspergillosis," Aspergillus & Aspergillosis Website, n.d: http://www.aspergillus.org.uk/content/marijuana-use-and-aspergillosis (accessed June 22, 2017).

69 Brooke Borel, "The Wild West of Pesticides," *Atlantic*, August 31, 2015.

70 Colorado Department of Agriculture, "Criteria for Pesticides Used in the Production of Marijuana In Colorado," March 25, 2015, https://www.colorado.gov/pacific/sites/default/files/atoms/files/Criteria%20for%20pesticides%20used%20in%20the%20production%20of%20marijuana%20in%20Colorado_0.pdf.

71 Ibid.

72 Silvaggio, conversation with author, July 26, 2014.

73 Thomas Mitchell, "Denver investigated 10 pot grows for use of banned pesticides, holds plants," *Westword*, May 18, 2015, http://www.westword.com/news/denver-investigated-10-pot-grows-for-use-of-banned-pesticides-holds-plants-6654706.

74 Dow Agrosciences, "Safety Data Sheet, Product Name: EAGLE 20EW Fungicide," May 12, 2015, http://www.cdms.net/ldat/mp6DG001.pdf.

75 Eagle20EW, for instance, has not undergone combustion/inhalation testing; see Colorado Green Lab, "Eagle 20 and Myclobutanil in the Context of Cannabis Cultivation and Consumption," coloradogreenlab.com: http://www.coloradogreenlab.com/blog/eagle-20-and-myclobutanil-in-the-context-of-cannabis-cultivation-and-consumption (accessed June 22, 2017).

76 John Hickenlooper, "Executive Order D 2015-015: Directing State Agencies to Address Threats to Public Safety Posed by Marijuana Contaminated by Pesticide," State of Colorado, November 12, 2015: https://www.colorado.gov/pacific/sites/default/files/atoms/files/D%202015-015%20Executive%20Order%20for%20Marijuana%20and%20Pesticides.pdf (accessed June 22, 2017).

77 Colorado Department of Agriculture, "Pesticide Applicators' Act Rules and Regulations, Part 17. The Use of Pesticides in the Production of Cannabis," March 30, 2016: https://www.colorado.gov/pacific/sites/default/files/atoms/files/3-30-2016%20PAA%20Cannabis%20Rule%20WEB.pdf (accessed June 22, 2017).

78 Colorado Department of Agriculture, "Pesticide Use in Cannabis Production Information tables."

79 Rodger Voelker and Mowgli Holmes, "Pesticide Use on Cannabis," Cannabis Safety Institute, June 2015, http://cannabissafetyinstitute.org/wp-content/uploads/2015/06/CSI-Pesticides-White-Paper.pdf.

80 Oregon Department of Agriculture, "Cannabis and Pesticides," last modified May 25, 2017: http://www.oregon.gov/ODA/programs/Pesticides/Pages/CannabisPesticides.aspx (accessed June 22, 2017); Oregon Department of Agriculture, "Cannabis and pesticides: Letter to Producers," November 21, 2016: http://www.oregon.gov/ODA/shared/Documents/Publications/PesticidesPARC/CannabisPesticidesLetter.pdf (accessed June 22, 2017).

81   "Oregon issues first marijuana recall over high pesticide levels," Associated Press via *The Cannabist* (*Denver Post*), March 21, 2017; "Pyrethrins General Fact Sheet," National Pesticide Information Center, Oregon State University, November 2014, p. 2: http://npic.orst.edu/factsheets/pyrethrins.pdf (accessed June 22, 2017).

82   Washington State Department of Agriculture, "Pesticide and Fertilizer Use on Marijuana in Washington," last modified June 1, 2017: https://agr.wa.gov/pest-fert/pesticides/pesticideuseonmarijuana.aspx (accessed June 22, 2017); "Medical Marijuana Pesticide Testing," Washington State Department of Health, n.d: http://www.doh.wa.gov/YouandYourFamily/Marijuana/MedicalMarijuana/ProductCompliance/PesticideTesting (accessed June 22, 2017).

83   Michelle Mart, Pesticides, *A Love Story: America's Enduring Embrace of Dangerous Chemicals* (Lawrence: University Press of Kansas, 2015), 6.

84   Adrian Devitt-Lee, "Pesticide Regulations Need Rethink," *Project CBD*, May 5, 2017: https://www.projectcbd.org/article/cannabis-pesticide-regulations-need-re-think-pyrethrins-eagle-20 (accessed June 22, 2017).

85   "Greening Corporate Cannabis," Seminar at the annual convention of the National Cannabis Industry Association (author attended), Denver, Colorado, June 29, 2015.

86   Aron Swan, Silver State Relief, conversation with author, August 5, 2015; See, for example, "Grow Lights—LED vs. HID Operating Costs," *The Weed Blog*, posted by Johnny Green on January 26, 2014, http://www.theweedblog.com/grow-lights-led-vs-hid-operating-costs/ (accessed December 30, 2015).

87   Will Yakowicz, "Willie Nelson Would Like to Grow Some Marijuana for You," Inc., August 8, 2016: www.inc.com/will-yakowicz/willie-nelson-denver-relief-marijuana.html (accessed June 19, 2017).

88   "Introducing Icarus," *BIOS Lighting*, http://bioslighting.com/icarus-2/ (accessed December 31, 2015).

89   Nick Hice, conversation with author, August 19, 2015.

90   Nick Hice, conversation with author, August 19, 2015.

91   Nick Hice, conversation with author, May 22, 2017.

92   Ibid.

93   Resource Innovation Institute, 2017: resourceinnovationinstitute.org (accessed June 20, 2017).

94   Nick Hice, conversation with author, May 22, 2017; the *Denver Post* reported in 2016 that more than half of the city's 329 marijuana licenses went to cultivators, see "A revealing map of Denver marijuana facilities," *Denver Post*, January 4, 2016 (updated April 18, 2016: denverpost.com/2016/01/04/a-revealing-map-of-denver-marijuana-facilities/ (accessed June 20, 2017).

95   Oregon Sungrown Growers' Guild, home page, http://oregonsungrown.org/ (accessed January 1, 2016).

96   Sarah Aitchison, "Sun grown and rain watered: First sustainable pot farm certified in Washington," *Puget Sound Business Journal*, December 3, 2014, http://www.bizjournals.com/seattle/news/2014/12/03/sun-grown-and-rain-watered-first-sustainable-pot.html (accessed December 31, 2015).

97 Greening Corporate Cannabis, home page, http://greeningcorporatecannabis.com/ (accessed January 1, 2016).

98 "Greening Corporate Cannabis," Seminar, National Cannabis Industry Association, Denver, Colorado, June 29, 2015 (author attended).

99 John-Paul Maxfield, Organic Cannabis Association, conversation with author, July 17, 2015.

100 Christi Turner, "A Greener Weed: Certified Pesticide-Free Cannabis Comes to Colorado," *Modern Farmer*, August 24, 2016, http://modernfarmer.com/2016/08/pesticide-free-cannabis/.

101 Austa Somvichian-Clausen, "Organic Weed? Marijuana Growers Go Green," *National Geographic*, June 16, 2017: news.nationalgeographic.com/2017/06/marijuana-organic-cannabis-industry-goes-green-energy-water-pesticides (accessed June 20, 2017).

102 Andrew Kenney, "Dr. Bronner's wants to help you find organic marijuana in Colorado," *Denverite*, June 7, 2017.

103 Mitchell, "Denver investigated 10 pot grows . . ."

104 John-Paul Maxfield, conversation with author, July 17, 2015.

105 Noah Hirsch, conversation with author, August 6, 2015.

106 Scott Greacen, conversation with author, April 26, 2017.

107 Ibid.

108 Jon Brooks, "DEA Raids Pot Grower Licensed by Mendocino County; 'They Came in Guns Blazing,' Says Grower," KQED (San Francisco), October 13, 2011, http://ww2.kqed.org/news/2011/10/13/mendocino-county-raid-has-marijuana-advocates-riled; Mary Callahan, "Mendocino County to turn over medical marijuana records," *Press Democrat* (San Francisco), October 16, 2013, http://www.pressdemocrat.com/csp/mediapool/sites/PressDemocrat/News/story.csp?cid=2221120&sid=555&fid=181.

109 Silvaggio, conversation with author, July 26, 2014.

110 Greacen, conversation with author, April 26, 2017.

111 Ibid.

112 Greacen, conversation with author, June 5, 2015.

Conclusion

1 Guy Kovner, "New California water reporting rules worry Sonoma County grape growers," *Press Democrat* (Santa Rosa, CA), January 20, 2016, http://www.pressdemocrat.com/business/5104241-181/new-california-water-reporting-rules.

2 "Wine and Cannabis? Oregon Vineyards Give Marijuana Farming a Try," Associated Press via Leafly.com, May 25, 2017.

3 Greg Paneitz, conversation with author, August 8, 2015.

4 Eli McVey, "Map: The post-election U.S. marijuana landscape," *Marijuana Business Daily*, November 14, 2016: https://mjbizdaily.com/chart-majority-of-u-s-embraces-legal-marijuana/ (accessed June 22, 2017).

5 See Magalie Noebes, "Weed and Waste: What To Do With Your Empty Containers," *MassRoots*, May 17, 2016: www.massroots.com/news/weed-and-

waste-what-to-do-with-your-empty-containers (accessed June 21, 2017); on the viability of hemp as a replacement for petroleum-based plastic, see Fine, *Hemp Bound*, 42–43; see also "Doug Fine talks about plastic made from hemp," YouTube video, 0:53, posted by "J. Anthony Martinez" on June 14, 2016: www.youtube.com/watch?v=EOgPmdwMG5s (accessed June 21, 2017).

6   Angela Bacca, "The Unbearable Whiteness of the Marijuana Industry," *Alternet*, March 31, 2015, http://www.alternet.org/drugs/incredible-whiteness-colorado-cannabis-business; "German Lopez, "After Colorado legalized marijuana, arrests fell for white kids—but rose for black kids," *Vox*, May 11, 2016, http://www.vox.com/2016/5/11/11656582/colorado-marijuana-arrests-race.

7   Nat Stein, "Racial disparities persist in marijuana arrests," *Colorado Springs Independent*, May 4, 2016, http://www.csindy.com/coloradosprings/racial-disparities-persist-in-marijuana-arrests/Content?oid=3775503.

Select Books on Cannabis

Barcott, Bruce. *Weed the People: The Future of Legal Marijuana in America.* New York: Time Books, 2015.

Bonnie, Richard J. and Charles Whitebread. *The Marijuana Conviction: A History of Marijuana Prohibition in the United States.* New York: The Lindesmith Center, 1999.

Booth, Martin. *Cannabis: A History.* New York: St. Martin's Press, 2003.

Brady, Emily. *Humboldt: Life on America's Marijuana Frontier.* New York: Hachette, 2013.

Campos, Isaac. *Home Grown: Marijuana and the Origins of Mexico's War on Drugs.* Chapel Hill: University of North Carolina Press, 2013.

Caulkins, Jonathan P., Angela Hawken, Beau Kilmer, Mark A. R. Kleiman. *Marijuana Legalization: What Everyone Needs to Know.* New York: Oxford University Press, 2012.

Clarke, Robert C. and Mark Merlin. *Cannabis: Evolution and Ethnobotany.* Berkeley: University of California Press, 2013.

Drake, Bill. *The Cultivator's Handbook of Marijuana.* Berkeley, CA: Bill Drake c/o Book People, 1970.

Duvall, Chris. *Cannabis.* London: Reaktion Books, 2014.

Earlywine, Mitch. *Understanding Marijuana: A New Look at the Scientific Evidence.* New York: Oxford University Press, 2002.

Falck, Zachary. *Weeds: An Urban Environmental History.* Pennsylvania: University of Pittsburgh Press, 2010.

Fine, Doug. *Hemp Bound: Dispatches from the Front Lines of the Next Agricultural Revolution.* White River Junction, VT: Chelsea Green Publishing, 2014.

Frank, Mel, and Ed Rosenthal. *The Marijuana Grower's Guide.* Berkeley, CA: And/Or Press, 1978.

Hecht, Peter. *Weed Land: Inside America's Marijuana Epicenter and How Pot Went Legit.* Berkeley: University of California Press, 2014.

Hudak, John. *Marijuana: A Short History.* Washington, DC: Brookings Institution, 2016.

Jankowiak, William and Daniel Bradburd. *Drugs, Labor, and Colonial Expansion.* Tucson: University of Arizona Press, 2003.

Kuzmarov, Jeremy. *The Myth of the Addicted Army: Vietnam and the Modern War on Drugs.* Boston: University of Massachusetts Press, 2009.

Lee, Martin A. *Smoke Signals: A Social History of Marijuana—Medical, Recreational, Scientific.* New York: Scribner, 2012.

Mills, James H. *Cannabis Britannica: Empire, Nation, and Trade 1800-1928.* New York: Oxford University Press, 2003.

Pollan, Michael. *The Botany of Desire.* New York: Random House, 2001.

Raphael, Ray. *Cash Crop: An American Dream.* Mendocino, CA: Ridge Times Press, 1985.

Regan, Trish. *Joint Ventures: Inside America's Almost Legal Marijuana Industry.* New Jersey: John Wiley & Sons, 2011.

Rendon, Jim. *Super-Charged: How Outlaws, Hippies, and Scientists Reinvented Marijuana.* Portland, OR: Timber Press, 2012.

Rubin, Vera, and Lambros Comitas. *Ganja in Jamaica: A Medical Anthropological Study of Chronic Marihuana Use.* The Hague: New Babylon Studies in the Social Sciences, 1975.

Sloman, Larry. *Reefer Madness: A History of Marijuana.* New York: St. Martin's Griffin, 1979.

Index

National Institute on Drug Abuse
(NIDA), 103–104, 121, 127, 177–178
National Organization for the
Reform of Marijuana Laws
(NORML), 101, 120, 134, 136
Native American culture, 97–98
Nevada legalization, 145, 153, 161
New Mexico legalization, 146
newspaper reporting, 33–41
Nixon, Richard, 66, 102–103
Nuno, Ralph, 119

Oaksterdam University, 143–145, 180
Operation Green Merchant, 126
opiates, 31
opium, 17–19, 26, 30–32, 37, 49–50
Orabuena, Tony, 40–41
Oregon legalization, 145, 153, 155–156,
158–159, 160
Oregon Sungrown Growers' Guild,
165, 176, 180
Organic Cannabis Association
(OCA), 165–166
organic certification, 165–167

Panacea Chronicles, 110
Paneitz, Greg, 175–176, 178
paraquat, 120–122, 134–136
Parren, John, 79
Penhollow, W. L., 43–44
pesticides, 13, 124–125, 140, 156–160
Philadelphia Seed Company, 55–57
political support, 180–181
Pollan, Michael, 67
poverty, 78–79
Pratt, Henry, 70
Price, Roberta, 97
Progressive Movement, 151
Prohibition, 19, 39–41, 79–80

prohibition of marijuana, 39–41,
177–181. *See also* federal vs. state
regulations; legalization
Proposition 215, 149
psychoactive effects, 10–12, 14–16,
21–24
PTSD, 149
Pure Food and Drug Act (1906), 19

racism
blacks and, 37–38, 46, 49, 85, 146,
179–180
Chinese and, 19, 31–32, 73–74
legalization and, 179–180
Mexicans and, 17–20, 33–37, 39,
46–49
Randall, Robert, 85, 104–106, 118
Reagan, Nancy, 128
Reagan, Ronald, 121, 127–129
Reames, Richard, 123
recreational marijuana, 5
Reed, Daniel A., 56
reefer madness, 18, 48, 77
Reefer Madness (film), 48
Reefer Madness (Sloman), 48
research discoveries, 147–149, 177–178
Resource Innovation Institute (RII),
164, 180
Rice, David, 154, 165, 180
Robinson, Brittain, 60
rope, 59–62
Rose, Chelsea, 171–175
Rush, Daryl, 139–140

salmon, 4, 6, 167–168, 170, 177
A Sand County Almanac (Leopold),
89
San Juan Sun Grown, 165
Santos, Valdo, 79